JUSTIN JORDAN   ARIELA KRISTANTINA   BEN WILSONHAM

DEEP STATE

VOLUME TWO \ SYSTEMS OF CONTROL

BOOM! STUDIOS

DEEP STATE Volume Two, November 2015. Published by BOOM! Studios, a division of Boom Entertainment, Inc. Deep State is ™ & © 2015 Justin Jordan. Originally published in single magazine form as DEEP STATE No. 5-8. ™ & © 2015 Justin Jordan. All rights reserved. BOOM! Studios™ and the BOOM! Studios logo are trademarks of Boom Entertainment, Inc., registered in various countries and categories. All characters, events, and institutions depicted herein are fictional. Any similarity between any of the names, characters, persons, events, and/or institutions in this publication to actual names, characters, and persons, whether living or dead, events, and/or institutions is unintended and purely coincidental. BOOM! Studios does not read or accept unsolicited submissions of ideas, stories, or artwork.

A catalog record of this book is available from OCLC and from the BOOM! Studios website, www.boom-studios.com, on the Librarians page.

BOOM! Studios, 5670 Wilshire Boulevard, Suite 450, Los Angeles, CA 90036-5679. Printed in China. First Printing.

ISBN: 978-1-60886-741-7, eISBN: 978-1-61398-412-3

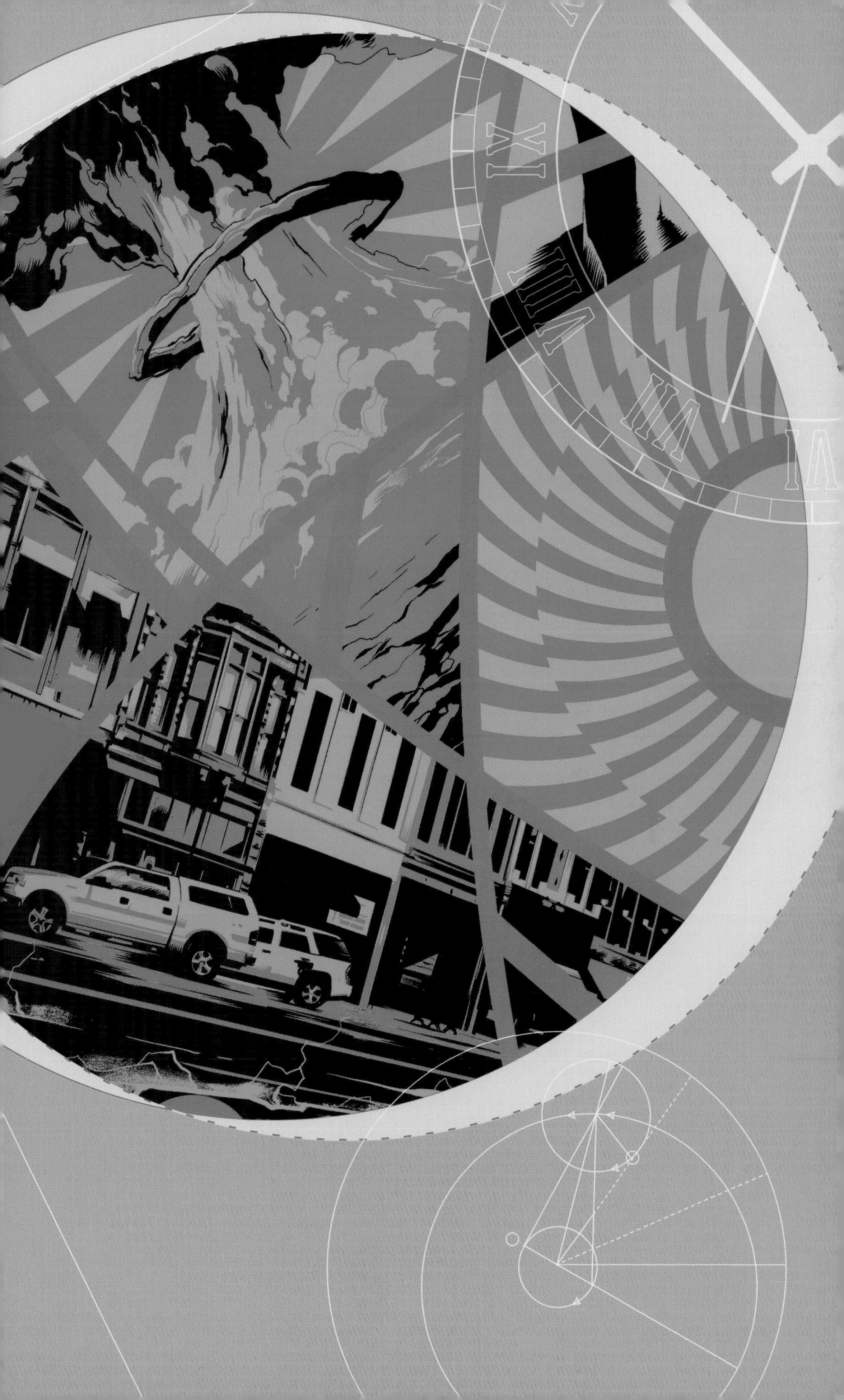

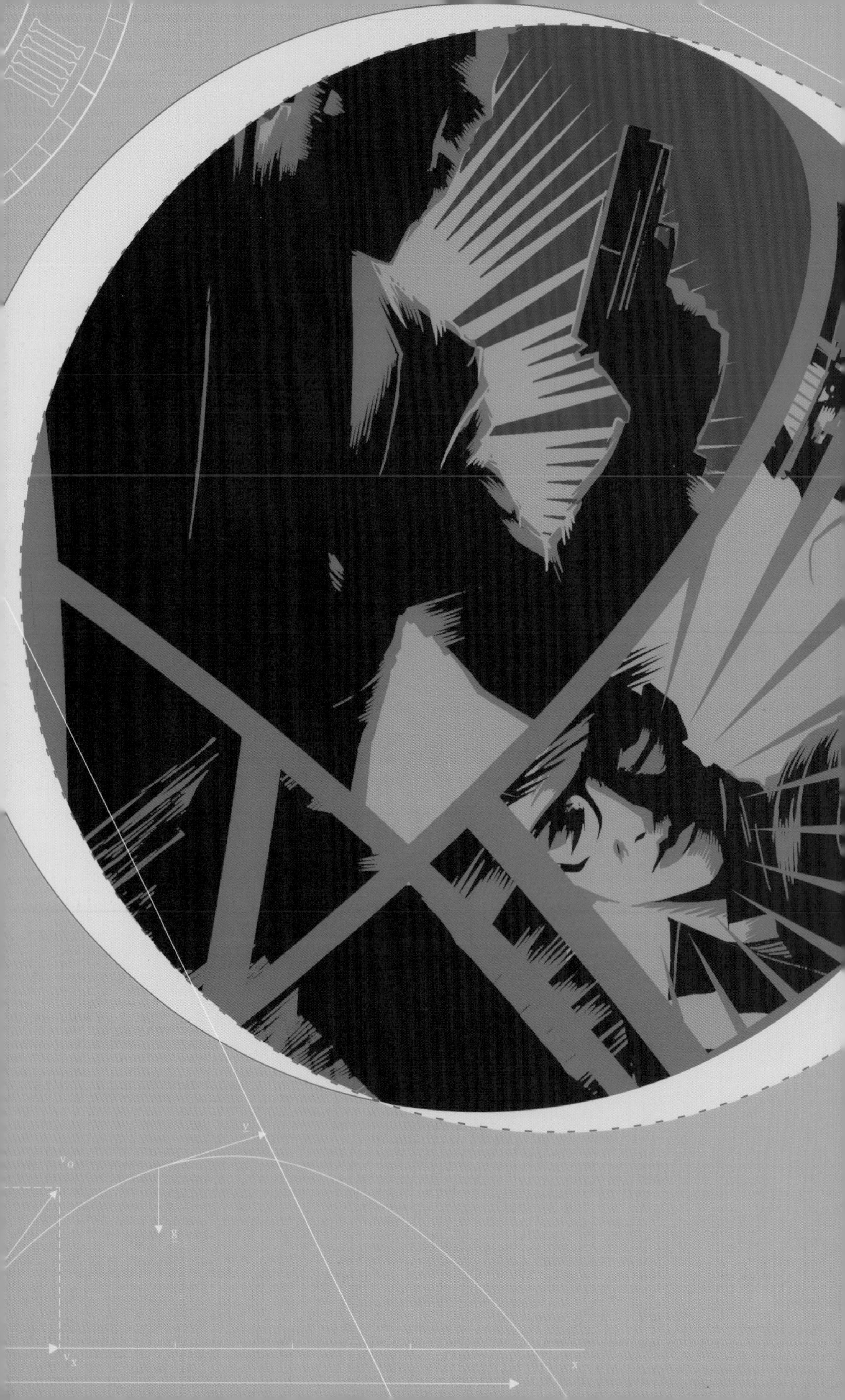

v
v0
g
vx
x

WRITTEN BY
JUSTIN JORDAN

ILLUSTRATED BY
ARIELA KRISTANTINA

COLORS BY
BEN WILSONHAM

LETTERS BY
ED DUKESHIRE

COVER BY
MATT TAYLOR

DESIGNER | KELSEY DIETERICH

ASSISTANT EDITOR | CAMERON CHITTOCK

EDITOR | Eric Harburn

DEEP STATE™
CREATED BY
JUSTIN JORDAN

CHAPTER FIVE

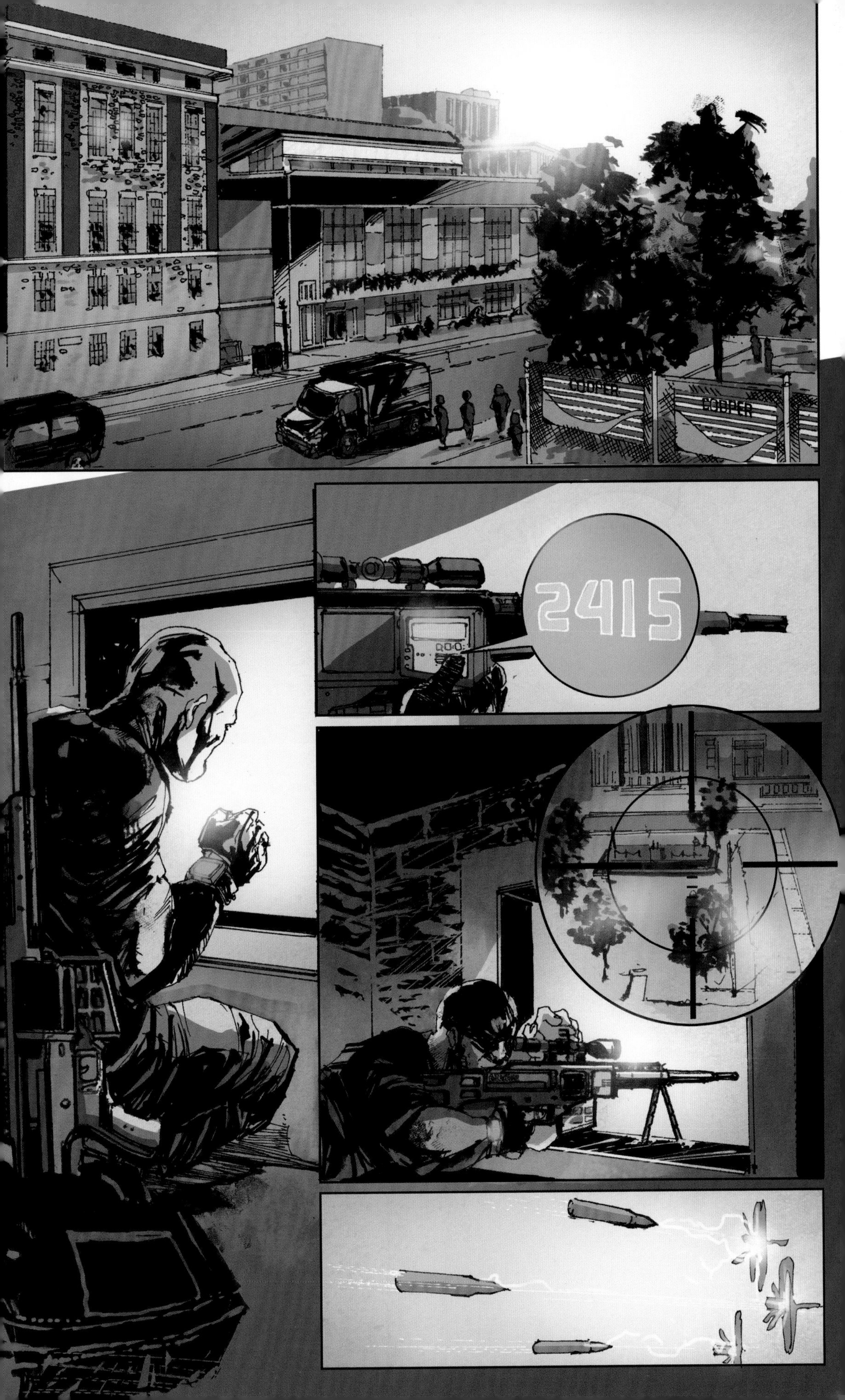

COOPER
COOPER
2415

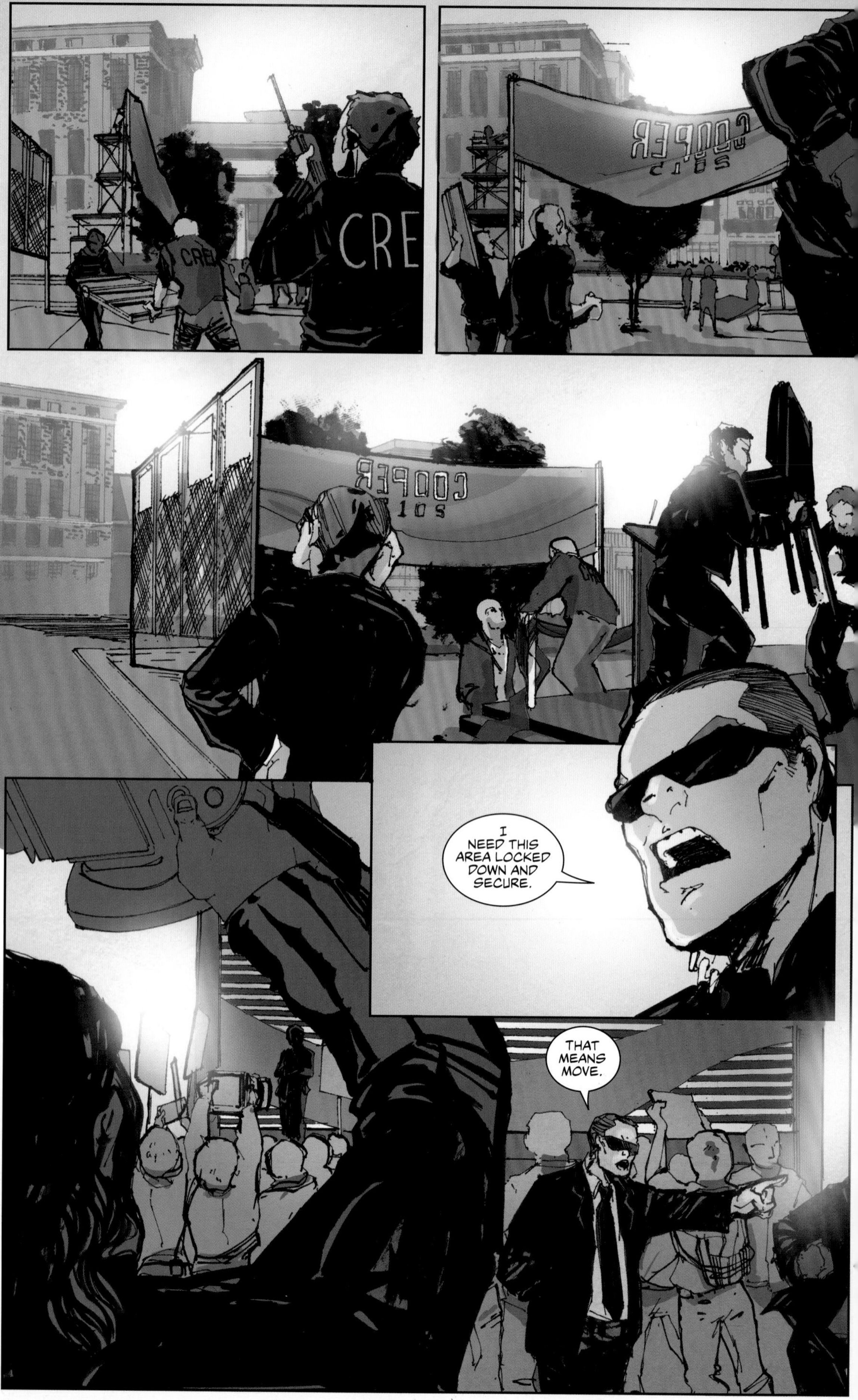
CRE
I NEED THIS AREA LOCKED DOWN AND SECURE.
THAT MEANS MOVE.

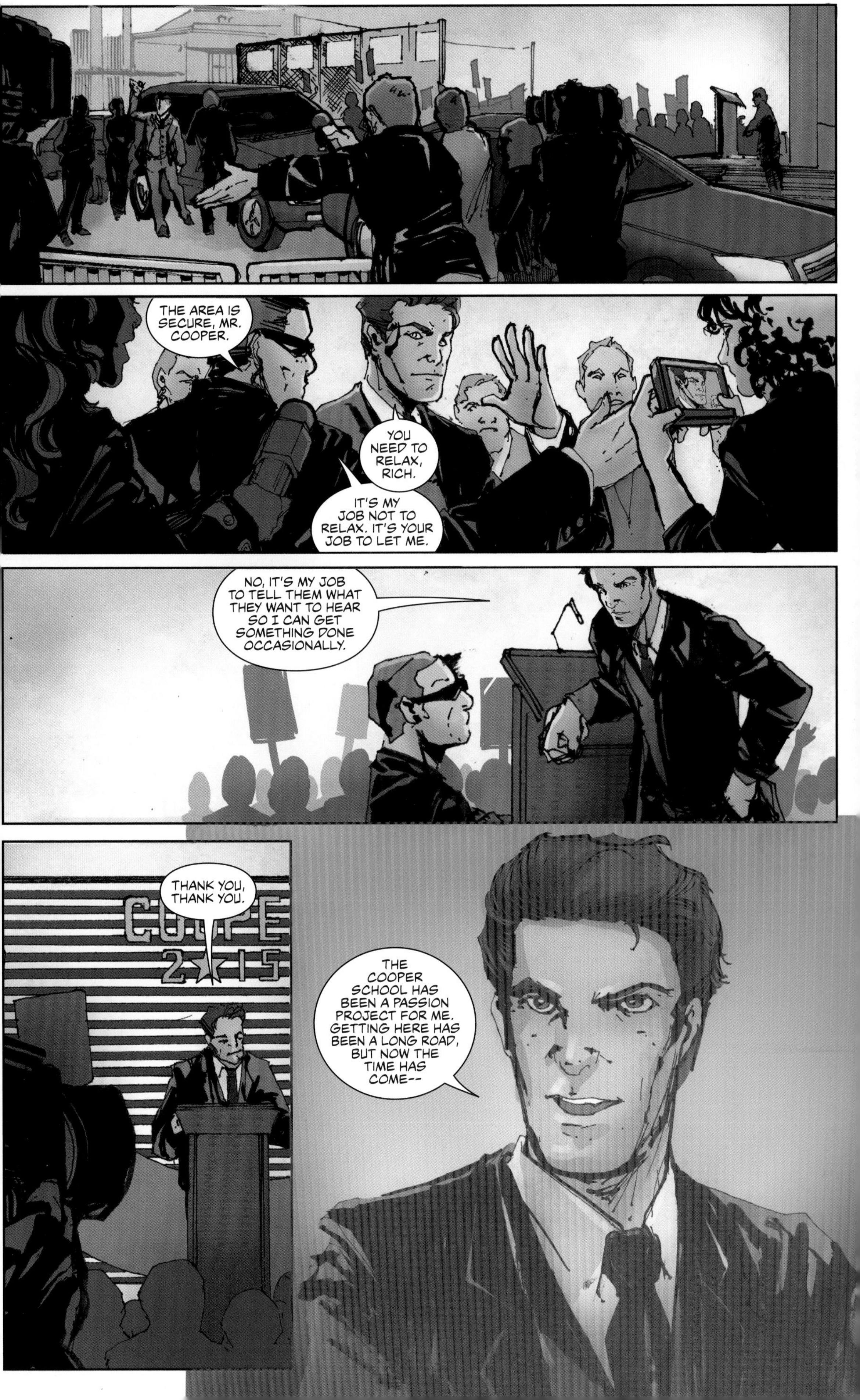
THE AREA IS SECURE, MR. COOPER.
YOU NEED TO RELAX, RICH.
IT'S MY JOB NOT TO RELAX. IT'S YOUR JOB TO LET ME.
NO, IT'S MY JOB TO TELL THEM WHAT THEY WANT TO HEAR SO I CAN GET SOMETHING DONE OCCASIONALLY.
THANK YOU, THANK YOU.
COOPE
2015
THE COOPER SCHOOL HAS BEEN A PASSION PROJECT FOR ME. GETTING HERE HAS BEEN A LONG ROAD, BUT NOW THE TIME HAS COME--

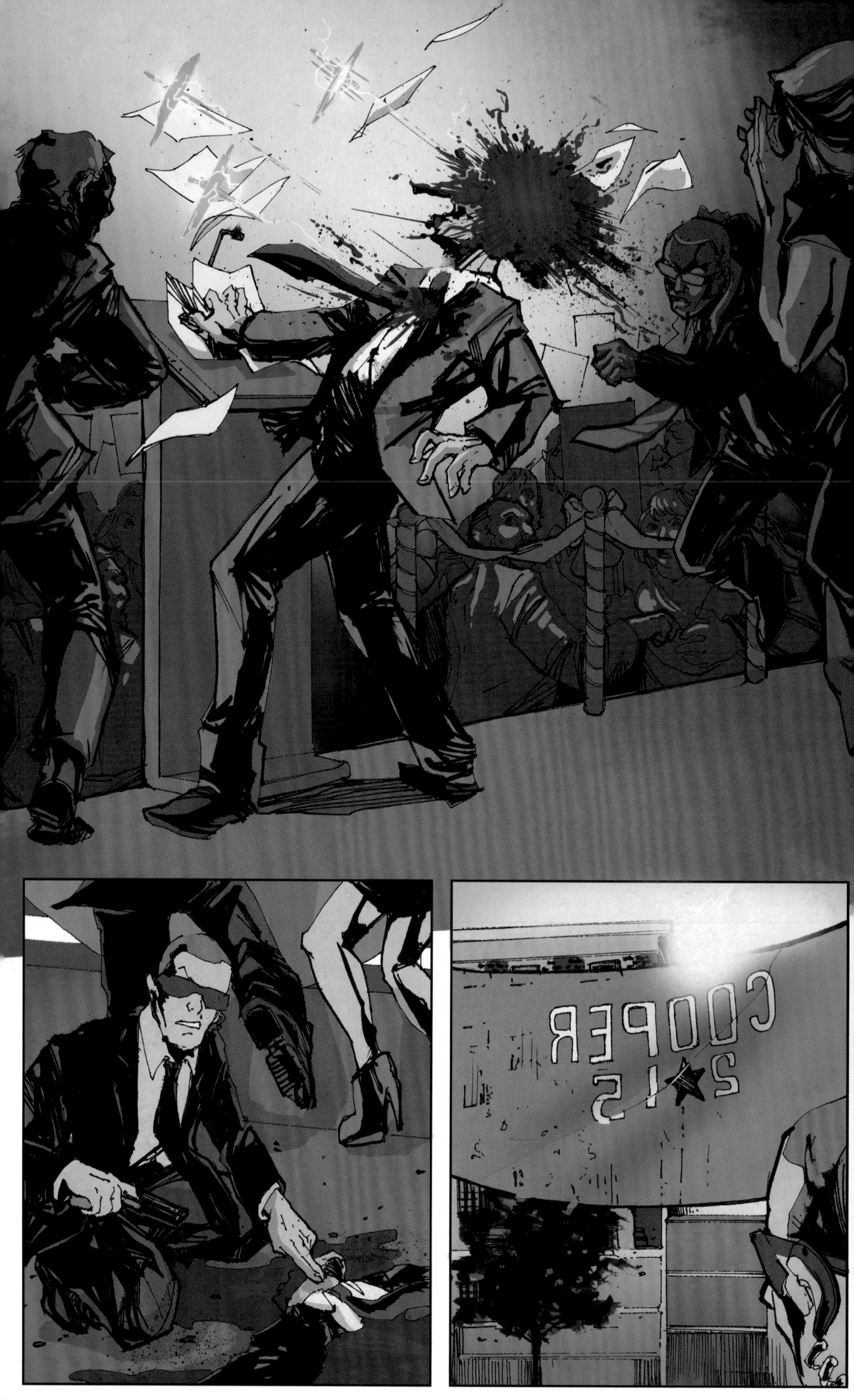
COOPER
2★15

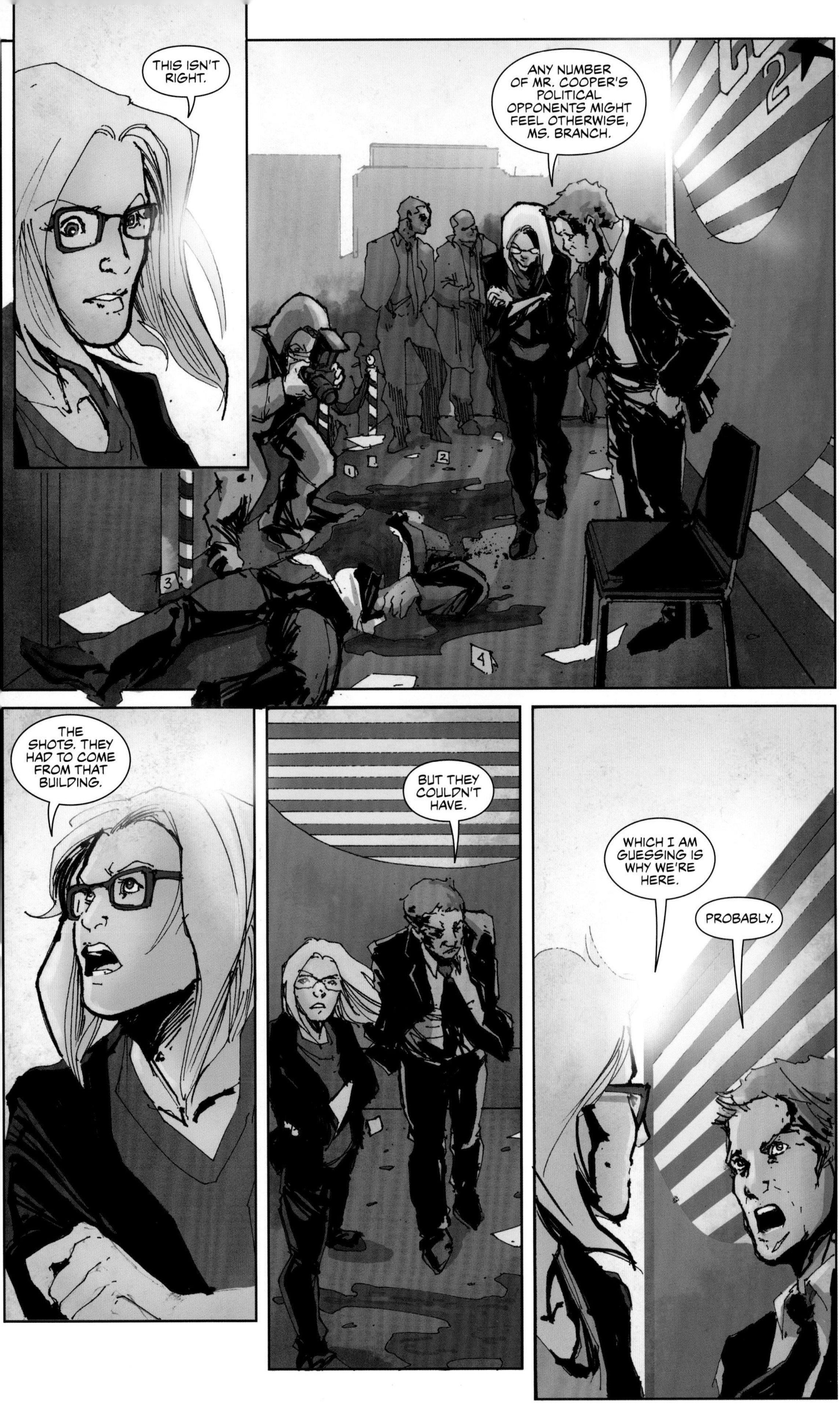
THIS ISN'T RIGHT.
ANY NUMBER OF MR. COOPER'S POLITICAL OPPONENTS MIGHT FEEL OTHERWISE, MS. BRANCH.
THE SHOTS. THEY HAD TO COME FROM THAT BUILDING.
BUT THEY COULDN'T HAVE.
WHICH I AM GUESSING IS WHY WE'RE HERE.
PROBABLY.

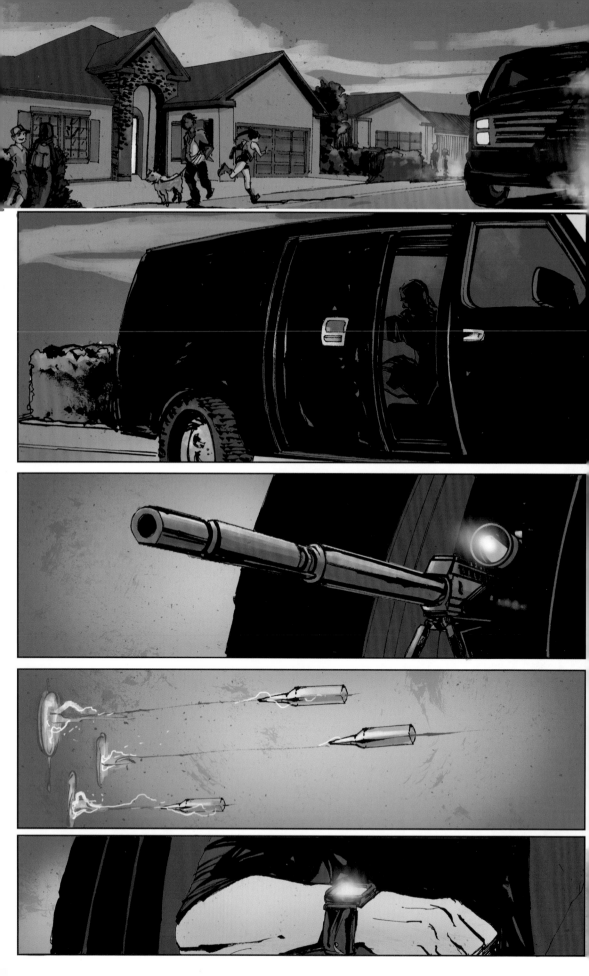

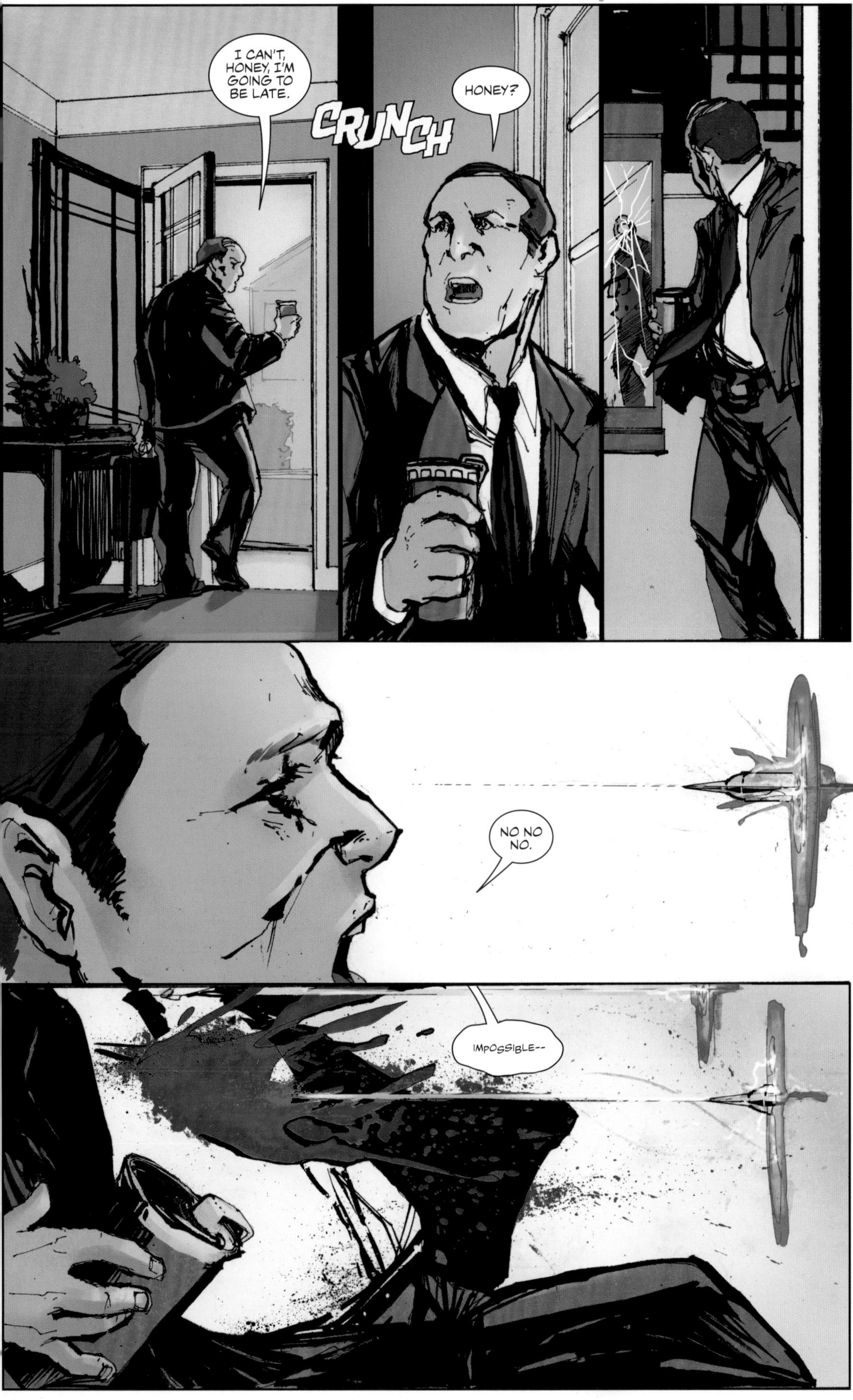
I CAN'T, HONEY, I'M GOING TO BE LATE.
CRUNCH
HONEY?
NO NO NO.
IMPOSSIBLE--

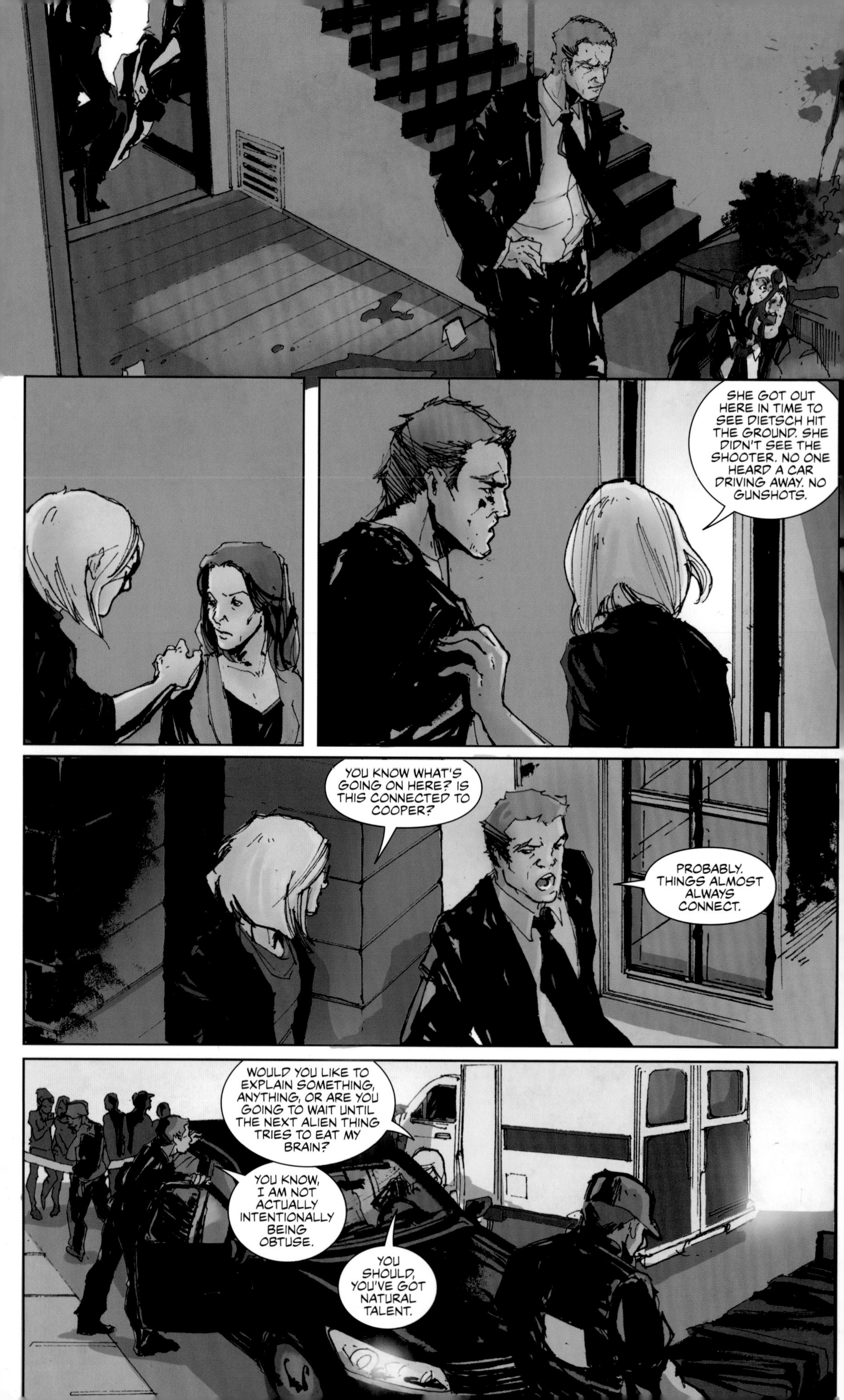
SHE GOT OUT HERE IN TIME TO SEE DIETSCH HIT THE GROUND. SHE DIDN'T SEE THE SHOOTER. NO ONE HEARD A CAR DRIVING AWAY. NO GUNSHOTS.
YOU KNOW WHAT'S GOING ON HERE? IS THIS CONNECTED TO COOPER?
PROBABLY. THINGS ALMOST ALWAYS CONNECT.
WOULD YOU LIKE TO EXPLAIN SOMETHING, ANYTHING, OR ARE YOU GOING TO WAIT UNTIL THE NEXT ALIEN THING TRIES TO EAT MY BRAIN?
YOU KNOW, I AM NOT ACTUALLY INTENTIONALLY BEING OBTUSE.
YOU SHOULD, YOU'VE GOT NATURAL TALENT.

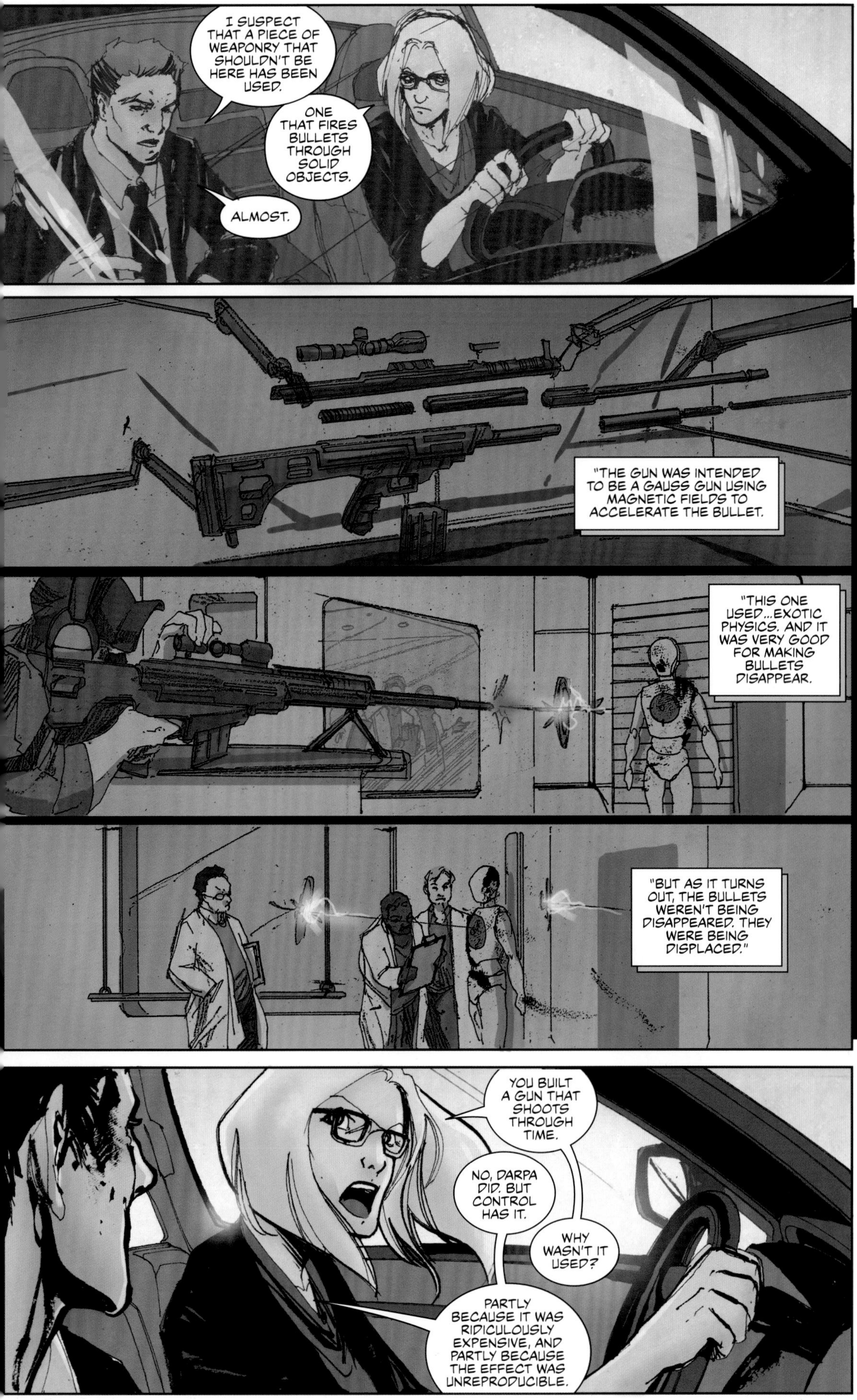
I SUSPECT THAT A PIECE OF WEAPONRY THAT SHOULDN'T BE HERE HAS BEEN USED.
ONE THAT FIRES BULLETS THROUGH SOLID OBJECTS.
ALMOST.
"THE GUN WAS INTENDED TO BE A GAUSS GUN USING MAGNETIC FIELDS TO ACCELERATE THE BULLET.
"THIS ONE USED...EXOTIC PHYSICS. AND IT WAS VERY GOOD FOR MAKING BULLETS DISAPPEAR.
"BUT AS IT TURNS OUT, THE BULLETS WEREN'T BEING DISAPPEARED. THEY WERE BEING DISPLACED."
YOU BUILT A GUN THAT SHOOTS THROUGH TIME.
NO, DARPA DID. BUT CONTROL HAS IT.
WHY WASN'T IT USED?
PARTLY BECAUSE IT WAS RIDICULOUSLY EXPENSIVE, AND PARTLY BECAUSE THE EFFECT WAS UNREPRODUCIBLE.

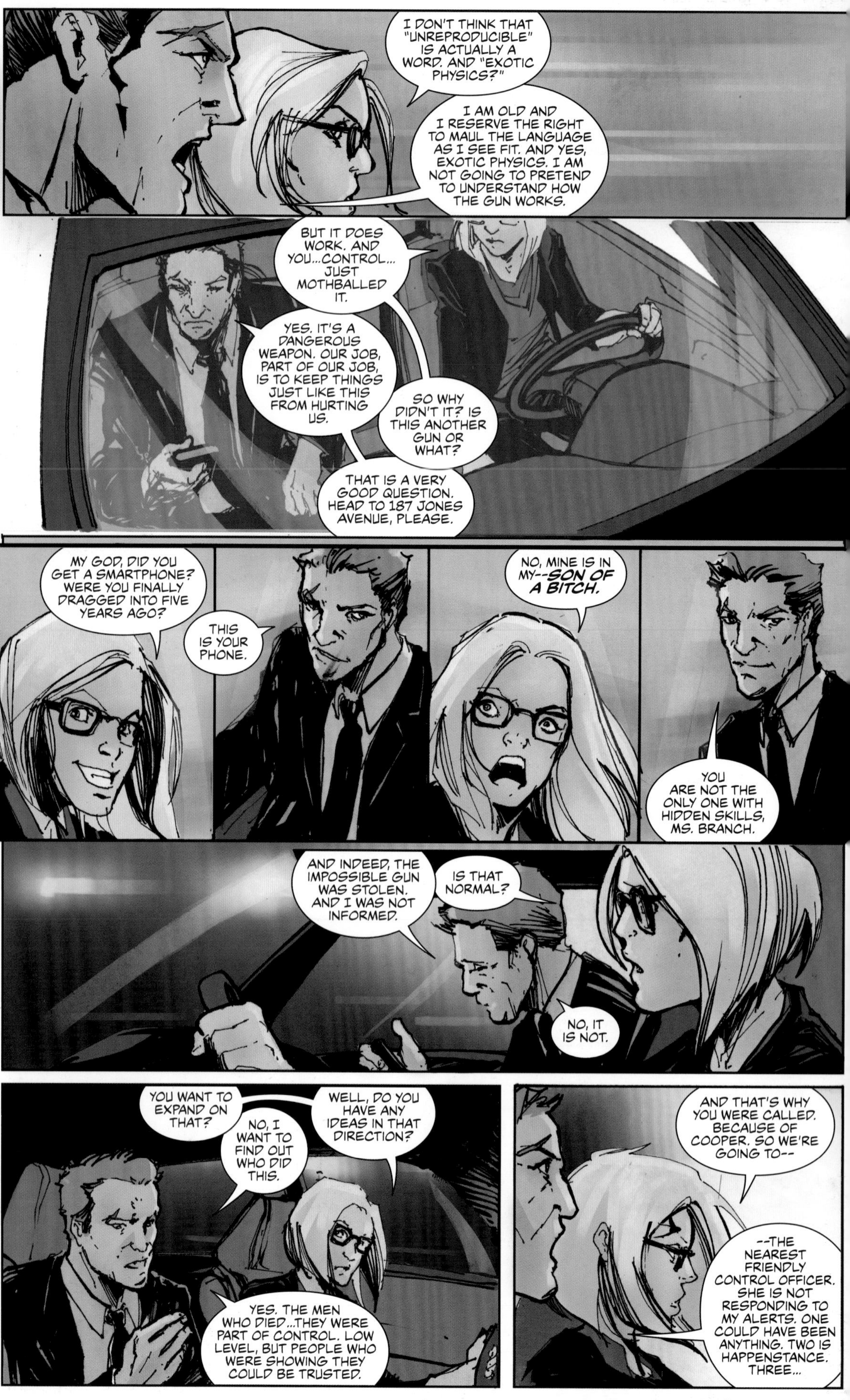

I DON'T THINK THAT "UNREPRODUCIBLE" IS ACTUALLY A WORD. AND "EXOTIC PHYSICS?"
I AM OLD AND I RESERVE THE RIGHT TO MAUL THE LANGUAGE AS I SEE FIT. AND YES, EXOTIC PHYSICS. I AM NOT GOING TO PRETEND TO UNDERSTAND HOW THE GUN WORKS.
BUT IT DOES WORK. AND YOU...CONTROL... JUST MOTHBALLED IT.
YES. IT'S A DANGEROUS WEAPON. OUR JOB, PART OF OUR JOB, IS TO KEEP THINGS JUST LIKE THIS FROM HURTING US.
SO WHY DIDN'T IT? IS THIS ANOTHER GUN OR WHAT?
THAT IS A VERY GOOD QUESTION. HEAD TO 187 JONES AVENUE, PLEASE.
MY GOD, DID YOU GET A SMARTPHONE? WERE YOU FINALLY DRAGGED INTO FIVE YEARS AGO?
THIS IS YOUR PHONE.
NO, MINE IS IN MY--*SON OF A BITCH.*
YOU ARE NOT THE ONLY ONE WITH HIDDEN SKILLS, MS. BRANCH.
AND INDEED, THE IMPOSSIBLE GUN WAS STOLEN. AND I WAS NOT INFORMED.
IS THAT NORMAL?
NO, IT IS NOT.
YOU WANT TO EXPAND ON THAT?
WELL, DO YOU HAVE ANY IDEAS IN THAT DIRECTION?
NO, I WANT TO FIND OUT WHO DID THIS.
YES. THE MEN WHO DIED...THEY WERE PART OF CONTROL. LOW LEVEL, BUT PEOPLE WHO WERE SHOWING THEY COULD BE TRUSTED.
AND THAT'S WHY YOU WERE CALLED. BECAUSE OF COOPER. SO WE'RE GOING TO--
--THE NEAREST FRIENDLY CONTROL OFFICER. SHE IS NOT RESPONDING TO MY ALERTS. ONE COULD HAVE BEEN ANYTHING. TWO IS HAPPENSTANCE. THREE...

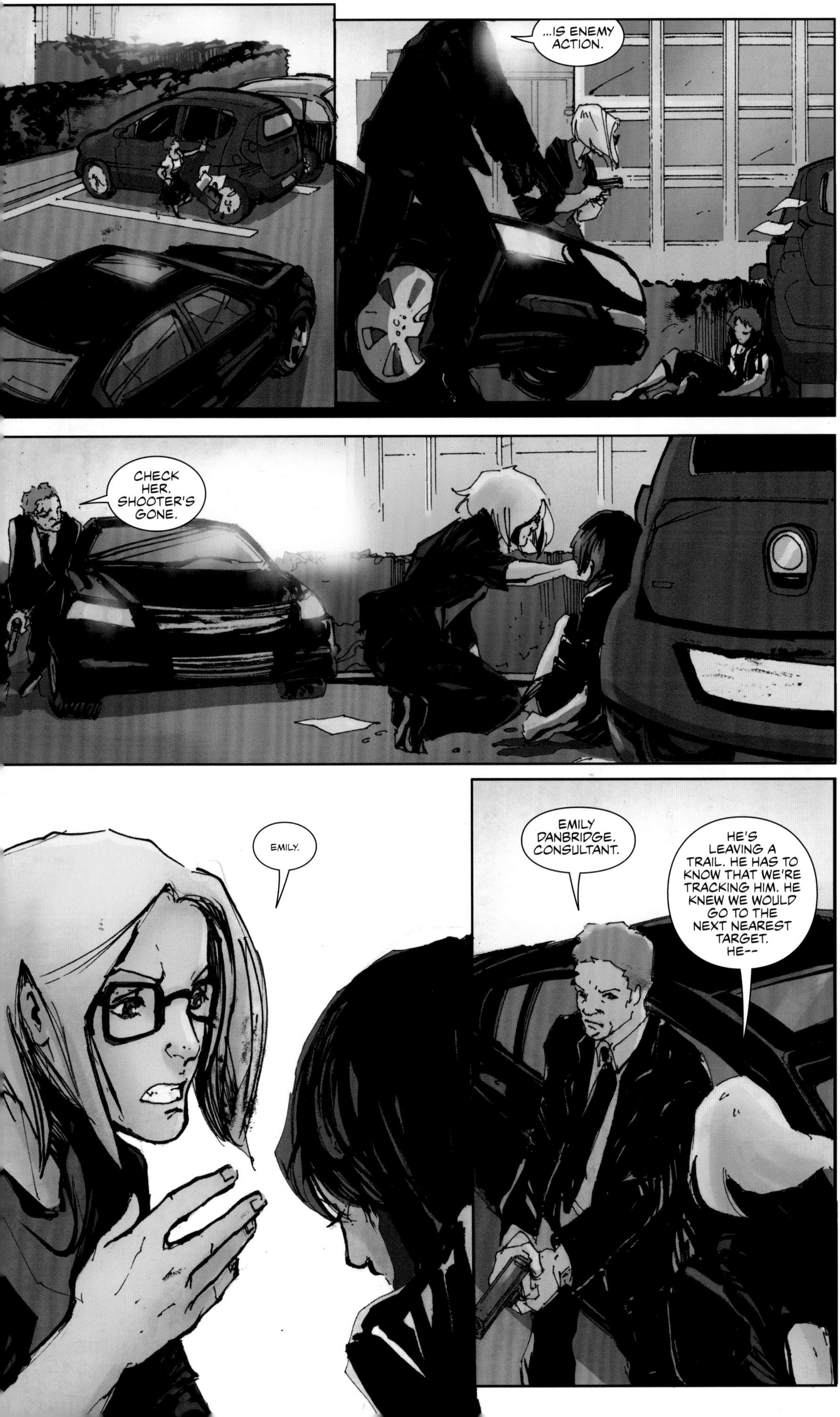
...IS ENEMY ACTION.
CHECK HER. SHOOTER'S GONE.
EMILY.
EMILY DANBRIDGE. CONSULTANT.
HE'S LEAVING A TRAIL. HE HAS TO KNOW THAT WE'RE TRACKING HIM. HE KNEW WE WOULD GO TO THE NEXT NEAREST TARGET. HE--

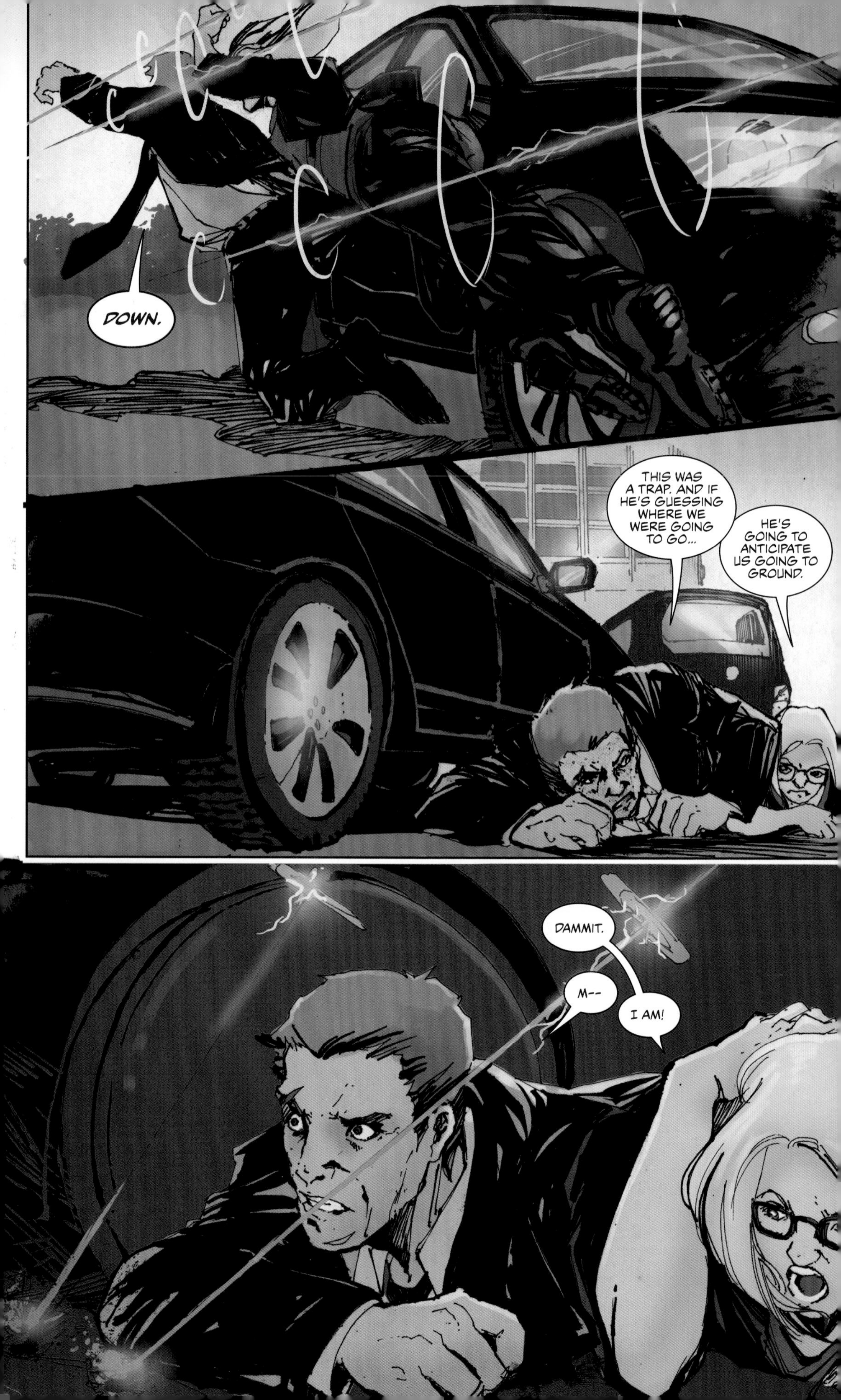
DOWN.
THIS WAS A TRAP. AND IF HE'S GUESSING WHERE WE WERE GOING TO GO...
HE'S GOING TO ANTICIPATE US GOING TO GROUND.
DAMMIT.
M--
I AM!

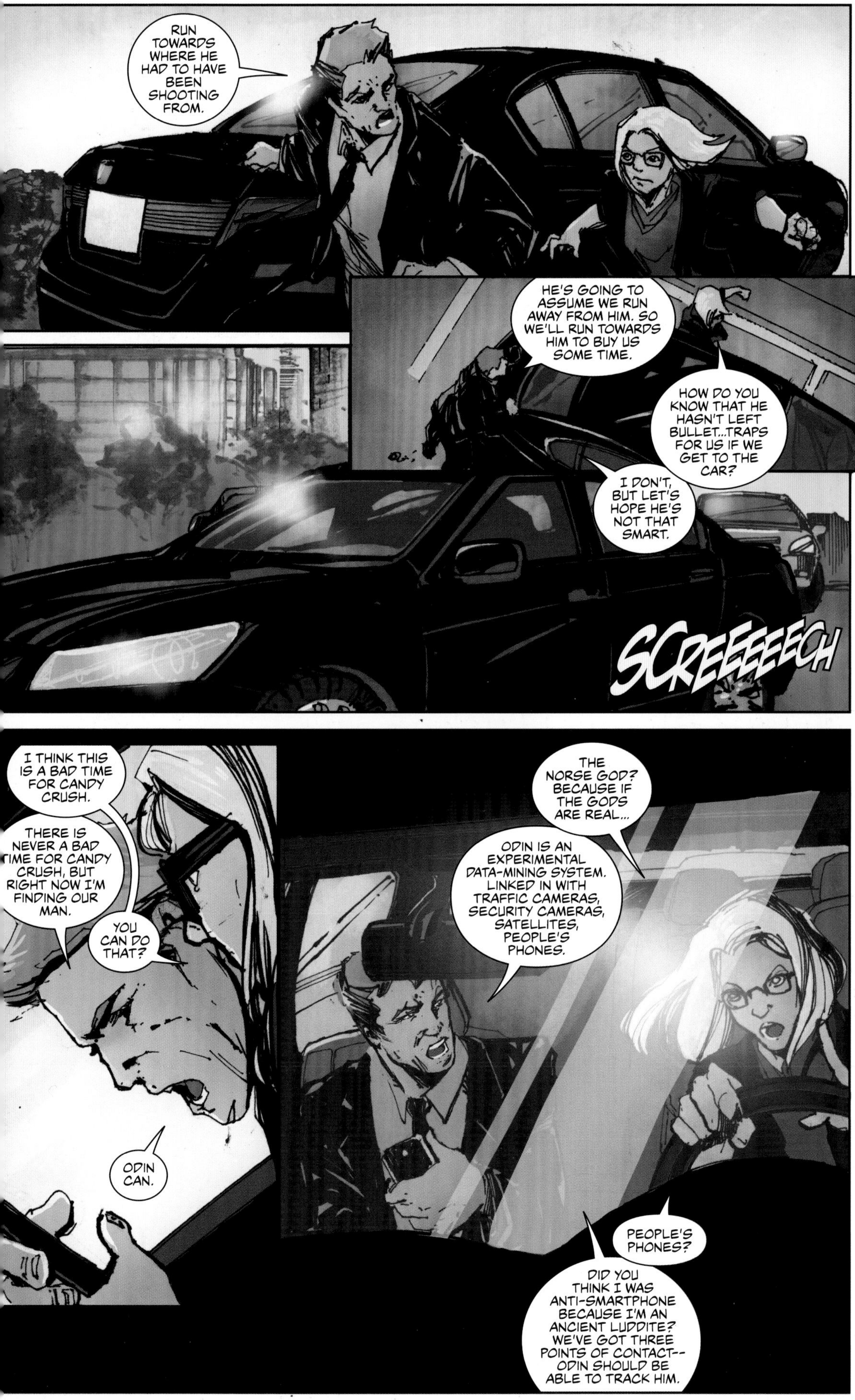
RUN TOWARDS WHERE HE HAD TO HAVE BEEN SHOOTING FROM.
HE'S GOING TO ASSUME WE RUN AWAY FROM HIM. SO WE'LL RUN TOWARDS HIM TO BUY US SOME TIME.
HOW DO YOU KNOW THAT HE HASN'T LEFT BULLET...TRAPS FOR US IF WE GET TO THE CAR?
I DON'T, BUT LET'S HOPE HE'S NOT THAT SMART.
SCREEEEEECH
I THINK THIS IS A BAD TIME FOR CANDY CRUSH.
THERE IS NEVER A BAD TIME FOR CANDY CRUSH, BUT RIGHT NOW I'M FINDING OUR MAN.
YOU CAN DO THAT?
ODIN CAN.
THE NORSE GOD? BECAUSE IF THE GODS ARE REAL...
ODIN IS AN EXPERIMENTAL DATA-MINING SYSTEM. LINKED IN WITH TRAFFIC CAMERAS, SECURITY CAMERAS, SATELLITES, PEOPLE'S PHONES.
PEOPLE'S PHONES?
DID YOU THINK I WAS ANTI-SMARTPHONE BECAUSE I'M AN ANCIENT LUDDITE? WE'VE GOT THREE POINTS OF CONTACT--ODIN SHOULD BE ABLE TO TRACK HIM.

"WITH JUST ONE, WE HAD TOO MUCH NOISE.

"BUT TWO IS A PATTERN.

"AND WE CAN FIND THE COMMONALITY.

"WHICH MEANS WE CAN FIND HIM.

SEARCHING...

"WHICH MEANS HE CAN'T HIDE.

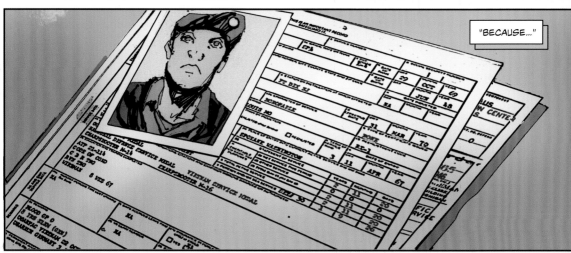

"BECAUSE..."

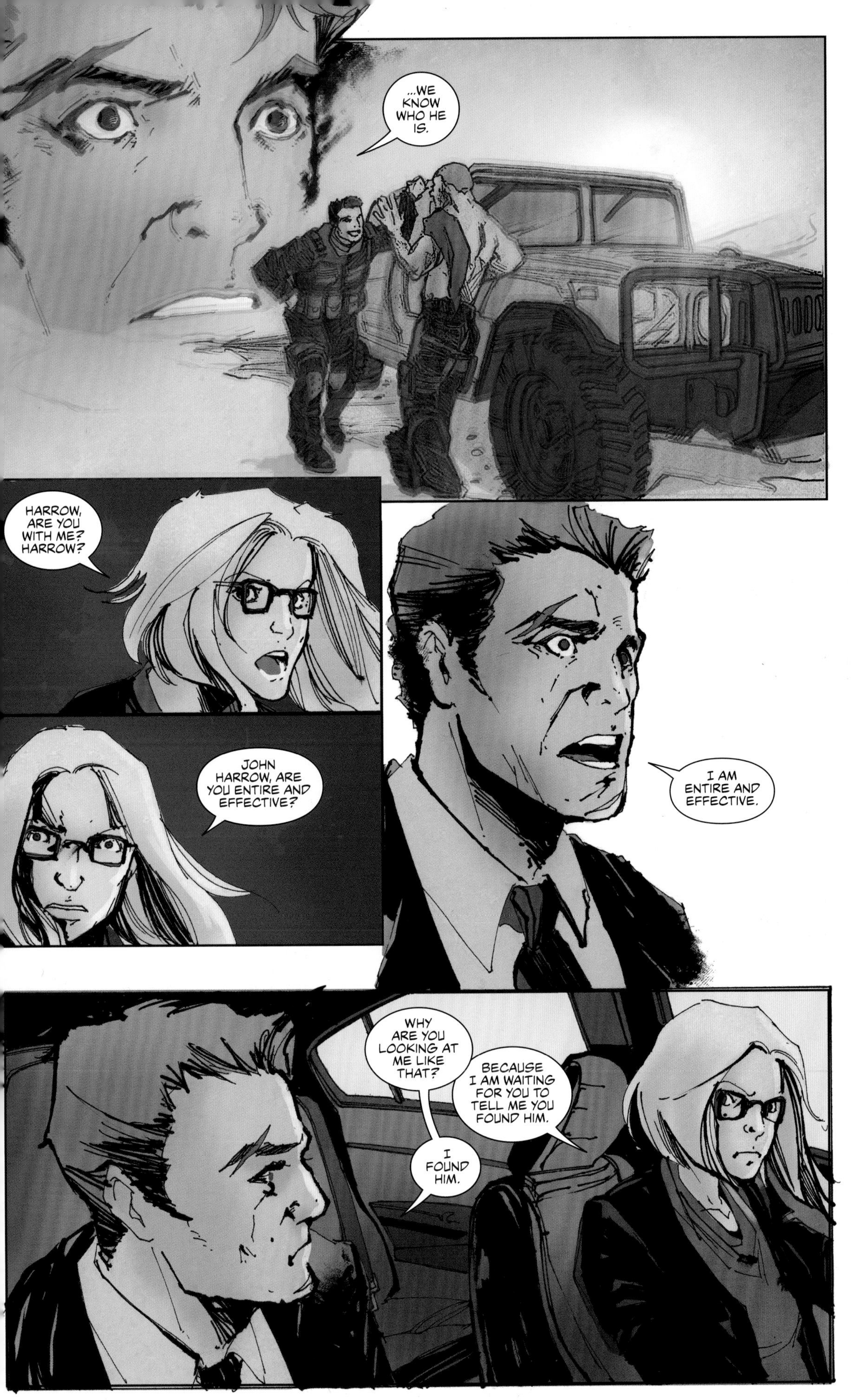
...WE KNOW WHO HE IS.
HARROW, ARE YOU WITH ME? HARROW?
JOHN HARROW, ARE YOU ENTIRE AND EFFECTIVE?
I AM ENTIRE AND EFFECTIVE.
WHY ARE YOU LOOKING AT ME LIKE THAT?
BECAUSE I AM WAITING FOR YOU TO TELL ME YOU FOUND HIM.
I FOUND HIM.

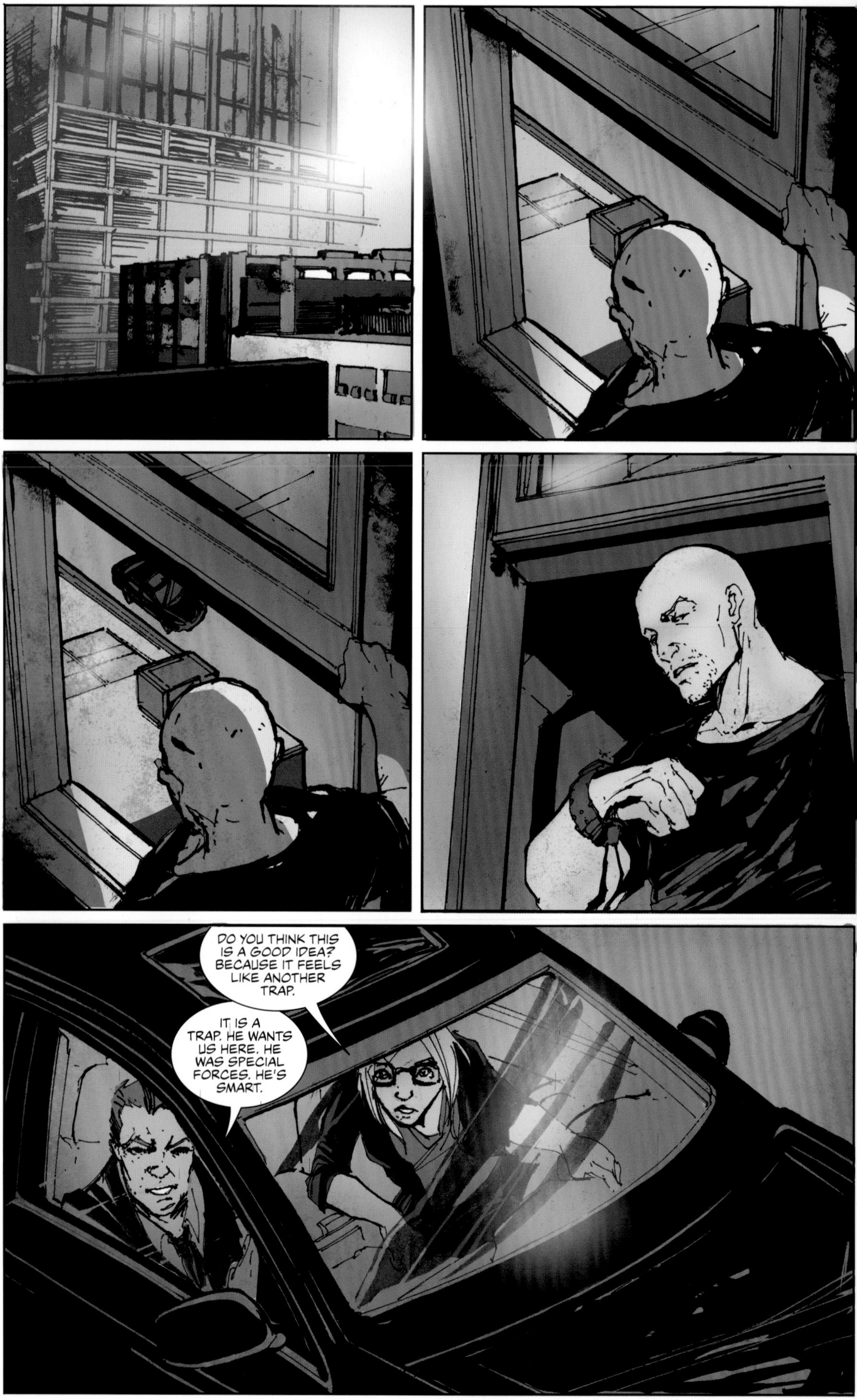
DO YOU THINK THIS IS A GOOD IDEA? BECAUSE IT FEELS LIKE ANOTHER TRAP.
IT IS A TRAP. HE WANTS US HERE. HE WAS SPECIAL FORCES. HE'S SMART.

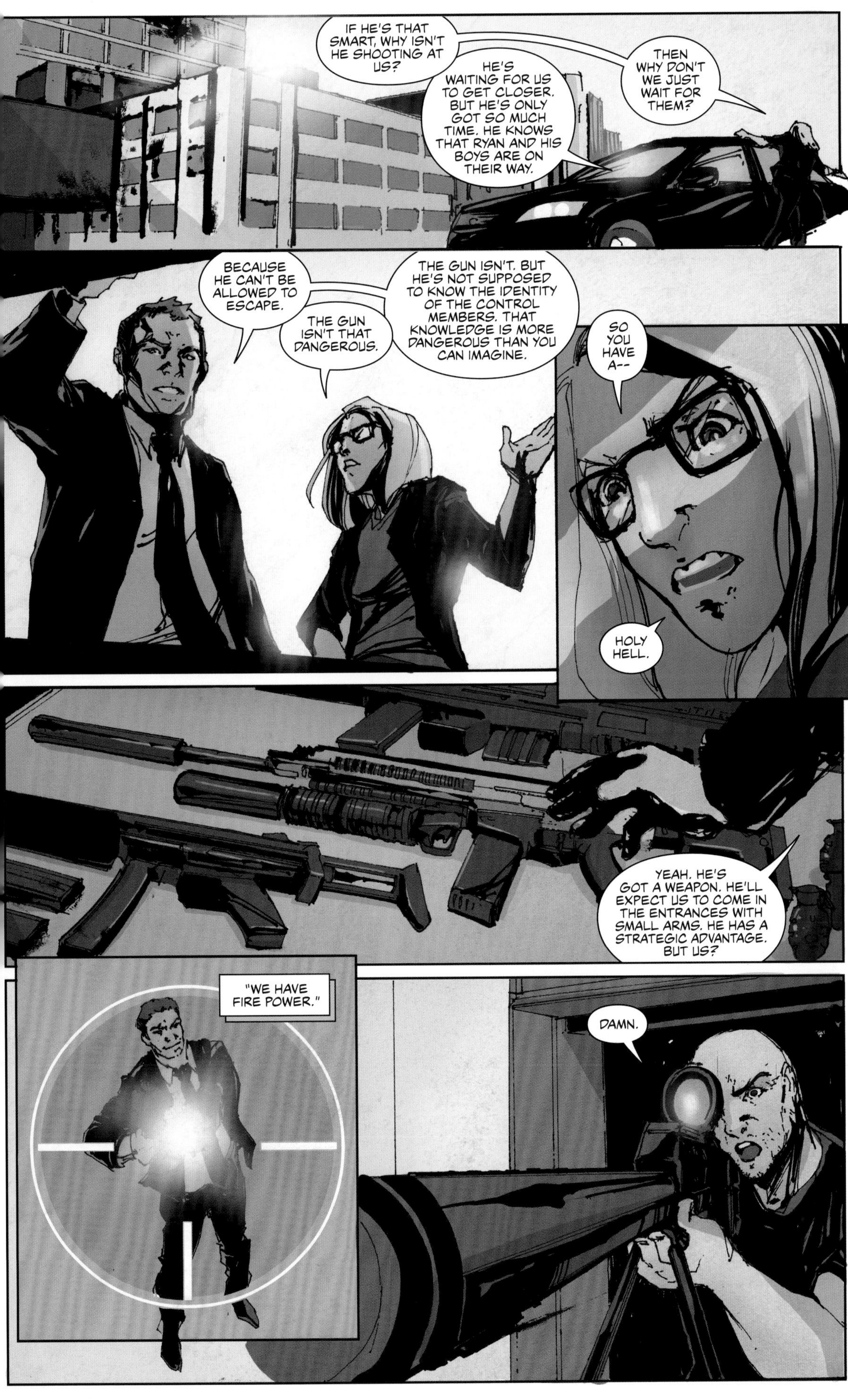
IF HE'S THAT SMART, WHY ISN'T HE SHOOTING AT US?
HE'S WAITING FOR US TO GET CLOSER. BUT HE'S ONLY GOT SO MUCH TIME. HE KNOWS THAT RYAN AND HIS BOYS ARE ON THEIR WAY.
THEN WHY DON'T WE JUST WAIT FOR THEM?
BECAUSE HE CAN'T BE ALLOWED TO ESCAPE.
THE GUN ISN'T THAT DANGEROUS.
THE GUN ISN'T. BUT HE'S NOT SUPPOSED TO KNOW THE IDENTITY OF THE CONTROL MEMBERS. THAT KNOWLEDGE IS MORE DANGEROUS THAN YOU CAN IMAGINE.
SO YOU HAVE A--
HOLY HELL.
YEAH. HE'S GOT A WEAPON. HE'LL EXPECT US TO COME IN THE ENTRANCES WITH SMALL ARMS. HE HAS A STRATEGIC ADVANTAGE. BUT US?
"WE HAVE FIRE POWER."
DAMN.

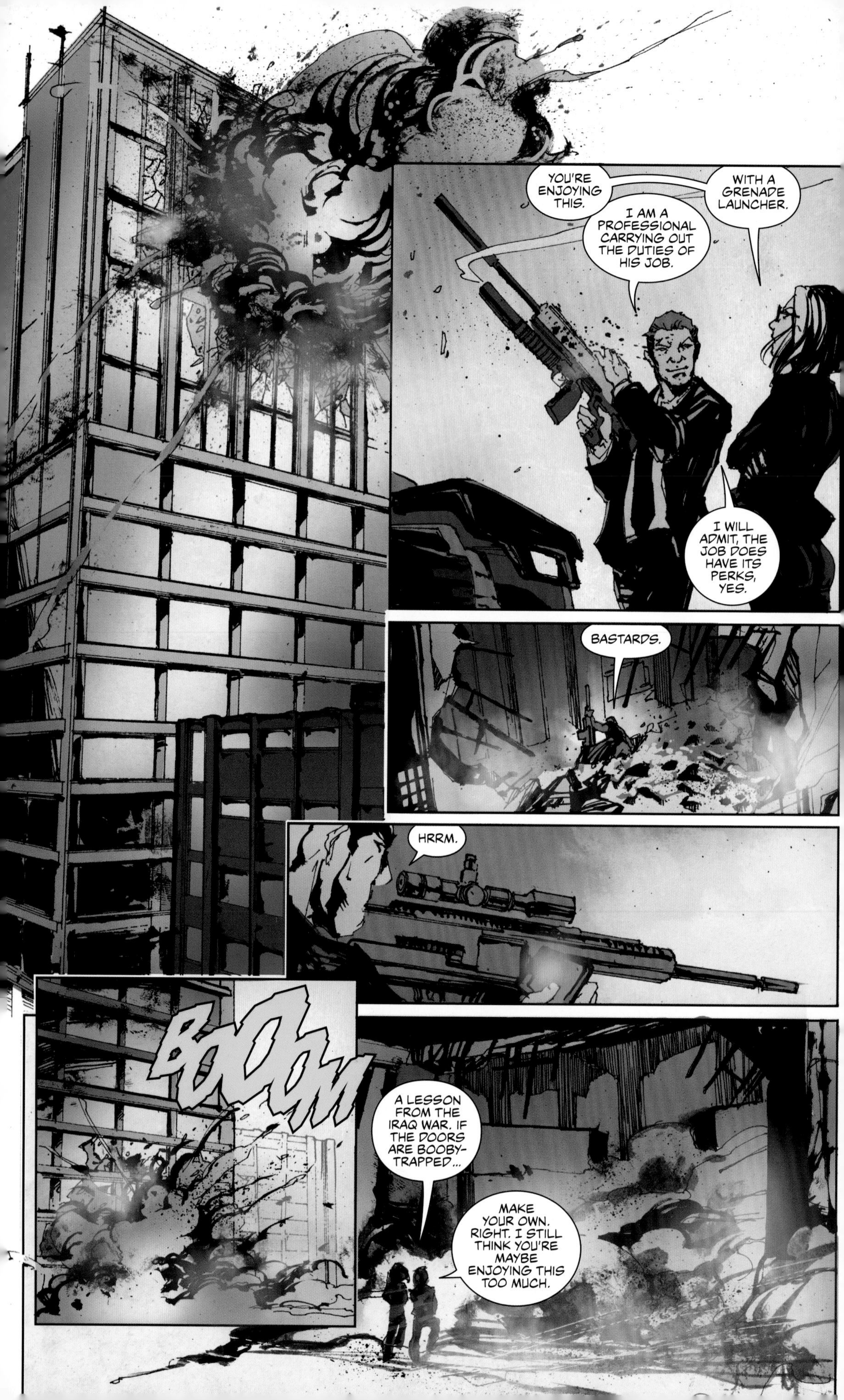
YOU'RE ENJOYING THIS.
I AM A PROFESSIONAL CARRYING OUT THE DUTIES OF HIS JOB.
WITH A GRENADE LAUNCHER.
I WILL ADMIT, THE JOB DOES HAVE ITS PERKS, YES.
BASTARDS.
HRRM.
BOOOM
A LESSON FROM THE IRAQ WAR. IF THE DOORS ARE BOOBY-TRAPPED...
MAKE YOUR OWN.
RIGHT. I STILL THINK YOU'RE MAYBE ENJOYING THIS TOO MUCH.

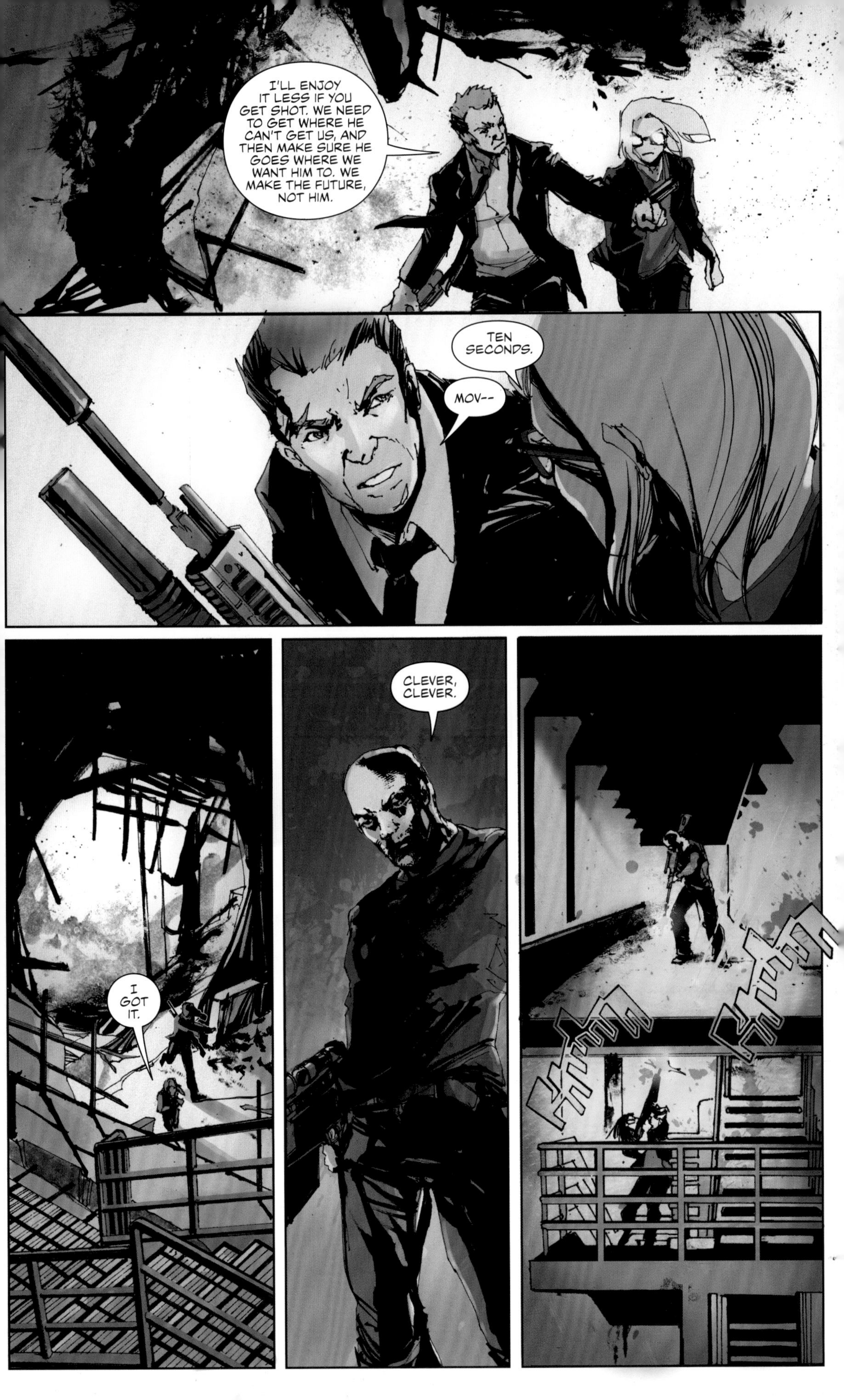
I'LL ENJOY IT LESS IF YOU GET SHOT. WE NEED TO GET WHERE HE CAN'T GET US, AND THEN MAKE SURE HE GOES WHERE WE WANT HIM TO. WE MAKE THE FUTURE, NOT HIM.
TEN SECONDS.
MOV--
I GOT IT.
CLEVER, CLEVER.

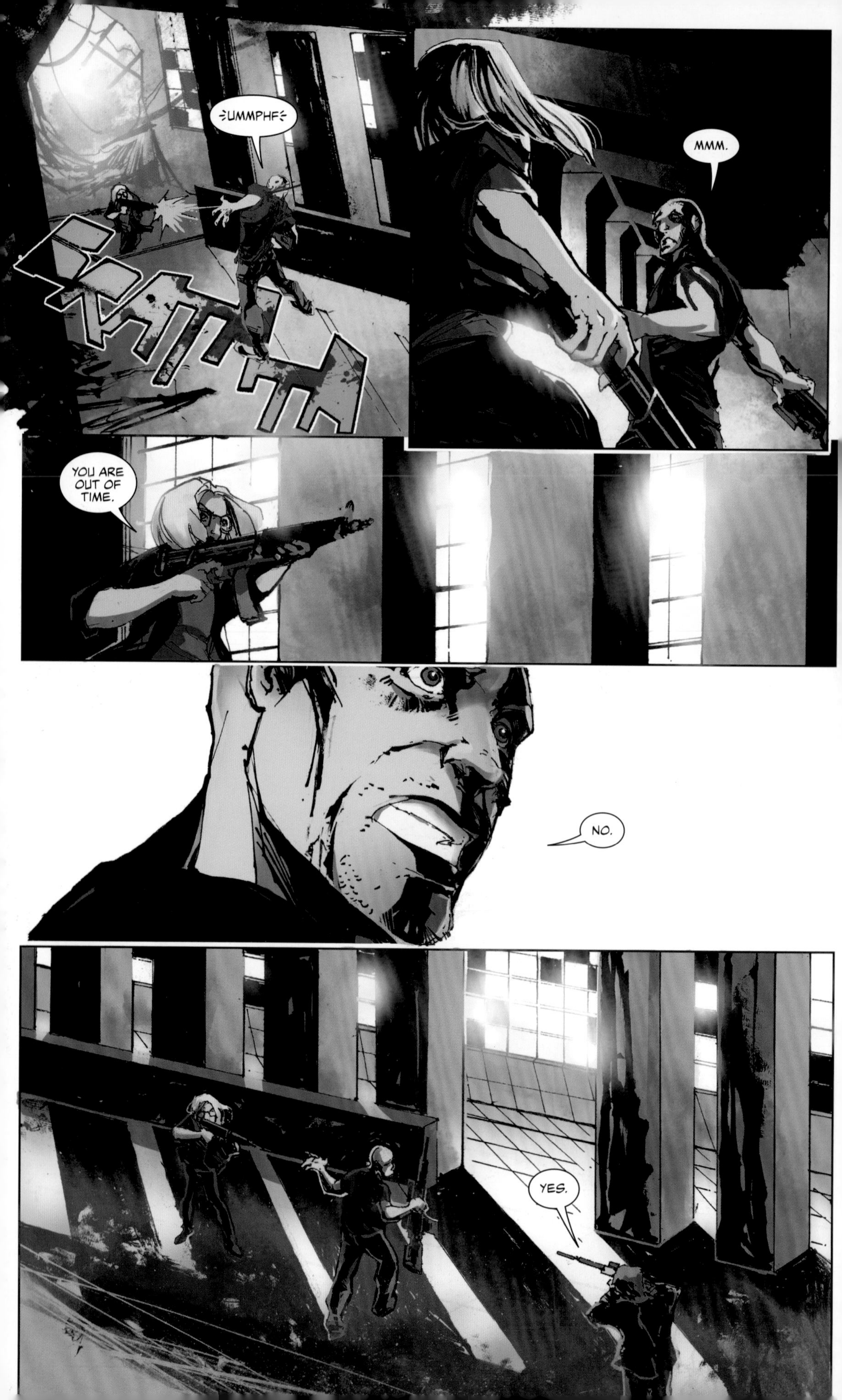

UMMPHF
SKLTCH
MMM.
YOU ARE OUT OF TIME.
NO.
YES.

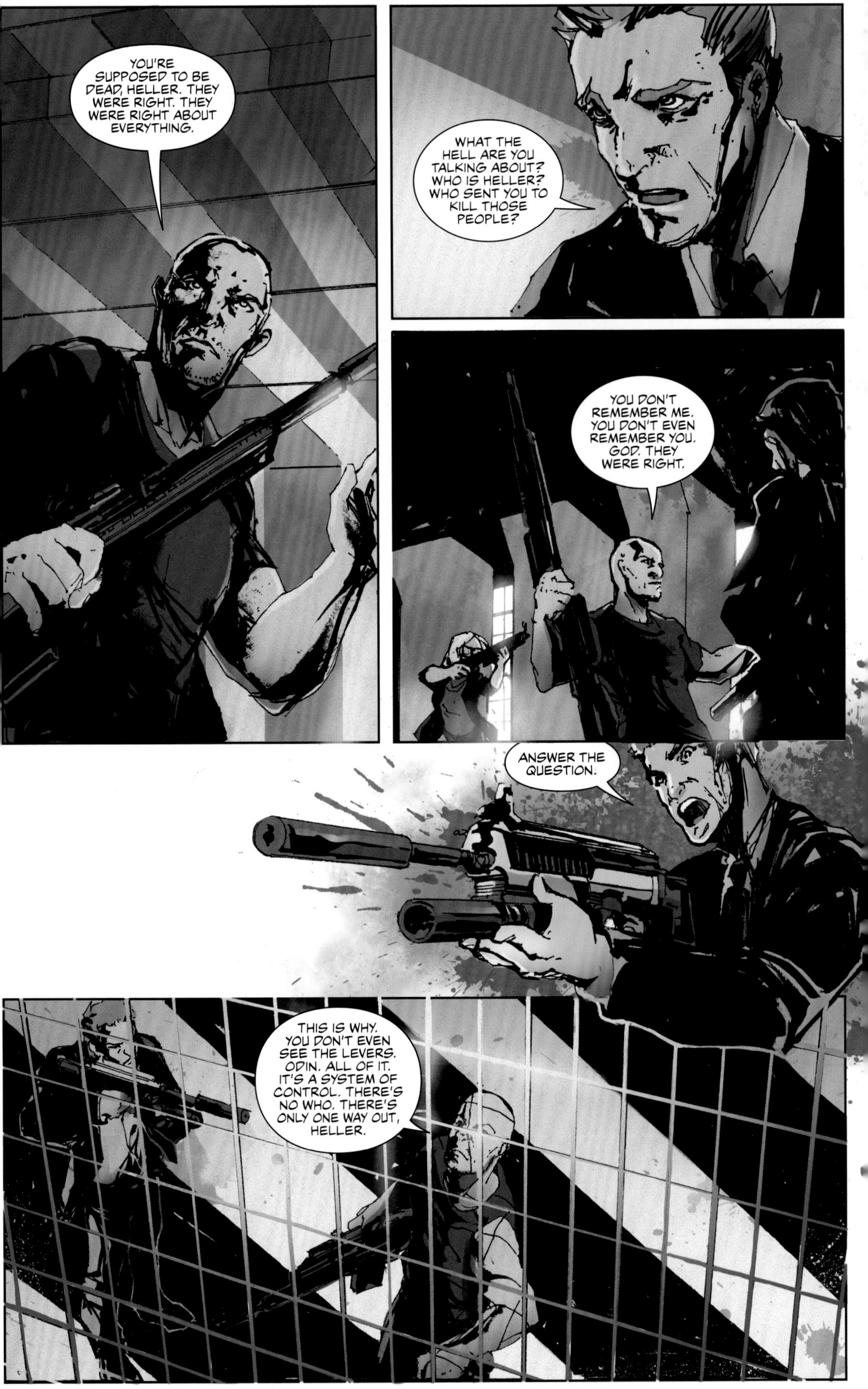
YOU'RE SUPPOSED TO BE DEAD, HELLER. THEY WERE RIGHT. THEY WERE RIGHT ABOUT EVERYTHING.
WHAT THE HELL ARE YOU TALKING ABOUT? WHO IS HELLER? WHO SENT YOU TO KILL THOSE PEOPLE?
YOU DON'T REMEMBER ME. YOU DON'T EVEN REMEMBER YOU. GOD. THEY WERE RIGHT.
ANSWER THE QUESTION.
THIS IS WHY. YOU DON'T EVEN SEE THE LEVERS. ODIN. ALL OF IT. IT'S A SYSTEM OF CONTROL. THERE'S NO WHO. THERE'S ONLY ONE WAY OUT, HELLER.

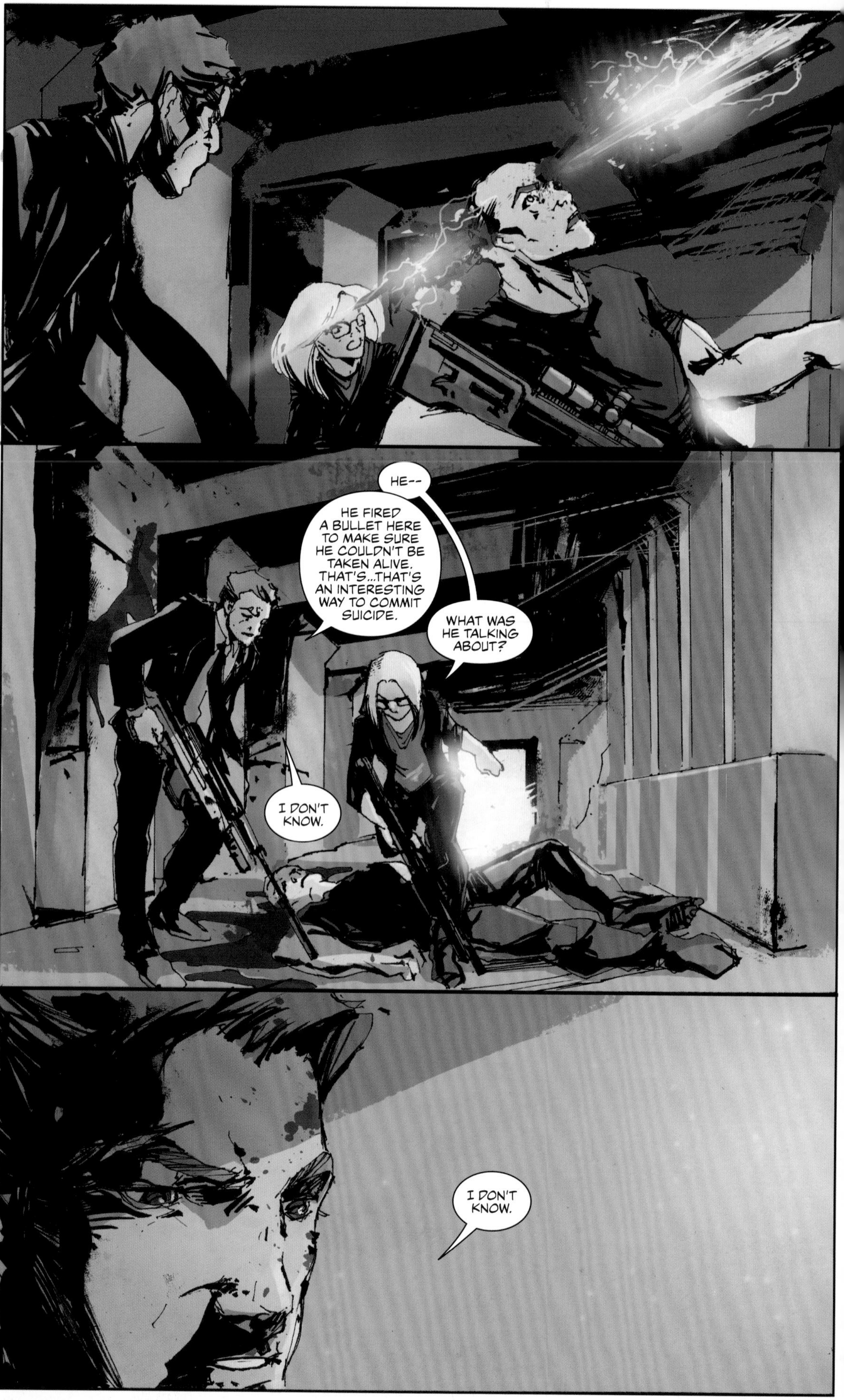
HE--
HE FIRED A BULLET HERE TO MAKE SURE HE COULDN'T BE TAKEN ALIVE. THAT'S...THAT'S AN INTERESTING WAY TO COMMIT SUICIDE.
WHAT WAS HE TALKING ABOUT?
I DON'T KNOW.
I DON'T KNOW.

CHAPTER SIX

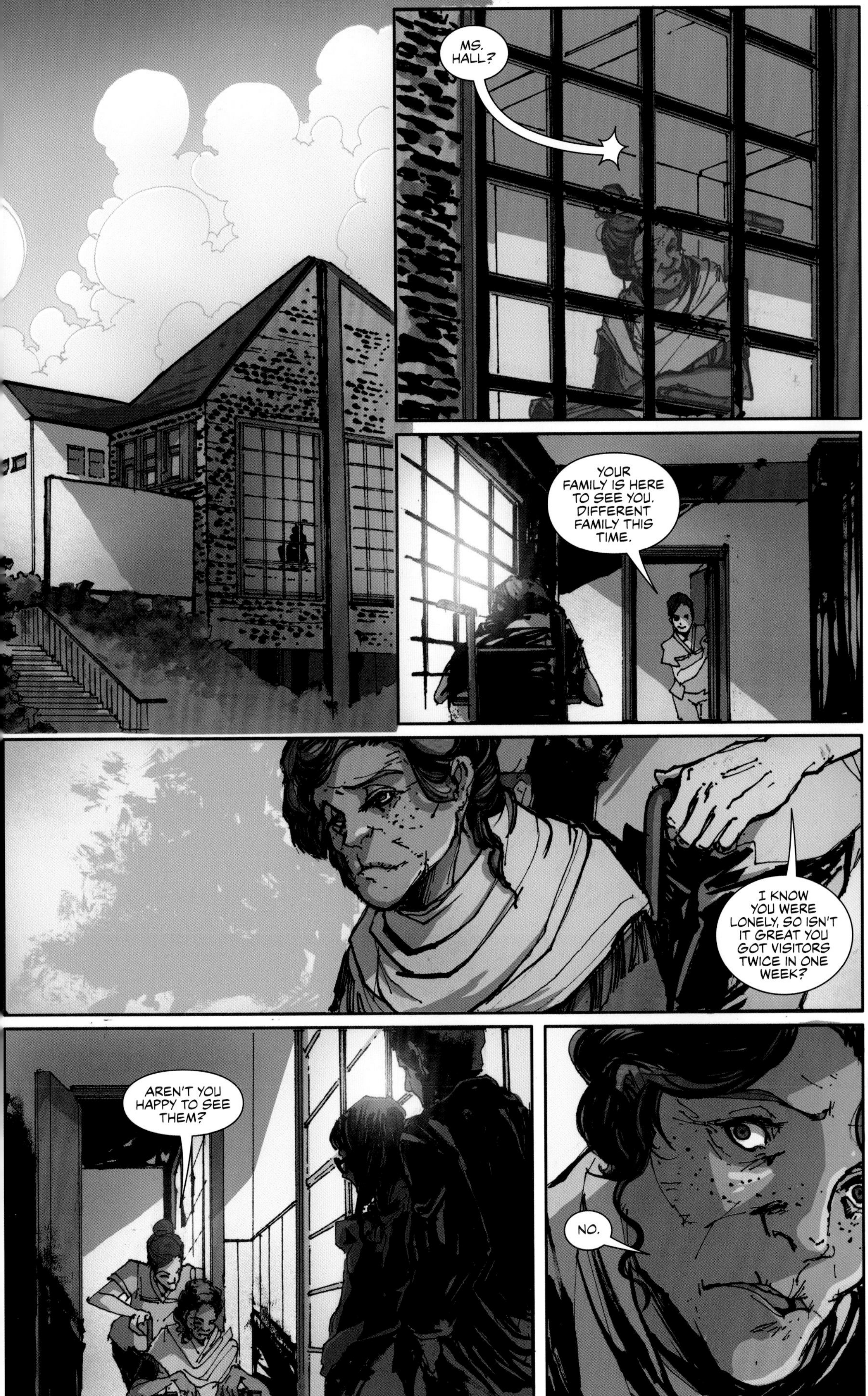
MS. HALL?
YOUR FAMILY IS HERE TO SEE YOU. DIFFERENT FAMILY THIS TIME.
I KNOW YOU WERE LONELY, SO ISN'T IT GREAT YOU GOT VISITORS TWICE IN ONE WEEK?
AREN'T YOU HAPPY TO SEE THEM?
NO.

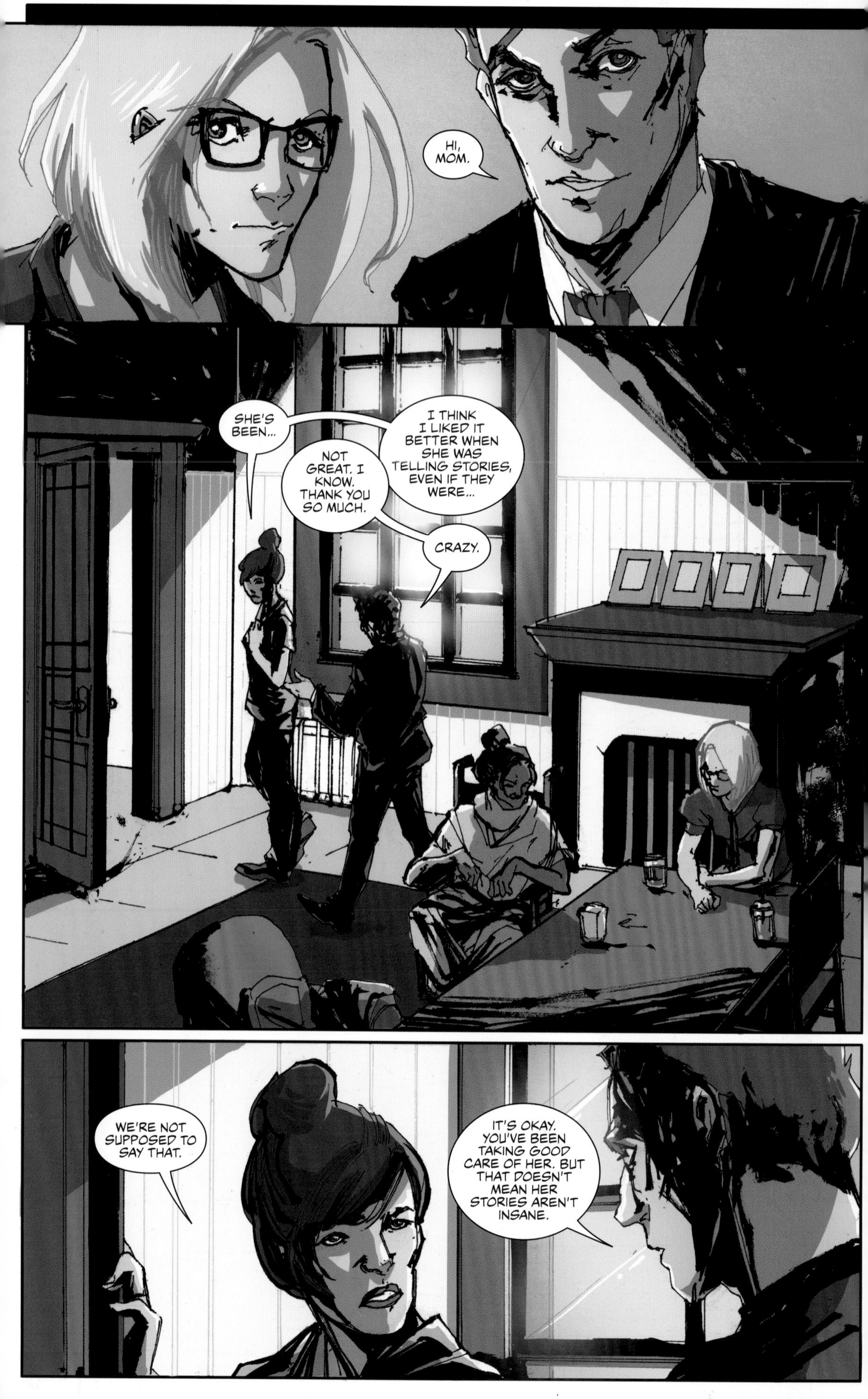
HI, MOM.
SHE'S BEEN...
I THINK I LIKED IT BETTER WHEN SHE WAS TELLING STORIES, EVEN IF THEY WERE...
NOT GREAT. I KNOW. THANK YOU SO MUCH.
CRAZY.
WE'RE NOT SUPPOSED TO SAY THAT.
IT'S OKAY. YOU'VE BEEN TAKING GOOD CARE OF HER. BUT THAT DOESN'T MEAN HER STORIES AREN'T INSANE.

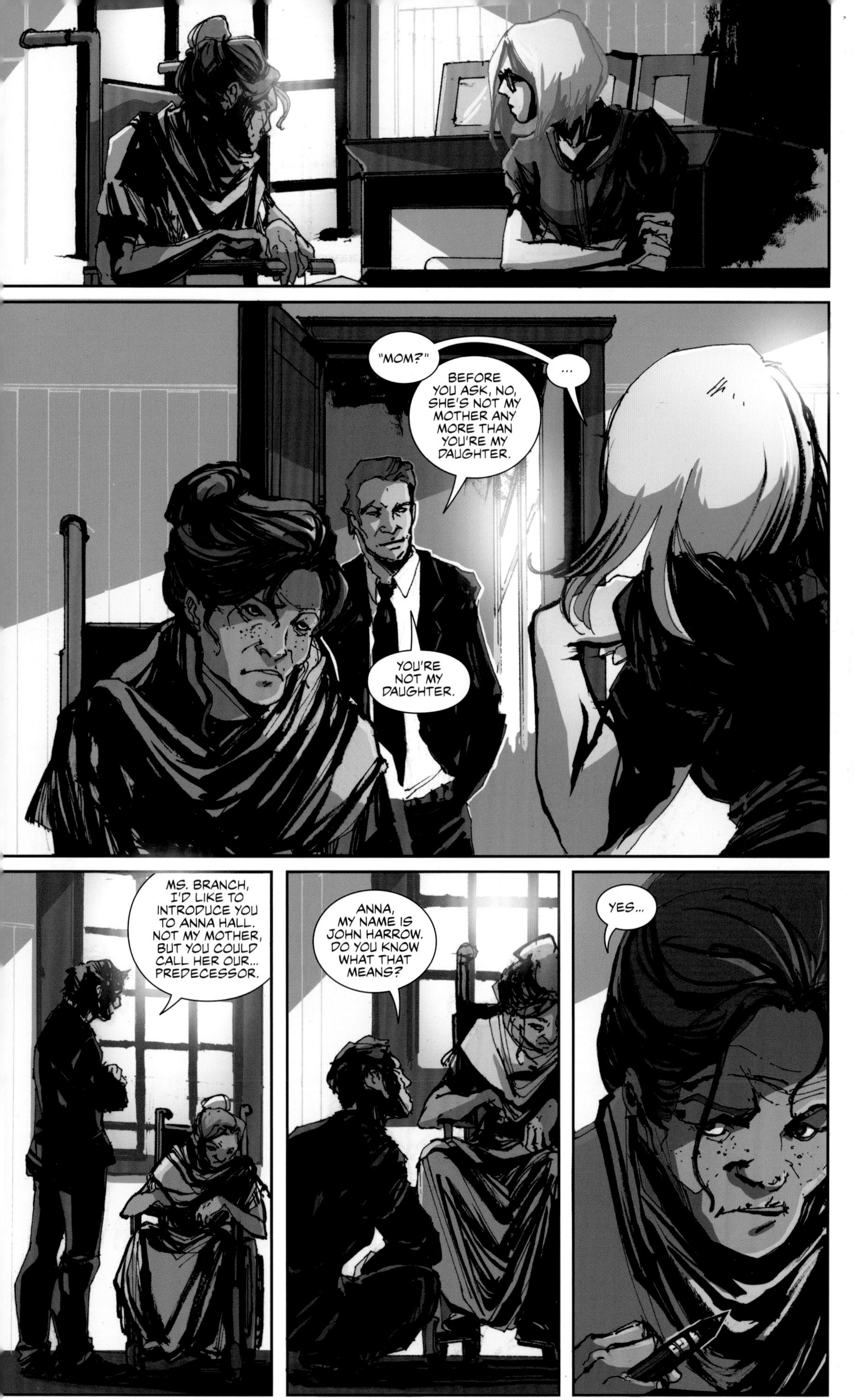
"MOM?"
...
BEFORE YOU ASK, NO, SHE'S NOT MY MOTHER ANY MORE THAN YOU'RE MY DAUGHTER.
YOU'RE NOT MY DAUGHTER.
MS. BRANCH, I'D LIKE TO INTRODUCE YOU TO ANNA HALL. NOT MY MOTHER, BUT YOU COULD CALL HER OUR... PREDECESSOR.
ANNA, MY NAME IS JOHN HARROW. DO YOU KNOW WHAT THAT MEANS?
YES...

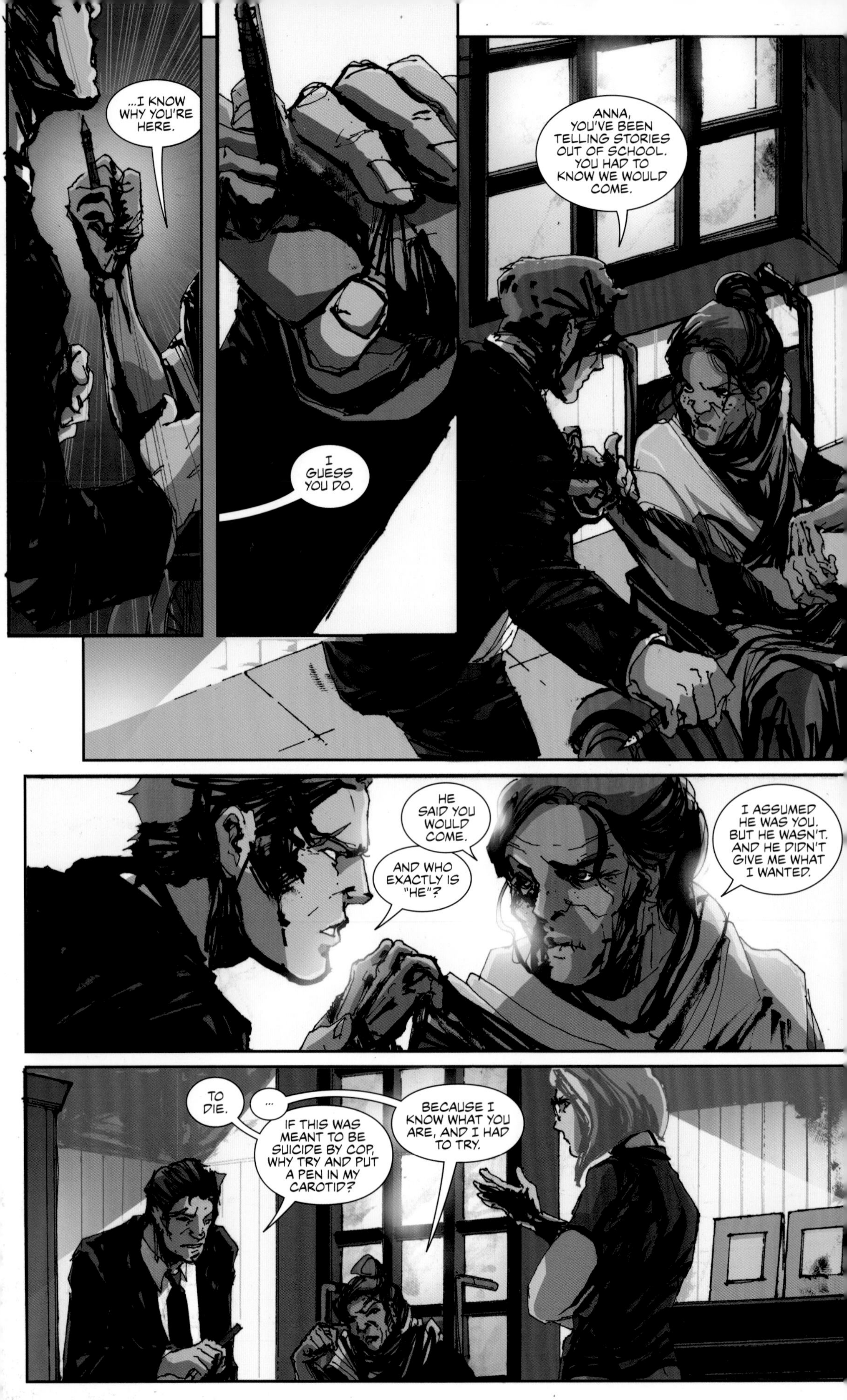
...I KNOW WHY YOU'RE HERE.
I GUESS YOU DO.
ANNA, YOU'VE BEEN TELLING STORIES OUT OF SCHOOL. YOU HAD TO KNOW WE WOULD COME.
HE SAID YOU WOULD COME.
AND WHO EXACTLY IS "HE"?
I ASSUMED HE WAS YOU. BUT HE WASN'T. AND HE DIDN'T GIVE ME WHAT I WANTED.
TO DIE.
...
IF THIS WAS MEANT TO BE SUICIDE BY COP, WHY TRY AND PUT A PEN IN MY CAROTID?
BECAUSE I KNOW WHAT YOU ARE, AND I HAD TO TRY.

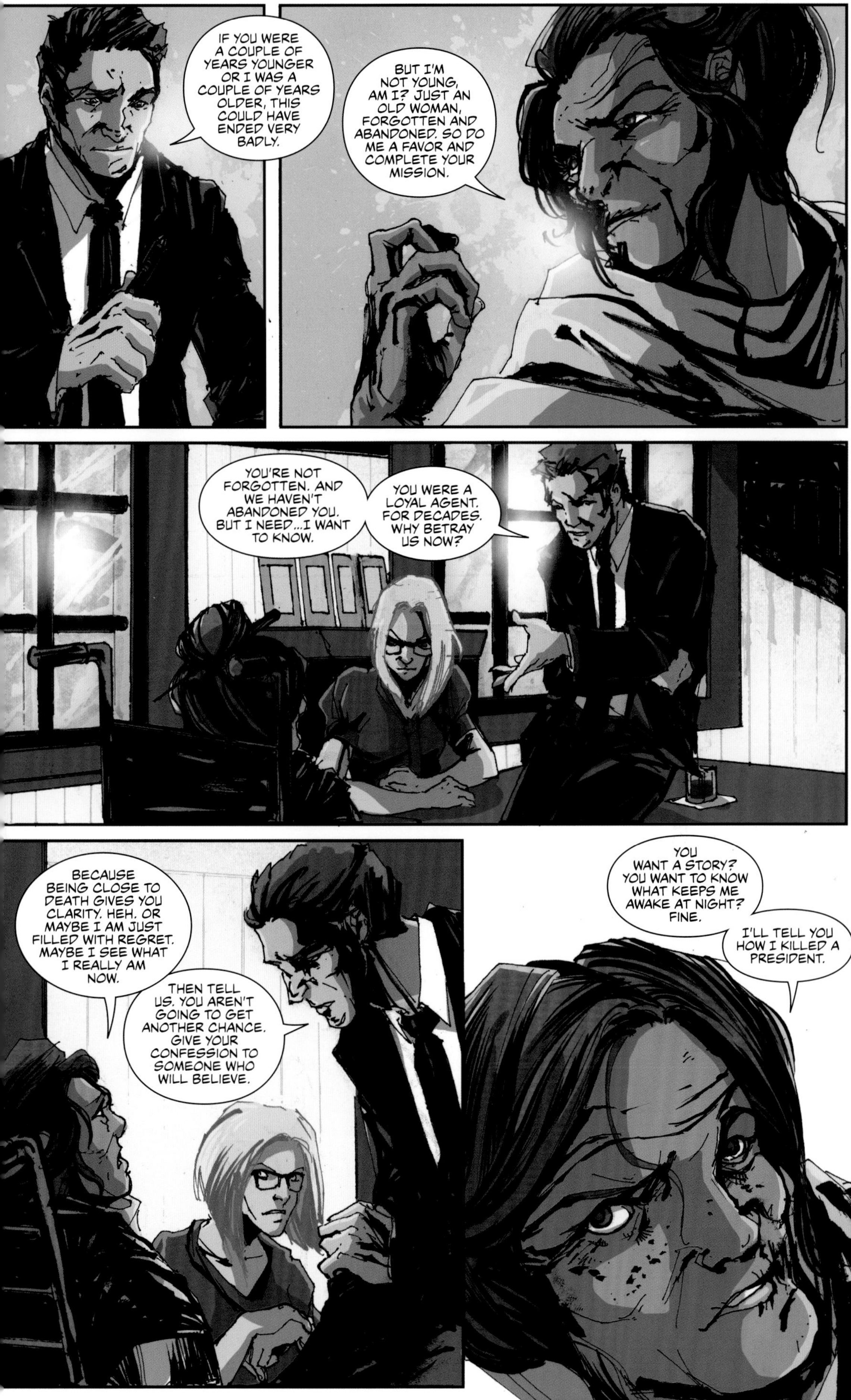
IF YOU WERE A COUPLE OF YEARS YOUNGER OR I WAS A COUPLE OF YEARS OLDER, THIS COULD HAVE ENDED VERY BADLY.
BUT I'M NOT YOUNG, AM I? JUST AN OLD WOMAN, FORGOTTEN AND ABANDONED. SO DO ME A FAVOR AND COMPLETE YOUR MISSION.
YOU'RE NOT FORGOTTEN. AND WE HAVEN'T ABANDONED YOU. BUT I NEED...I WANT TO KNOW.
YOU WERE A LOYAL AGENT. FOR DECADES. WHY BETRAY US NOW?
BECAUSE BEING CLOSE TO DEATH GIVES YOU CLARITY. HEH. OR MAYBE I AM JUST FILLED WITH REGRET. MAYBE I SEE WHAT I REALLY AM NOW.
THEN TELL US. YOU AREN'T GOING TO GET ANOTHER CHANCE. GIVE YOUR CONFESSION TO SOMEONE WHO WILL BELIEVE.
YOU WANT A STORY? YOU WANT TO KNOW WHAT KEEPS ME AWAKE AT NIGHT? FINE.
I'LL TELL YOU HOW I KILLED A PRESIDENT.

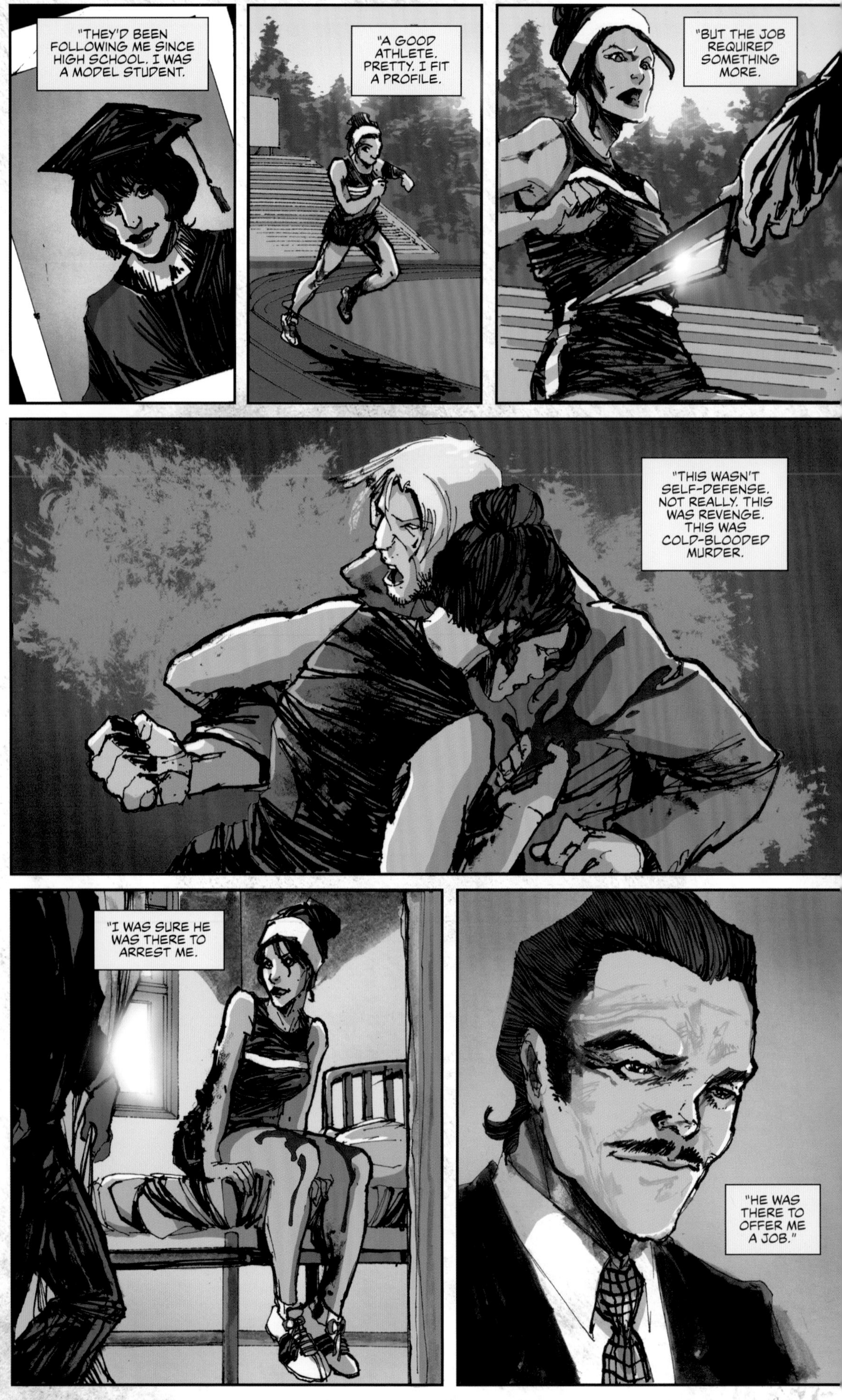
"THEY'D BEEN FOLLOWING ME SINCE HIGH SCHOOL. I WAS A MODEL STUDENT.
"A GOOD ATHLETE. PRETTY. I FIT A PROFILE.
"BUT THE JOB REQUIRED SOMETHING MORE.
"THIS WASN'T SELF-DEFENSE. NOT REALLY. THIS WAS REVENGE. THIS WAS COLD-BLOODED MURDER.
"I WAS SURE HE WAS THERE TO ARREST ME.
"HE WAS THERE TO OFFER ME A JOB."

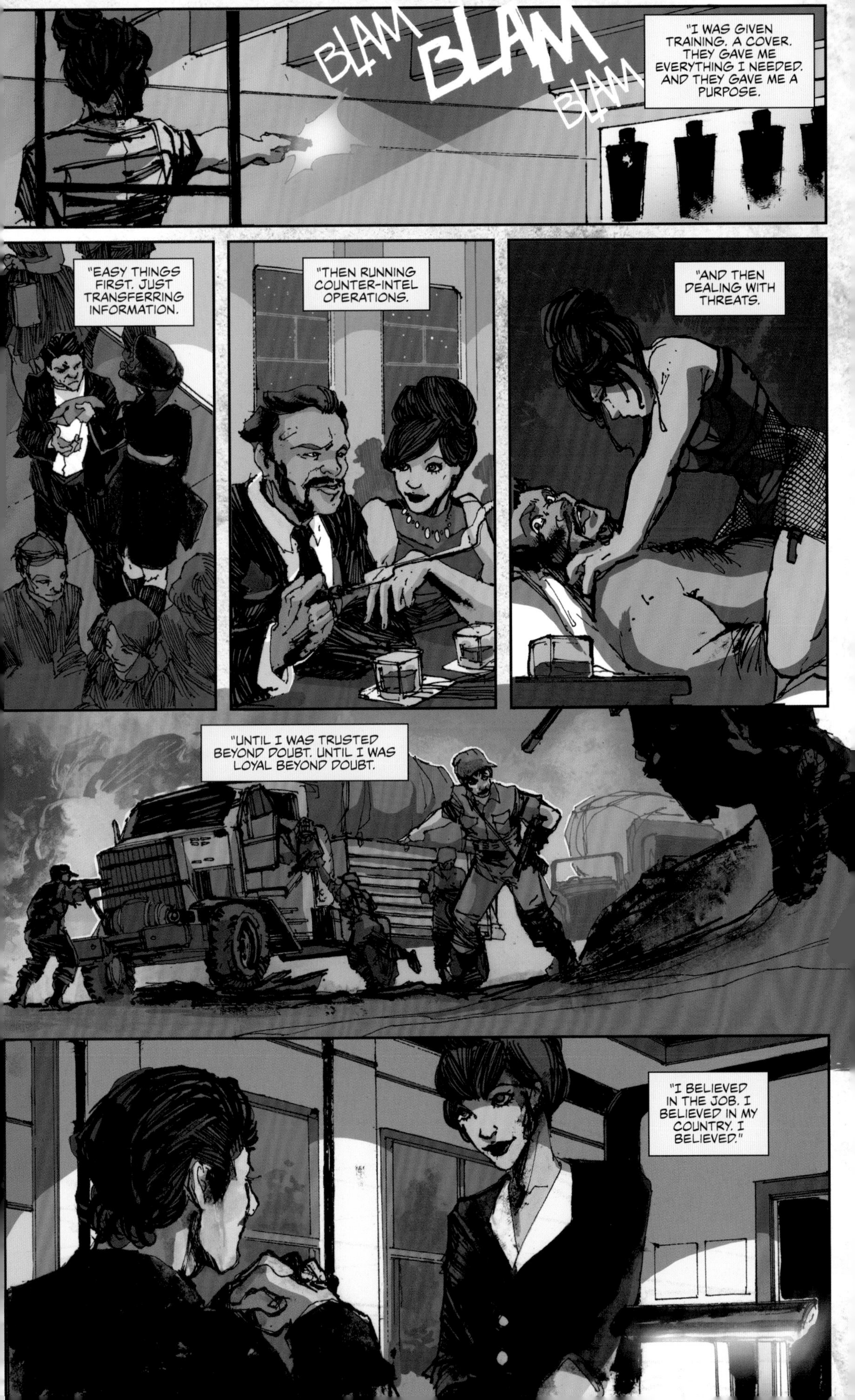
BLAM BLAM BLAM
"I WAS GIVEN TRAINING. A COVER. THEY GAVE ME EVERYTHING I NEEDED. AND THEY GAVE ME A PURPOSE.
"EASY THINGS FIRST. JUST TRANSFERRING INFORMATION.
"THEN RUNNING COUNTER-INTEL OPERATIONS.
"AND THEN DEALING WITH THREATS.
"UNTIL I WAS TRUSTED BEYOND DOUBT. UNTIL I WAS LOYAL BEYOND DOUBT.
"I BELIEVED IN THE JOB. I BELIEVED IN MY COUNTRY. I BELIEVED."

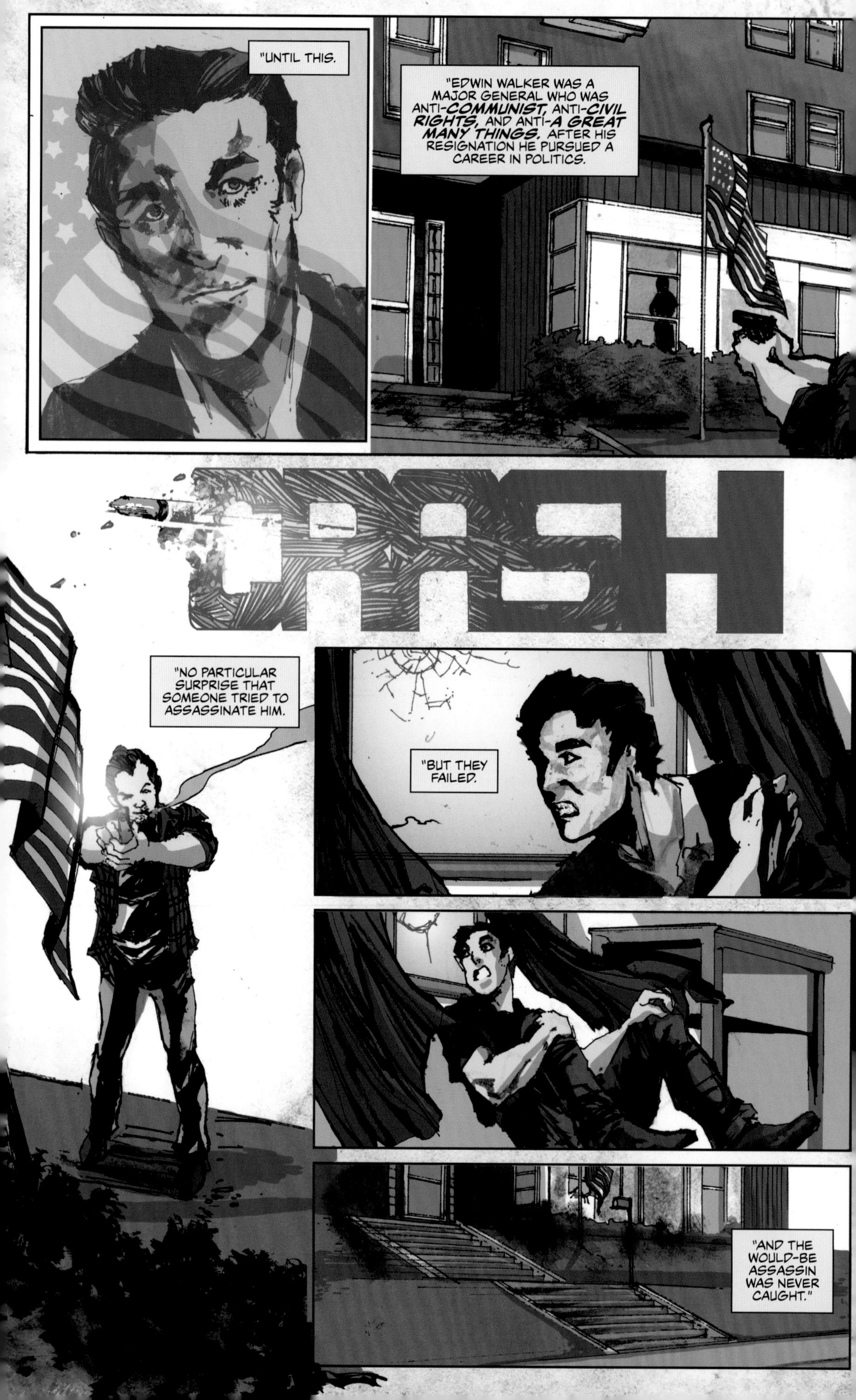

"UNTIL THIS.
"EDWIN WALKER WAS A MAJOR GENERAL WHO WAS ANTI-COMMUNIST, ANTI-CIVIL RIGHTS, AND ANTI-A GREAT MANY THINGS. AFTER HIS RESIGNATION HE PURSUED A CAREER IN POLITICS.
CRASH
"NO PARTICULAR SURPRISE THAT SOMEONE TRIED TO ASSASSINATE HIM.
"BUT THEY FAILED.
"AND THE WOULD-BE ASSASSIN WAS NEVER CAUGHT."

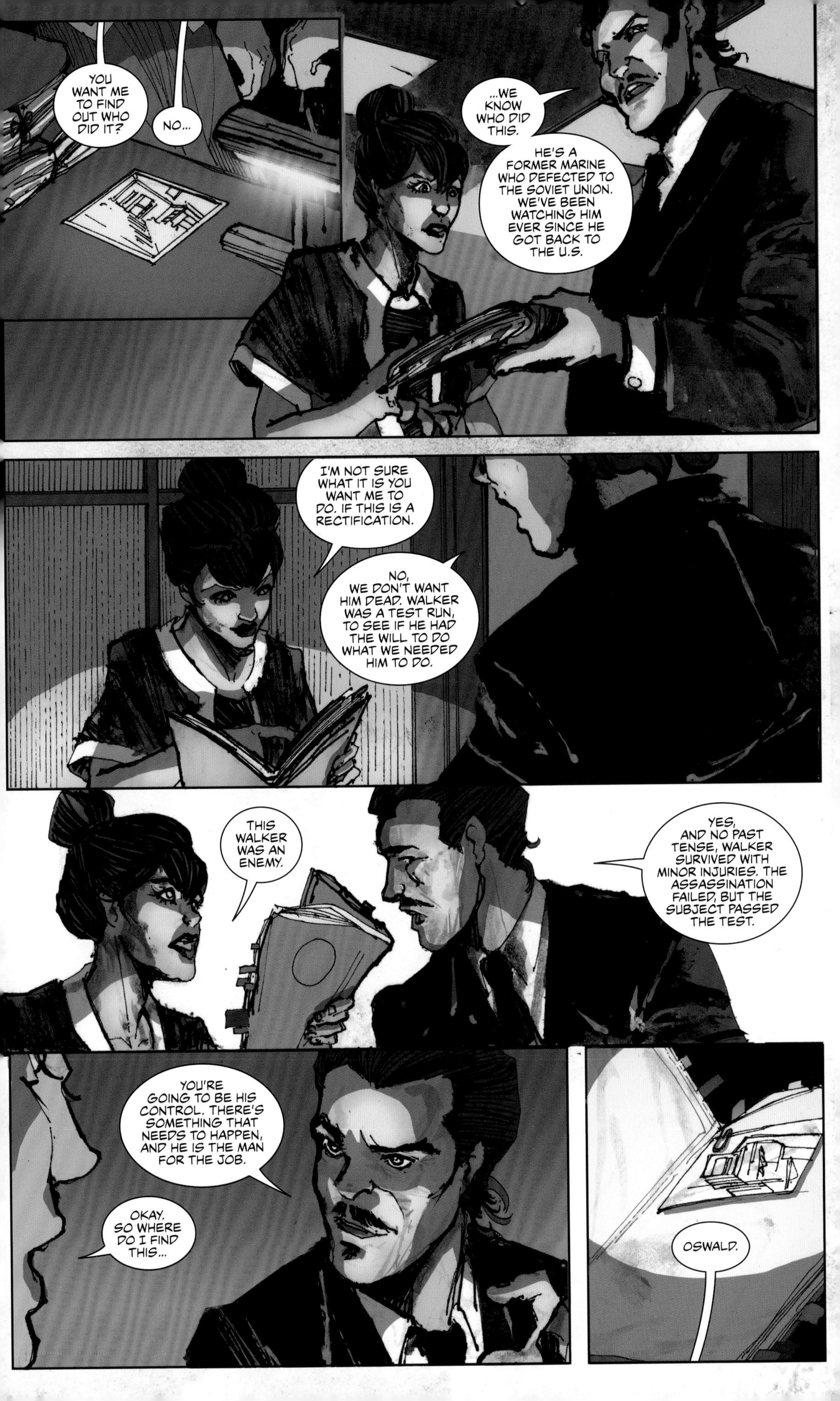

YOU WANT ME TO FIND OUT WHO DID IT?
NO...
...WE KNOW WHO DID THIS.
HE'S A FORMER MARINE WHO DEFECTED TO THE SOVIET UNION. WE'VE BEEN WATCHING HIM EVER SINCE HE GOT BACK TO THE U.S.
I'M NOT SURE WHAT IT IS YOU WANT ME TO DO. IF THIS IS A RECTIFICATION.
NO, WE DON'T WANT HIM DEAD. WALKER WAS A TEST RUN, TO SEE IF HE HAD THE WILL TO DO WHAT WE NEEDED HIM TO DO.
THIS WALKER WAS AN ENEMY.
YES, AND NO PAST TENSE, WALKER SURVIVED WITH MINOR INJURIES. THE ASSASSINATION FAILED, BUT THE SUBJECT PASSED THE TEST.
YOU'RE GOING TO BE HIS CONTROL. THERE'S SOMETHING THAT NEEDS TO HAPPEN, AND HE IS THE MAN FOR THE JOB.
OKAY. SO WHERE DO I FIND THIS...
OSWALD.

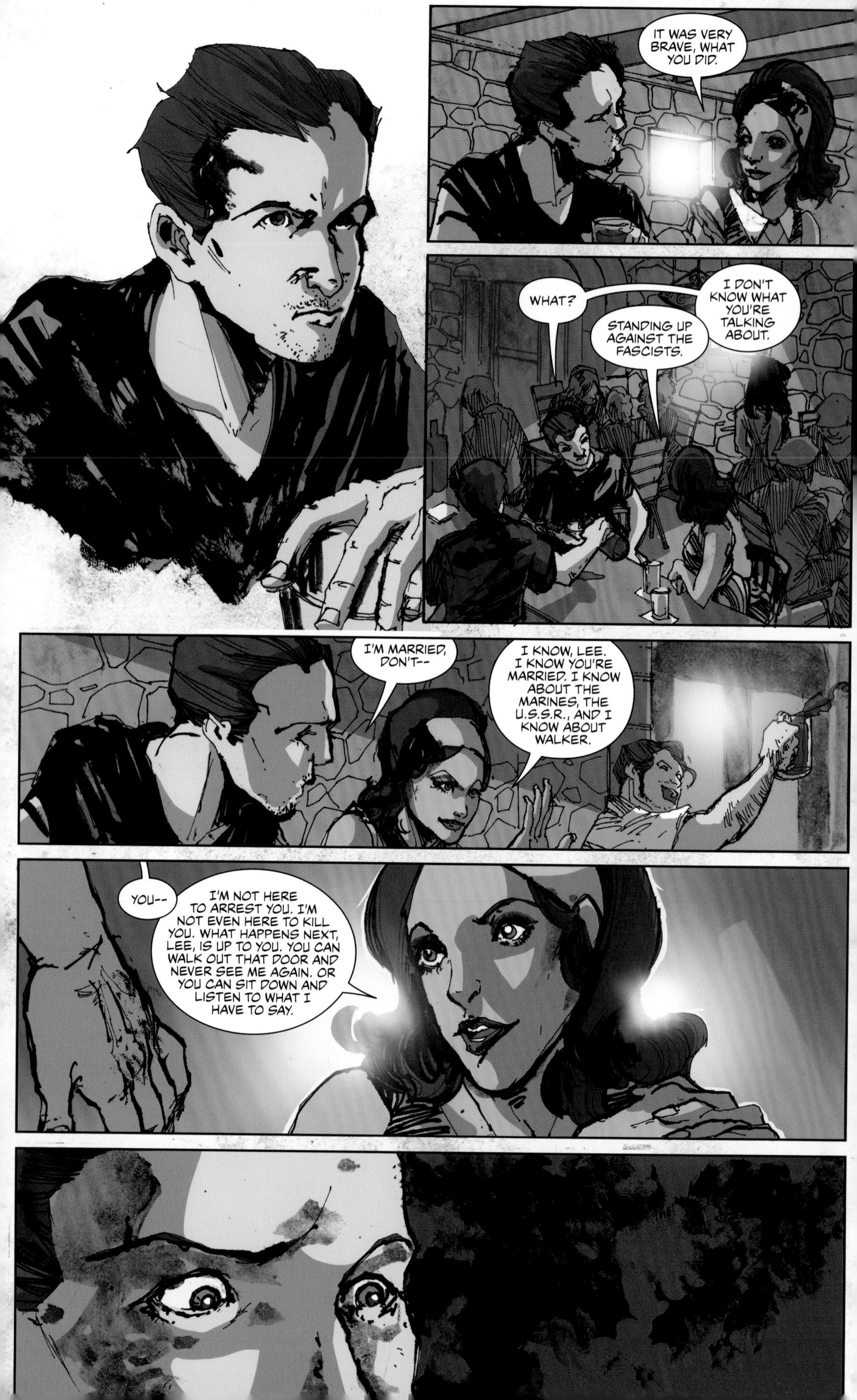
IT WAS VERY BRAVE, WHAT YOU DID.
WHAT?
STANDING UP AGAINST THE FASCISTS.
I DON'T KNOW WHAT YOU'RE TALKING ABOUT.
I'M MARRIED, DON'T--
I KNOW, LEE. I KNOW YOU'RE MARRIED. I KNOW ABOUT THE MARINES, THE U.S.S.R., AND I KNOW ABOUT WALKER.
YOU--
I'M NOT HERE TO ARREST YOU. I'M NOT EVEN HERE TO KILL YOU. WHAT HAPPENS NEXT, LEE, IS UP TO YOU. YOU CAN WALK OUT THAT DOOR AND NEVER SEE ME AGAIN. OR YOU CAN SIT DOWN AND LISTEN TO WHAT I HAVE TO SAY.

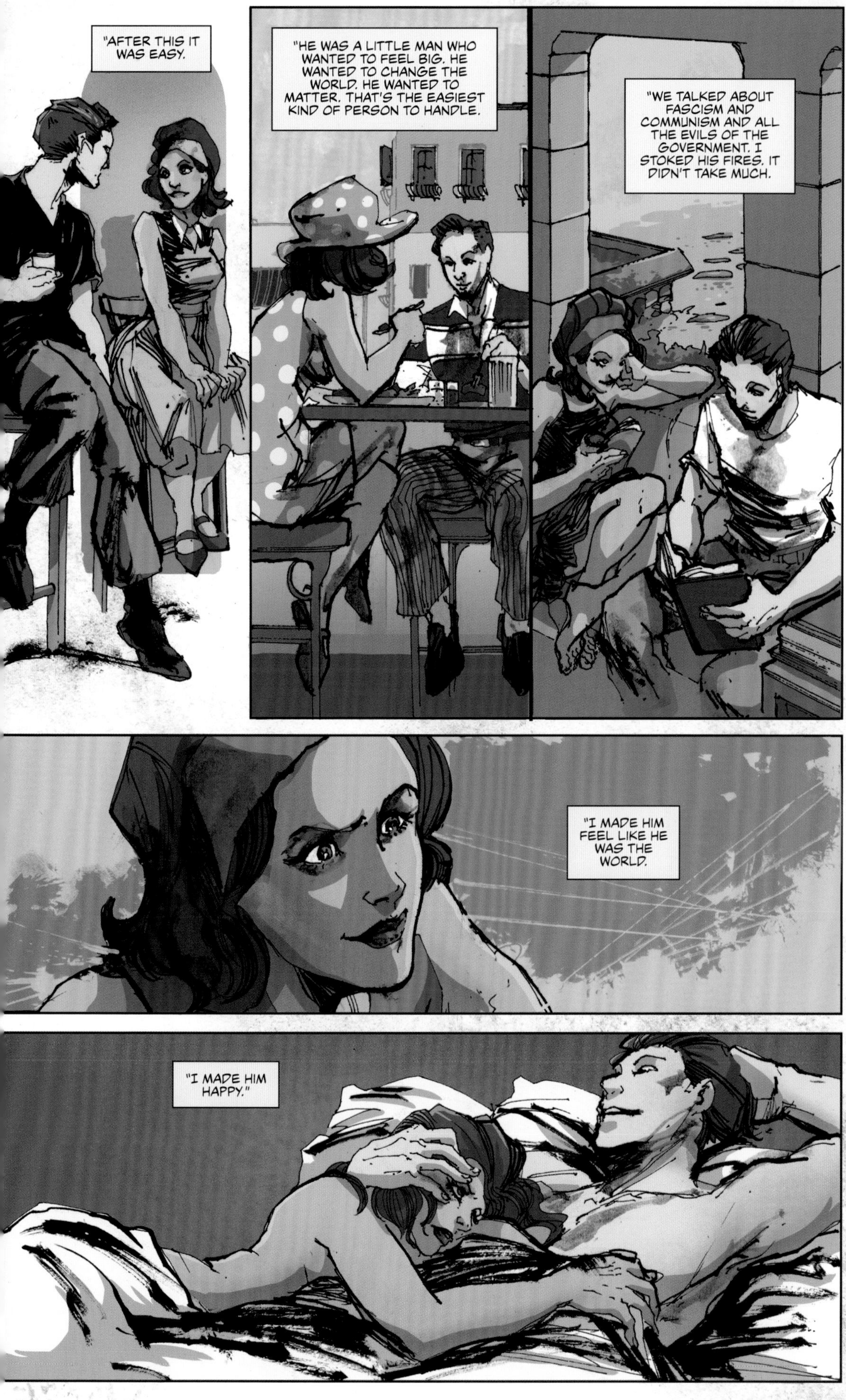
"AFTER THIS IT WAS EASY.
"HE WAS A LITTLE MAN WHO WANTED TO FEEL BIG. HE WANTED TO CHANGE THE WORLD. HE WANTED TO MATTER. THAT'S THE EASIEST KIND OF PERSON TO HANDLE.
"WE TALKED ABOUT FASCISM AND COMMUNISM AND ALL THE EVILS OF THE GOVERNMENT. I STOKED HIS FIRES. IT DIDN'T TAKE MUCH.
"I MADE HIM FEEL LIKE HE WAS THE WORLD.
"I MADE HIM HAPPY."

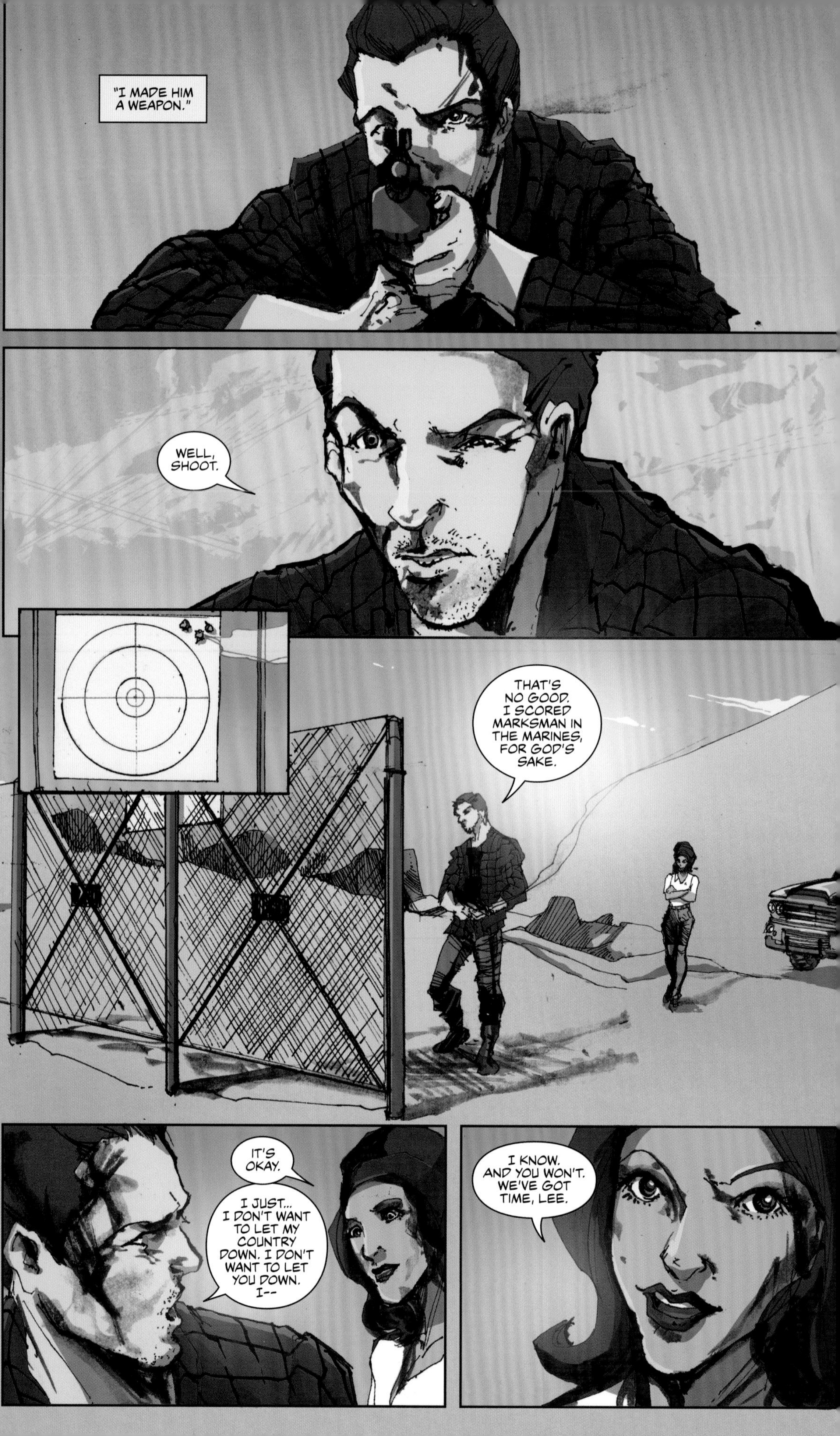
"I MADE HIM A WEAPON."
WELL, SHOOT.
THAT'S NO GOOD. I SCORED MARKSMAN IN THE MARINES, FOR GOD'S SAKE.
IT'S OKAY.
I JUST... I DON'T WANT TO LET MY COUNTRY DOWN. I DON'T WANT TO LET YOU DOWN. I--
I KNOW. AND YOU WON'T. WE'VE GOT TIME, LEE.

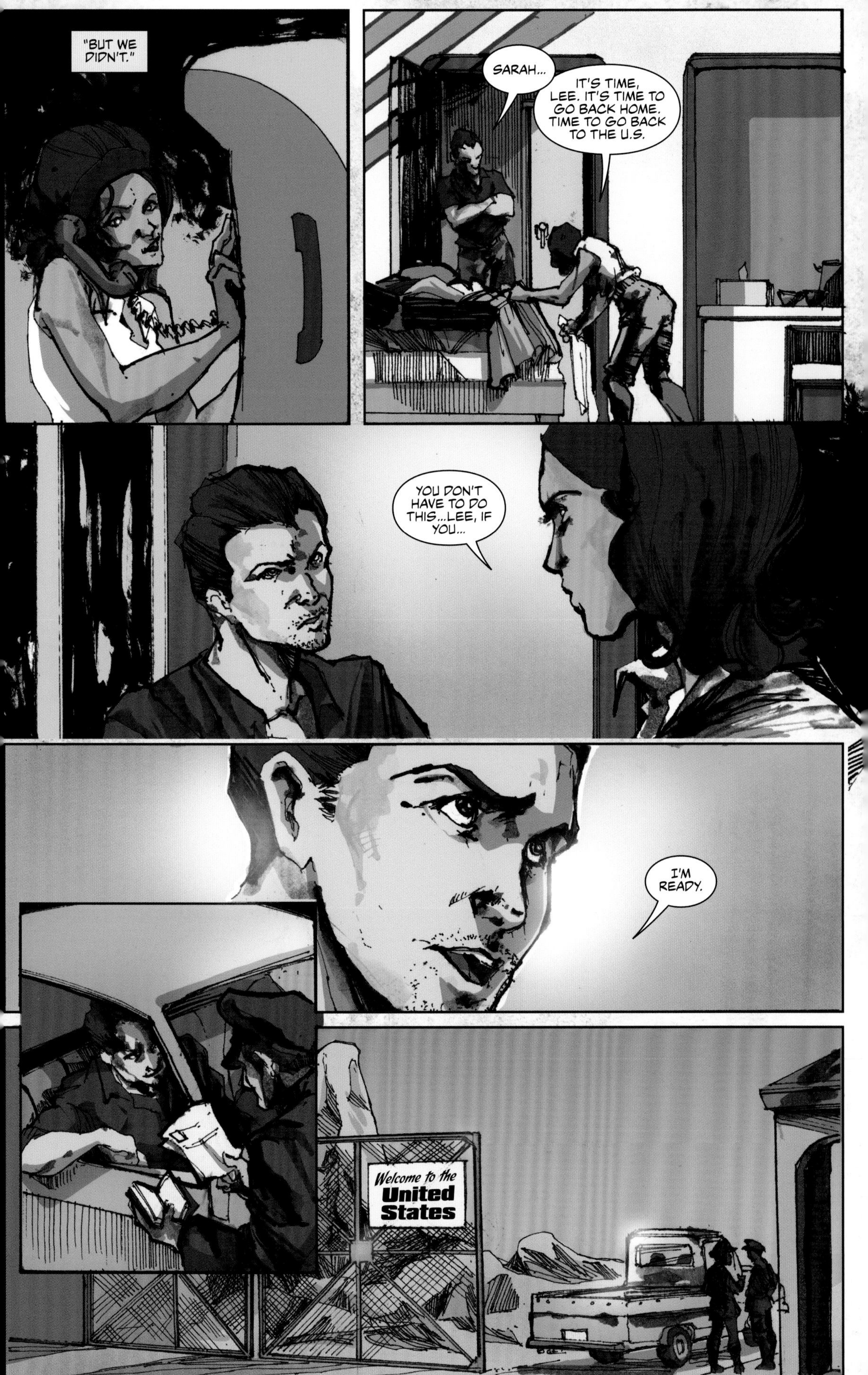
"BUT WE DIDN'T."
SARAH...
IT'S TIME, LEE. IT'S TIME TO GO BACK HOME. TIME TO GO BACK TO THE U.S.
YOU DON'T HAVE TO DO THIS...LEE, IF YOU...
I'M READY.
Welcome to the United States

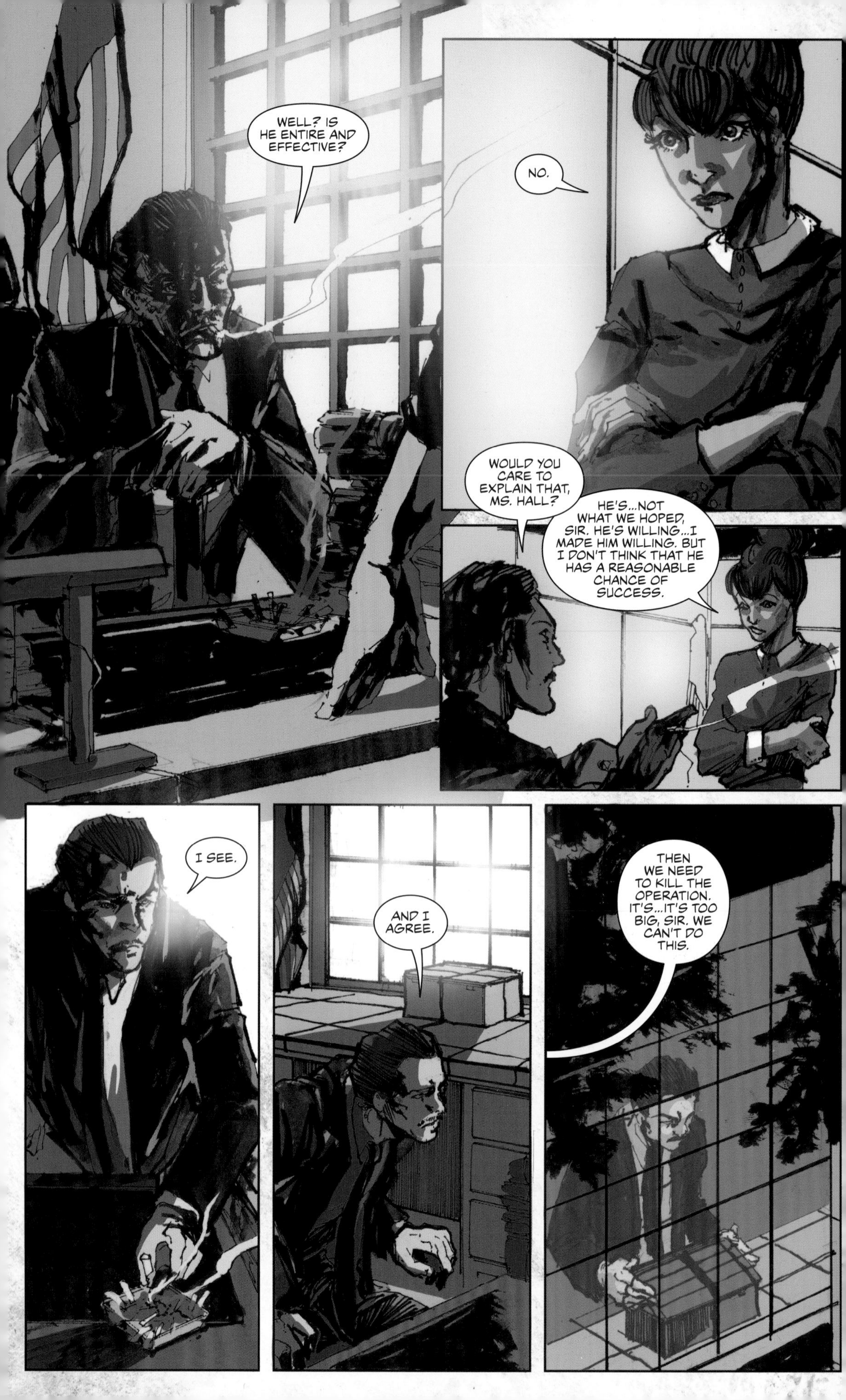
WELL? IS HE ENTIRE AND EFFECTIVE?
NO.
WOULD YOU CARE TO EXPLAIN THAT, MS. HALL?
HE'S...NOT WHAT WE HOPED, SIR. HE'S WILLING...I MADE HIM WILLING. BUT I DON'T THINK THAT HE HAS A REASONABLE CHANCE OF SUCCESS.
I SEE.
AND I AGREE.
THEN WE NEED TO KILL THE OPERATION. IT'S...IT'S TOO BIG, SIR. WE CAN'T DO THIS.

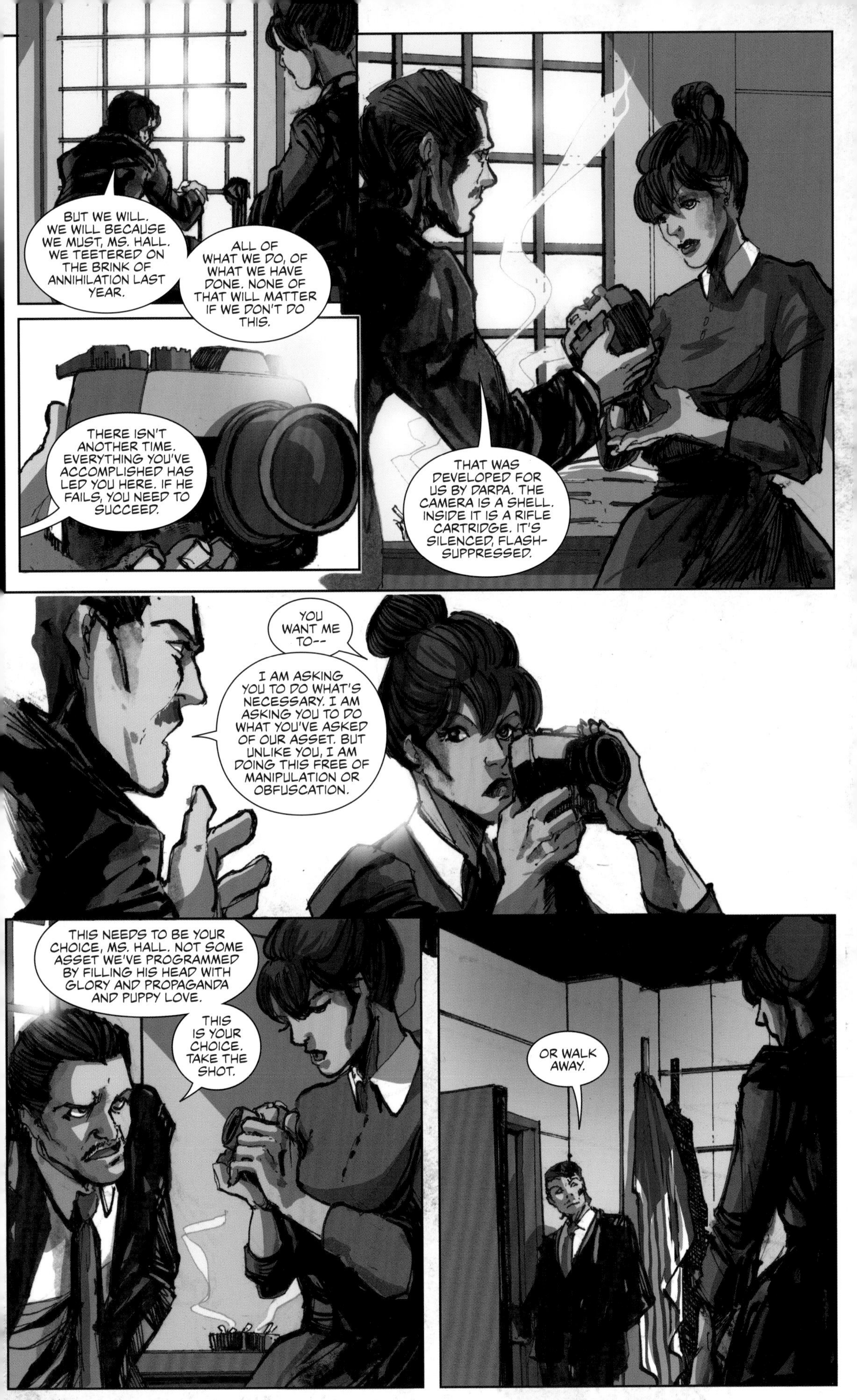
BUT WE WILL. WE WILL BECAUSE WE MUST, MS. HALL. WE TEETERED ON THE BRINK OF ANNIHILATION LAST YEAR.
ALL OF WHAT WE DO, OF WHAT WE HAVE DONE. NONE OF THAT WILL MATTER IF WE DON'T DO THIS.
THERE ISN'T ANOTHER TIME. EVERYTHING YOU'VE ACCOMPLISHED HAS LED YOU HERE. IF HE FAILS, YOU NEED TO SUCCEED.
THAT WAS DEVELOPED FOR US BY DARPA. THE CAMERA IS A SHELL. INSIDE IT IS A RIFLE CARTRIDGE. IT'S SILENCED, FLASH-SUPPRESSED.
YOU WANT ME TO--
I AM ASKING YOU TO DO WHAT'S NECESSARY. I AM ASKING YOU TO DO WHAT YOU'VE ASKED OF OUR ASSET. BUT UNLIKE YOU, I AM DOING THIS FREE OF MANIPULATION OR OBFUSCATION.
THIS NEEDS TO BE YOUR CHOICE, MS. HALL. NOT SOME ASSET WE'VE PROGRAMMED BY FILLING HIS HEAD WITH GLORY AND PROPAGANDA AND PUPPY LOVE.
THIS IS YOUR CHOICE. TAKE THE SHOT.
OR WALK AWAY.

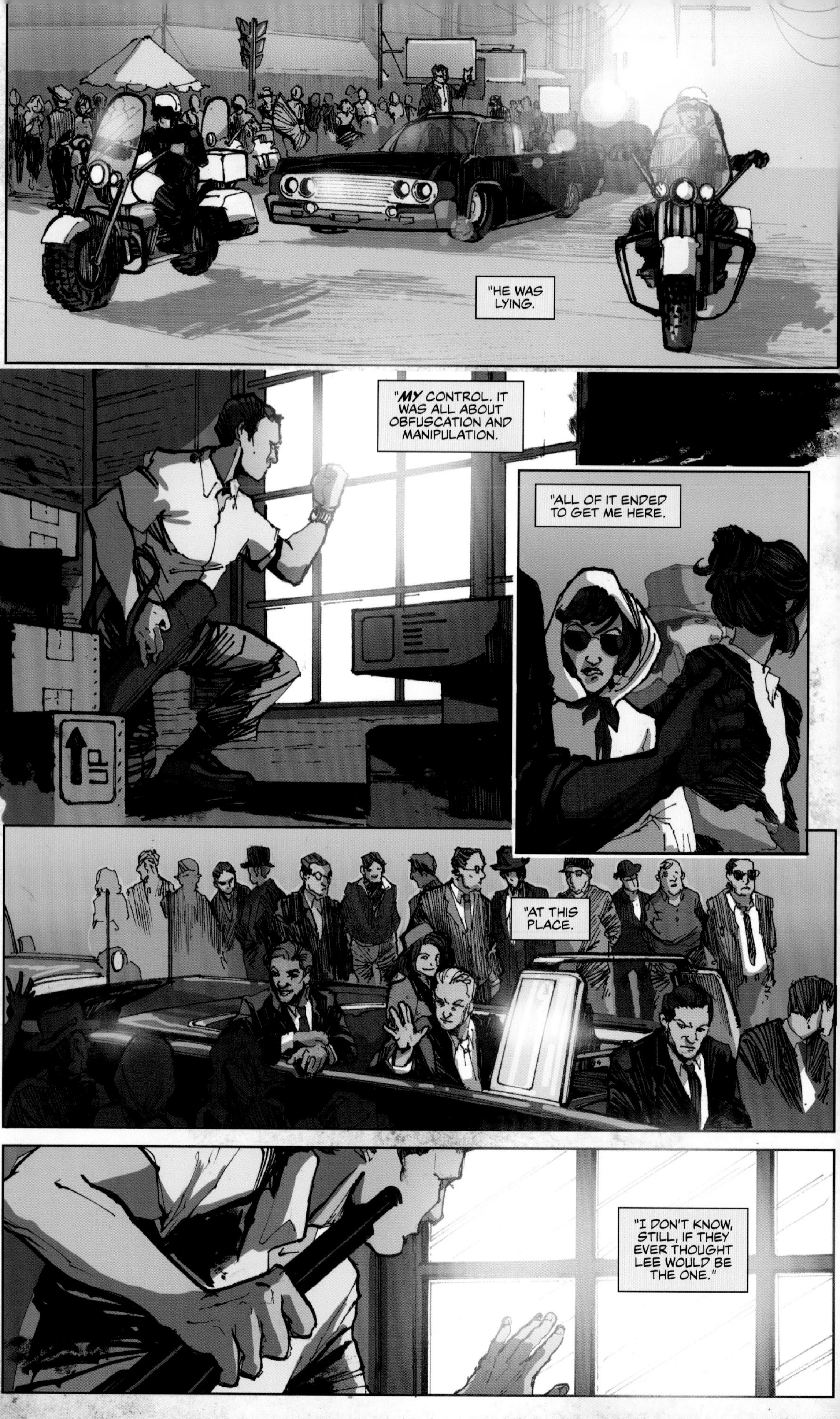
"HE WAS LYING.
"MY CONTROL. IT WAS ALL ABOUT OBFUSCATION AND MANIPULATION.
"ALL OF IT ENDED TO GET ME HERE.
"AT THIS PLACE.
"I DON'T KNOW, STILL, IF THEY EVER THOUGHT LEE WOULD BE THE ONE."
UP

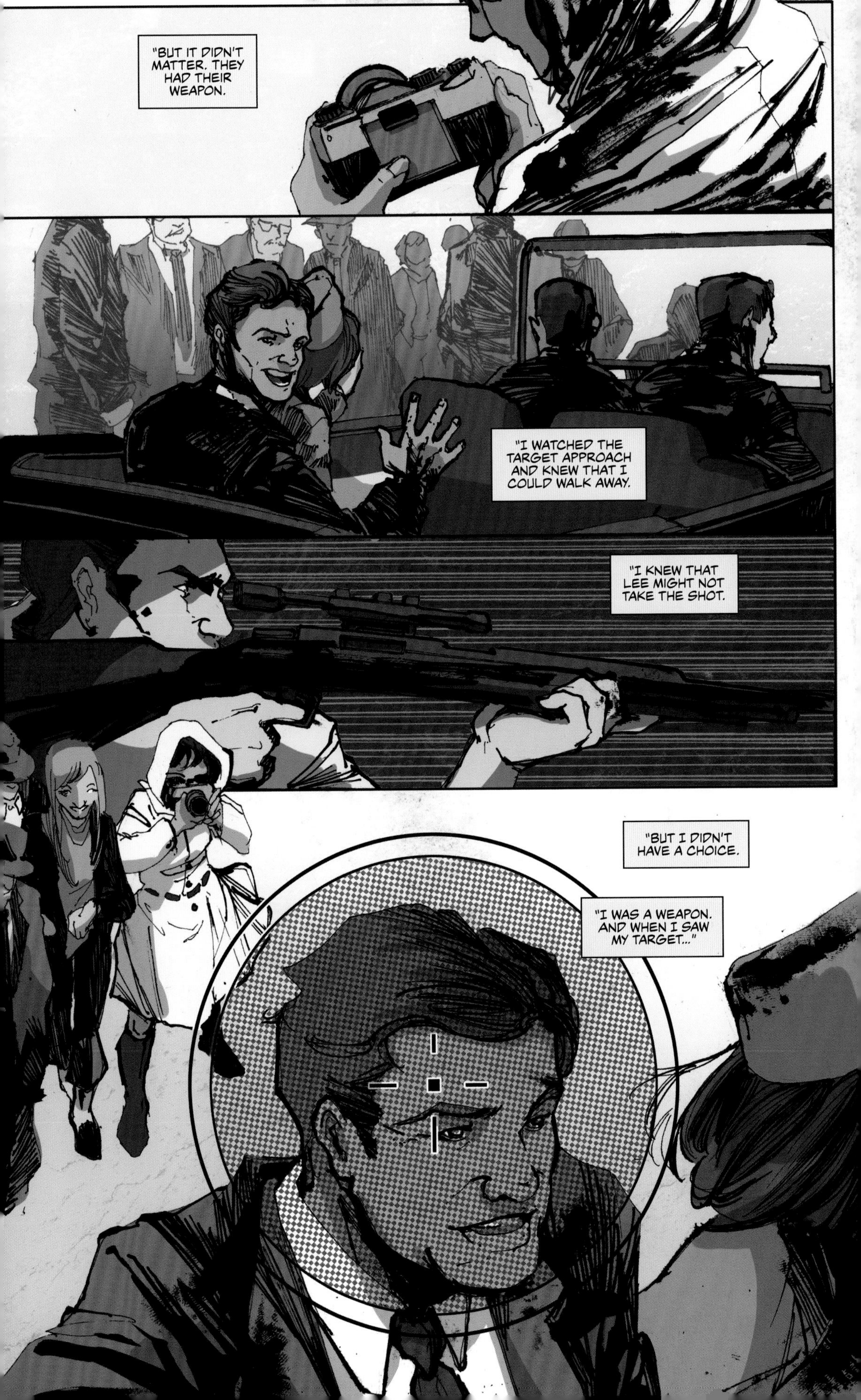
"BUT IT DIDN'T MATTER. THEY HAD THEIR WEAPON.
"I WATCHED THE TARGET APPROACH AND KNEW THAT I COULD WALK AWAY.
"I KNEW THAT LEE MIGHT NOT TAKE THE SHOT.
"BUT I DIDN'T HAVE A CHOICE.
"I WAS A WEAPON. AND WHEN I SAW MY TARGET..."

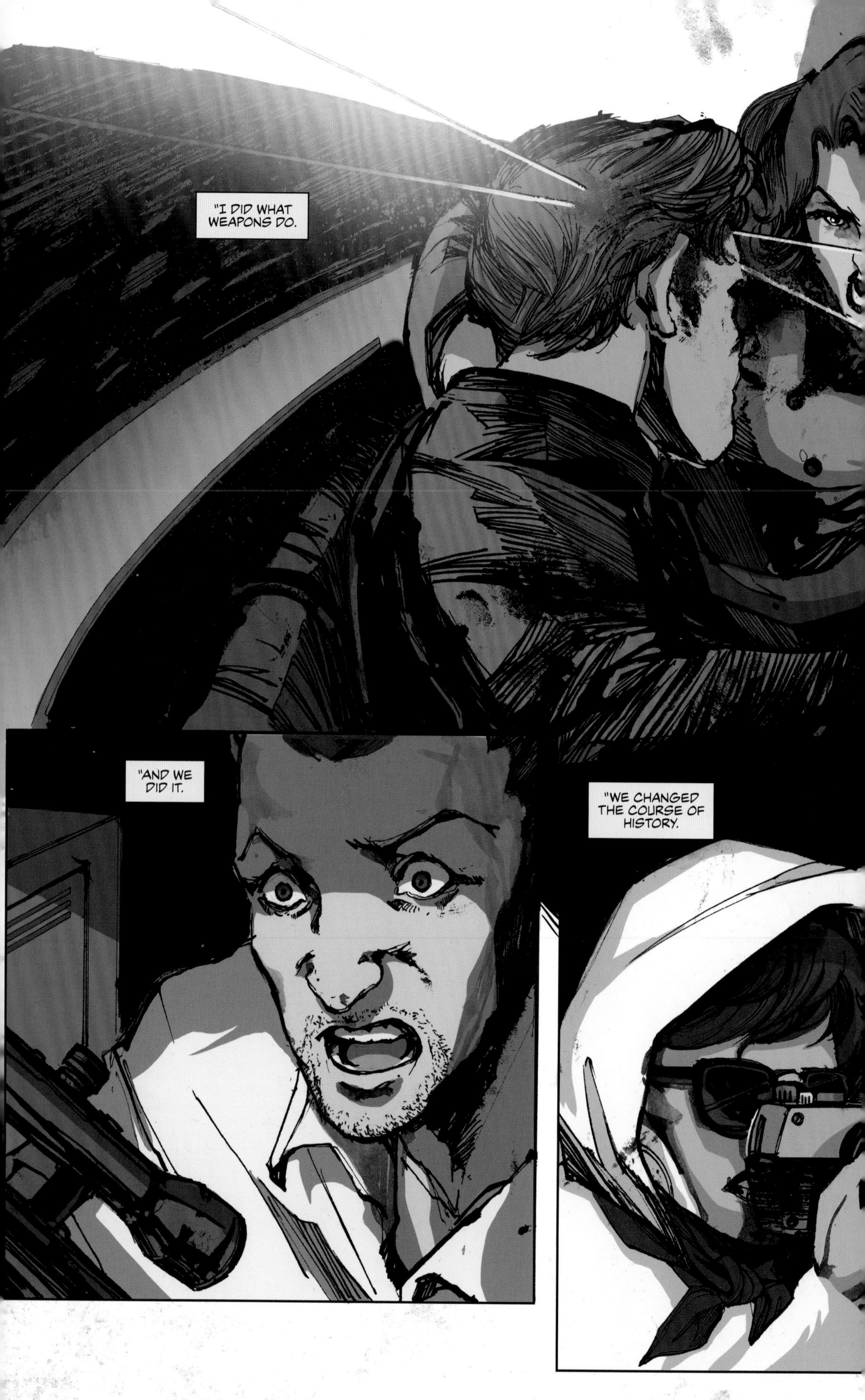
"I DID WHAT WEAPONS DO.
"AND WE DID IT.
"WE CHANGED THE COURSE OF HISTORY.

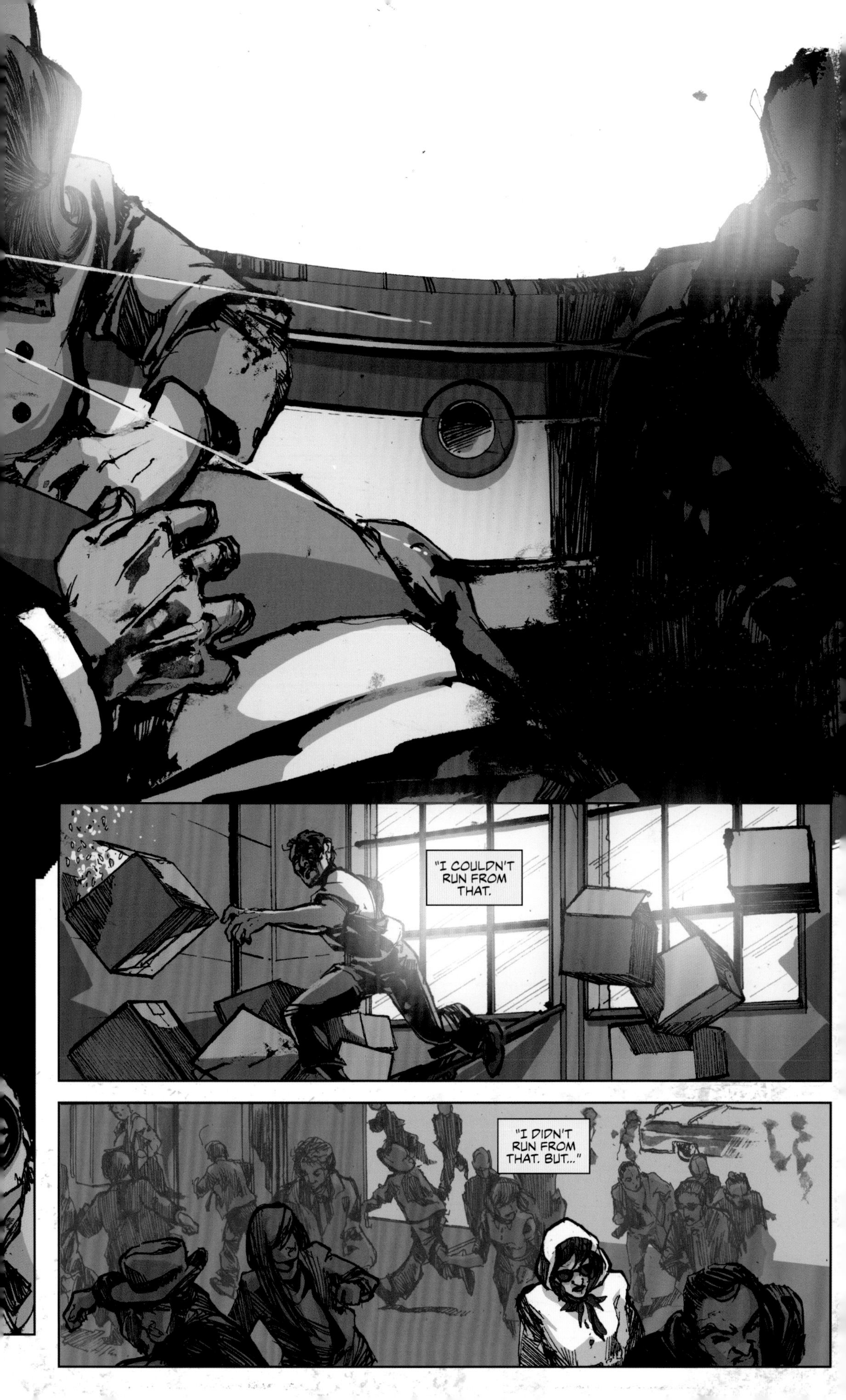
"I COULDN'T RUN FROM THAT.
"I DIDN'T RUN FROM THAT. BUT..."

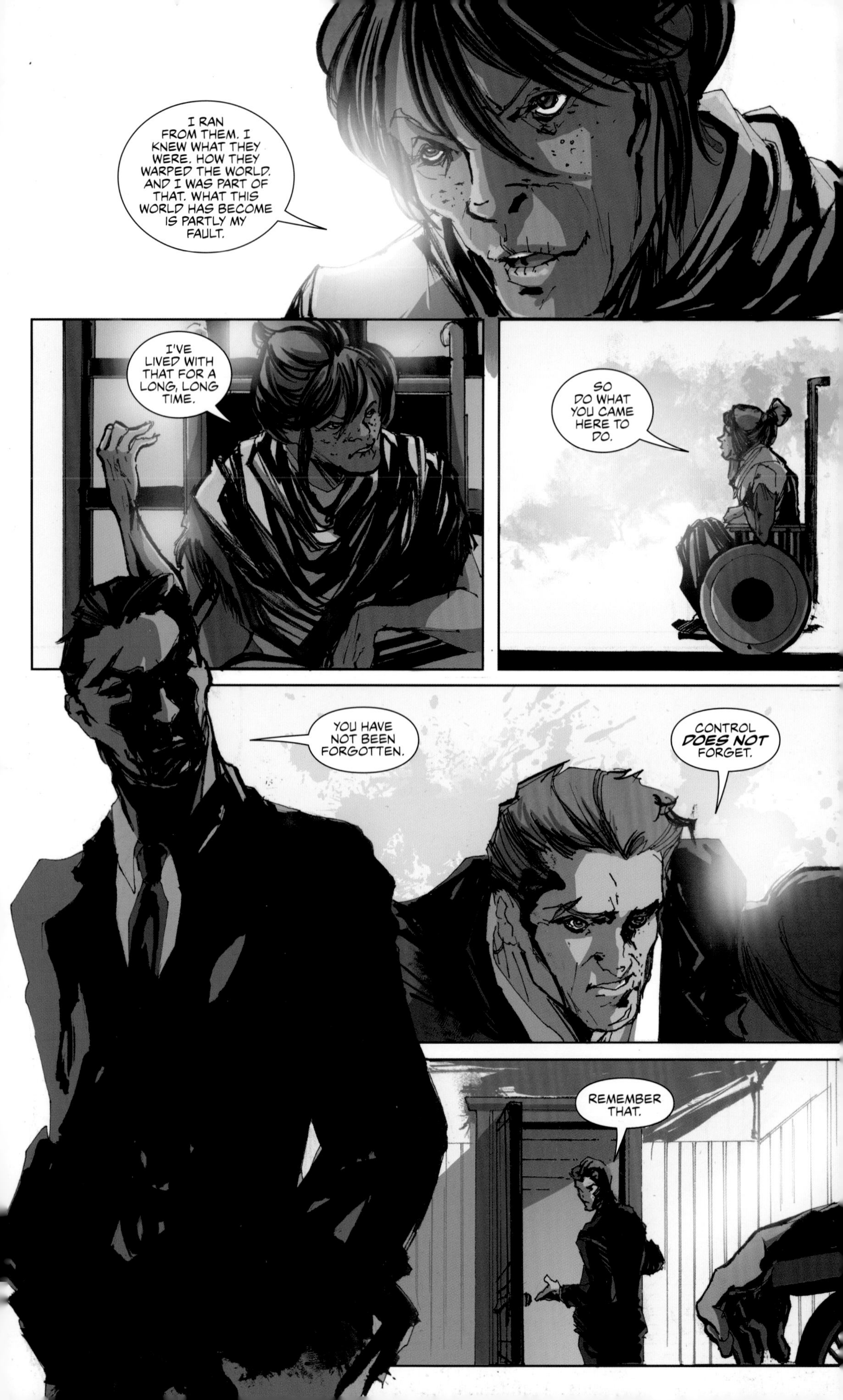
I RAN FROM THEM. I KNEW WHAT THEY WERE. HOW THEY WARPED THE WORLD. AND I WAS PART OF THAT. WHAT THIS WORLD HAS BECOME IS PARTLY MY FAULT.
I'VE LIVED WITH THAT FOR A LONG, LONG TIME.
SO DO WHAT YOU CAME HERE TO DO.
YOU HAVE NOT BEEN FORGOTTEN.
CONTROL **DOES NOT** FORGET.
REMEMBER THAT.

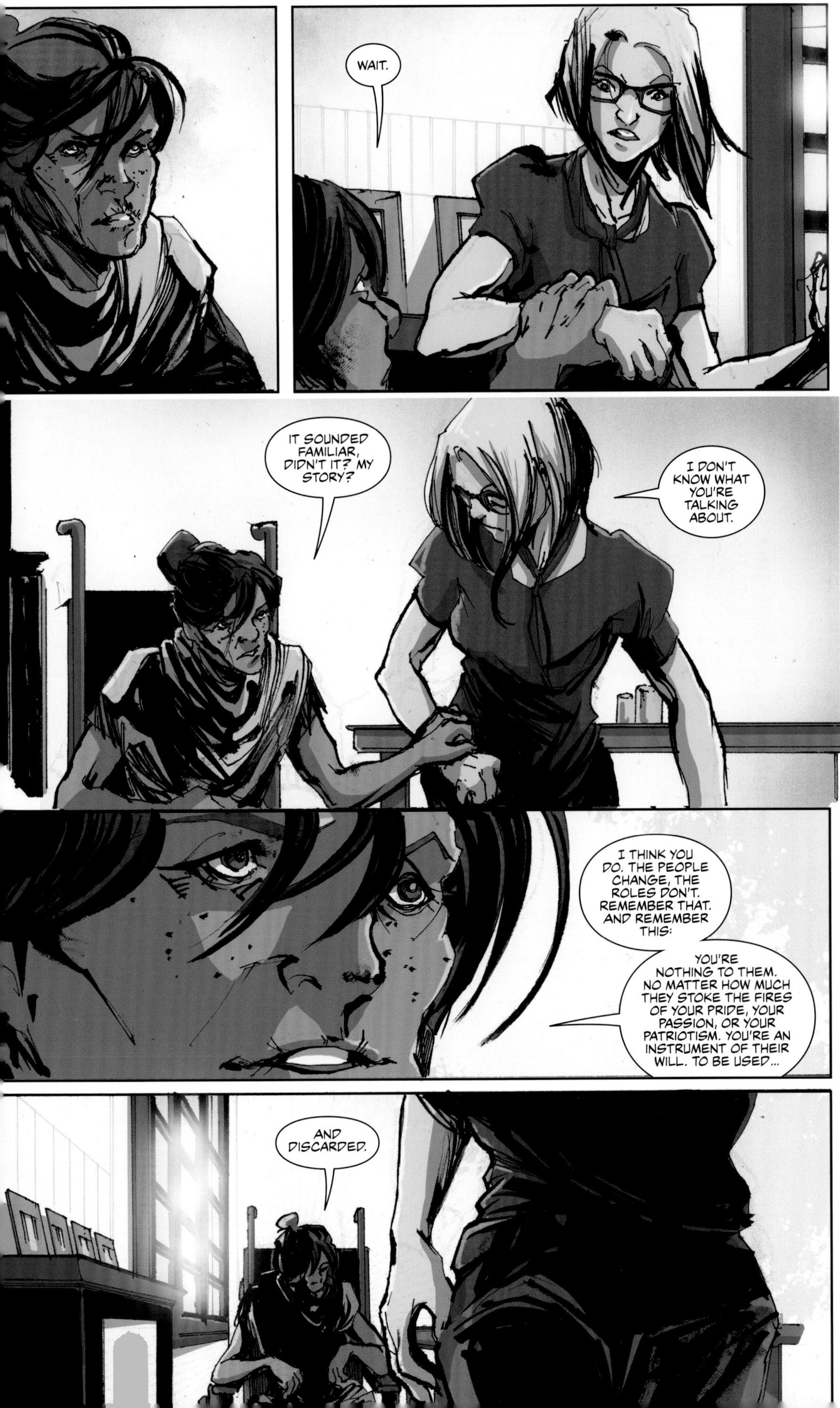
WAIT.
IT SOUNDED FAMILIAR, DIDN'T IT? MY STORY?
I DON'T KNOW WHAT YOU'RE TALKING ABOUT.
I THINK YOU DO. THE PEOPLE CHANGE, THE ROLES DON'T. REMEMBER THAT. AND REMEMBER THIS:
YOU'RE NOTHING TO THEM. NO MATTER HOW MUCH THEY STOKE THE FIRES OF YOUR PRIDE, YOUR PASSION, OR YOUR PATRIOTISM. YOU'RE AN INSTRUMENT OF THEIR WILL. TO BE USED...
AND DISCARDED.

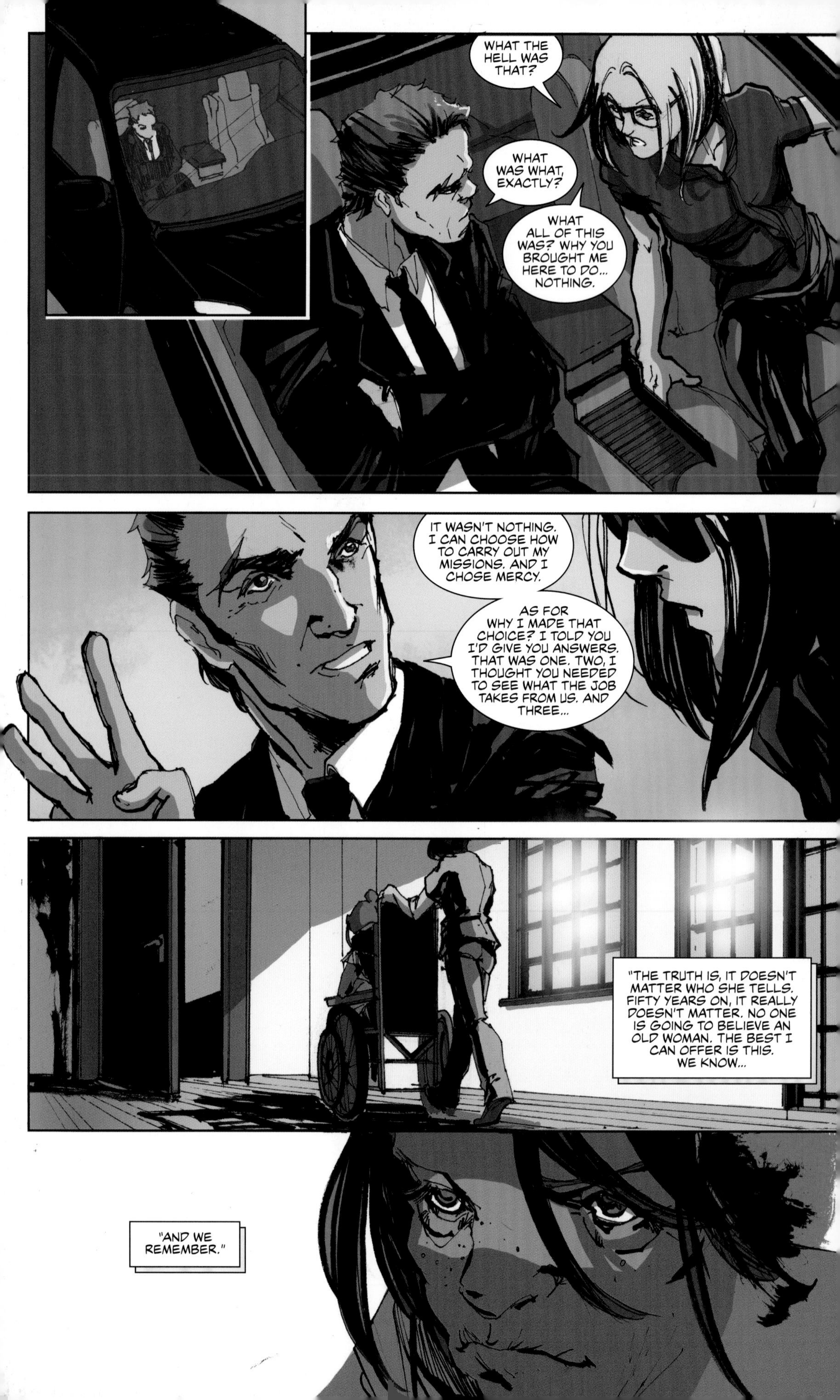
WHAT THE HELL WAS THAT?
WHAT WAS WHAT, EXACTLY?
WHAT ALL OF THIS WAS? WHY YOU BROUGHT ME HERE TO DO... NOTHING.
IT WASN'T NOTHING. I CAN CHOOSE HOW TO CARRY OUT MY MISSIONS. AND I CHOSE MERCY.
AS FOR WHY I MADE THAT CHOICE? I TOLD YOU I'D GIVE YOU ANSWERS. THAT WAS ONE. TWO, I THOUGHT YOU NEEDED TO SEE WHAT THE JOB TAKES FROM US. AND THREE...
"THE TRUTH IS, IT DOESN'T MATTER WHO SHE TELLS. FIFTY YEARS ON, IT REALLY DOESN'T MATTER. NO ONE IS GOING TO BELIEVE AN OLD WOMAN. THE BEST I CAN OFFER IS THIS. WE KNOW...
"AND WE REMEMBER."

CHAPTER SEVEN

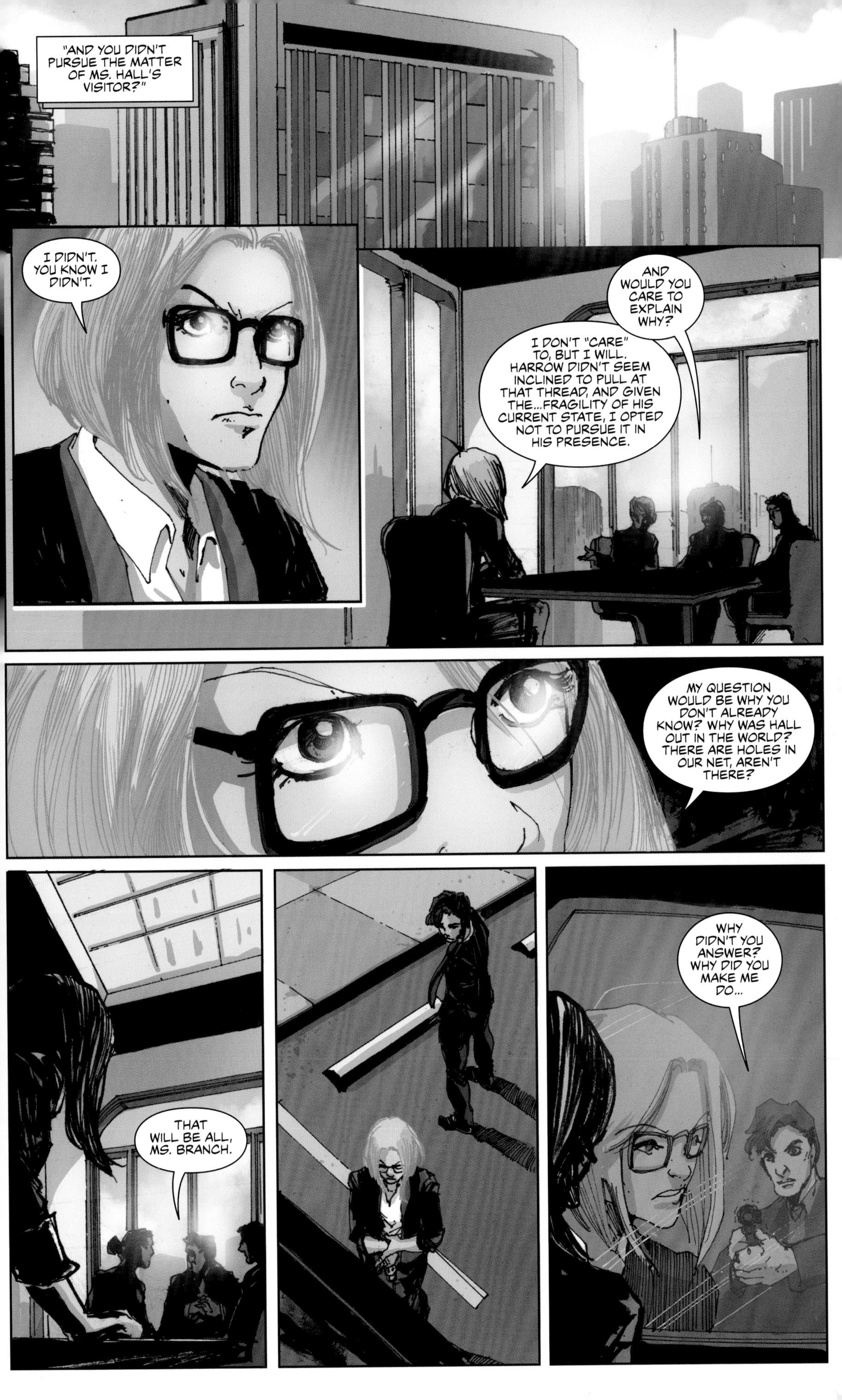
"AND YOU DIDN'T PURSUE THE MATTER OF MS. HALL'S VISITOR?"
I DIDN'T. YOU KNOW I DIDN'T.
AND WOULD YOU CARE TO EXPLAIN WHY?
I DON'T "CARE" TO, BUT I WILL. HARROW DIDN'T SEEM INCLINED TO PULL AT THAT THREAD, AND GIVEN THE...FRAGILITY OF HIS CURRENT STATE, I OPTED NOT TO PURSUE IT IN HIS PRESENCE.
MY QUESTION WOULD BE WHY YOU DON'T ALREADY KNOW? WHY WAS HALL OUT IN THE WORLD? THERE ARE HOLES IN OUR NET, AREN'T THERE?
THAT WILL BE ALL, MS. BRANCH.
WHY DIDN'T YOU ANSWER? WHY DID YOU MAKE ME DO...

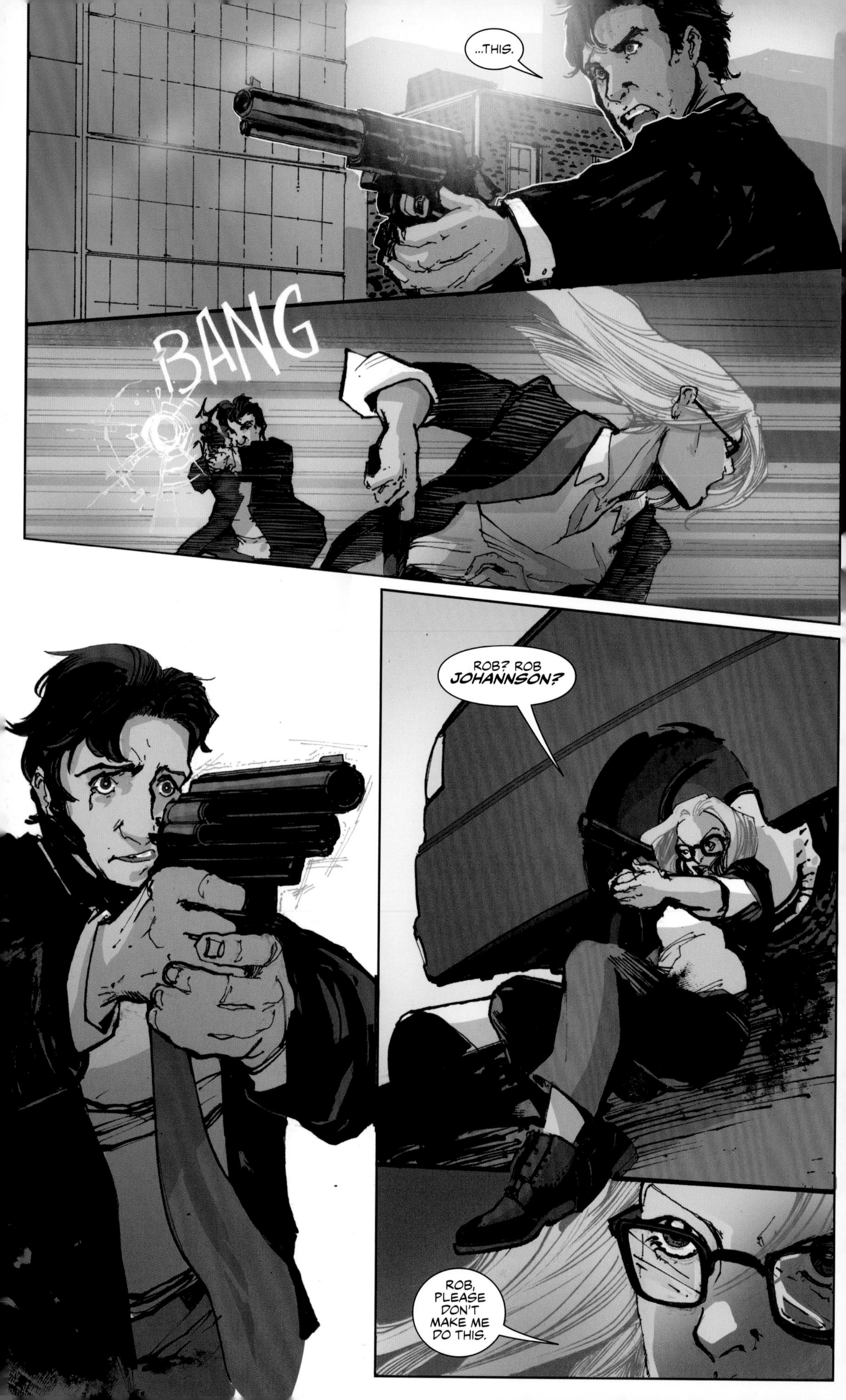

...THIS.
BANG
ROB? ROB JOHANNSON?
ROB, PLEASE DON'T MAKE ME DO THIS.

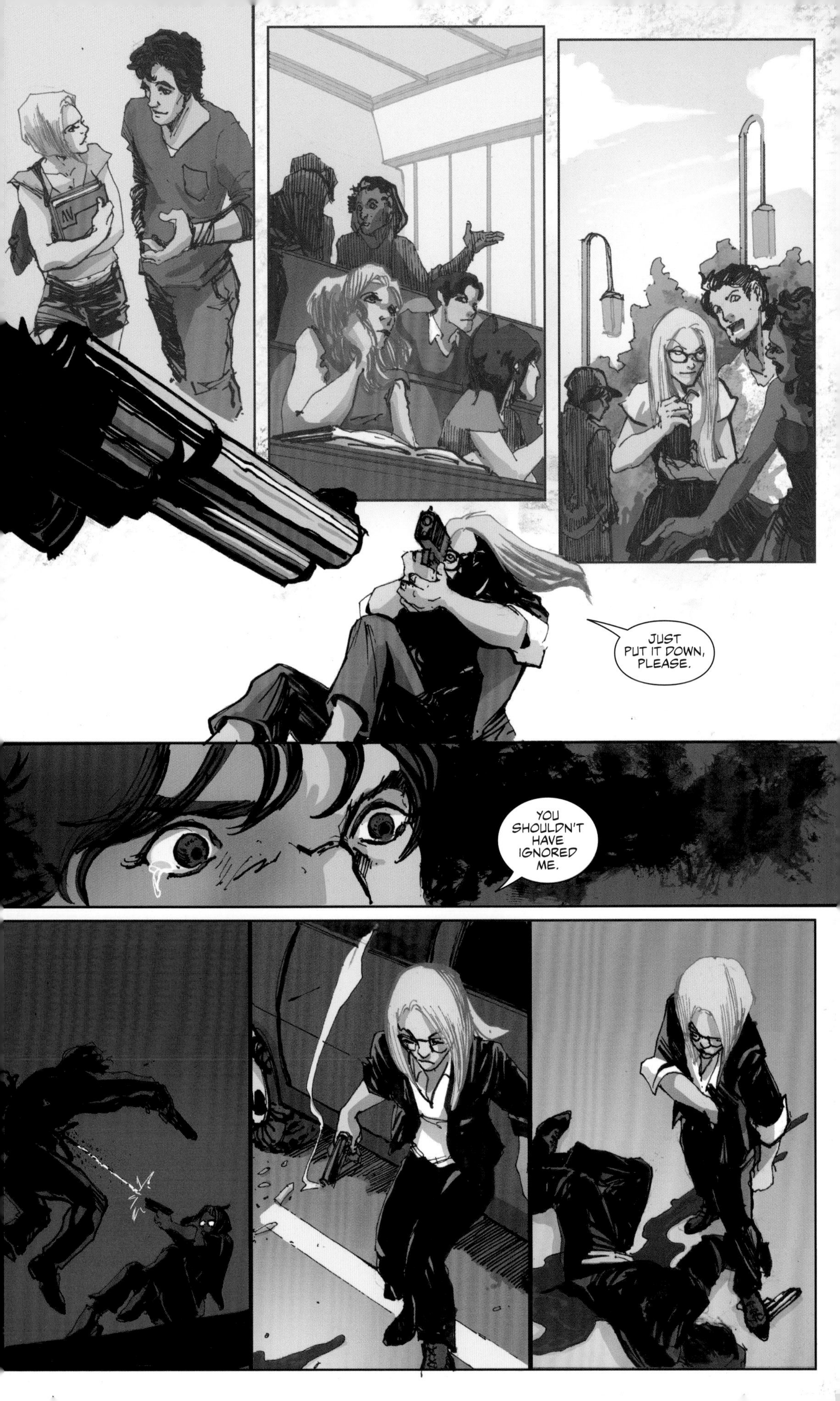
AV
JUST PUT IT DOWN, PLEASE.
YOU SHOULDN'T HAVE IGNORED ME.

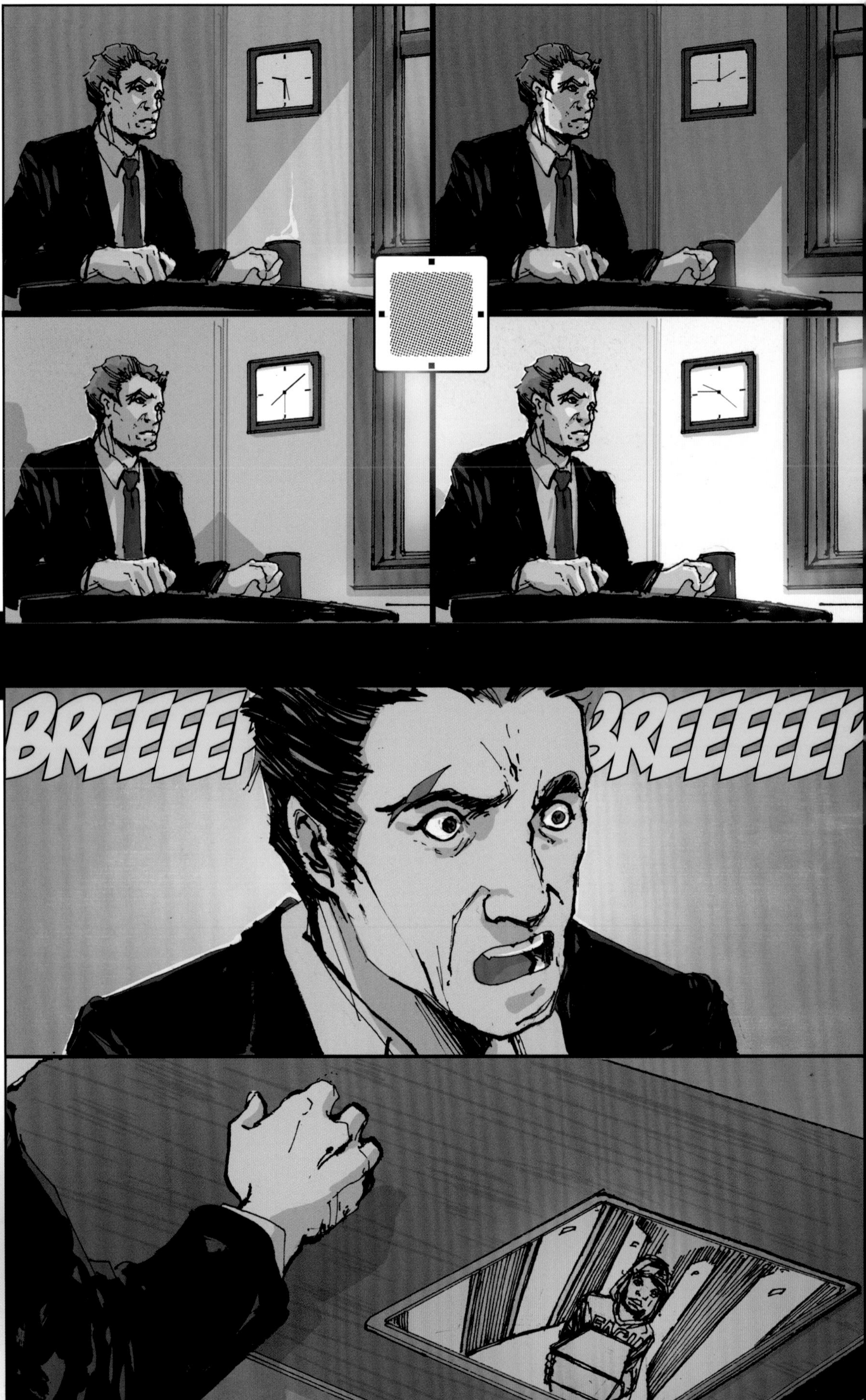
BREEEEP
BREEEEEEP

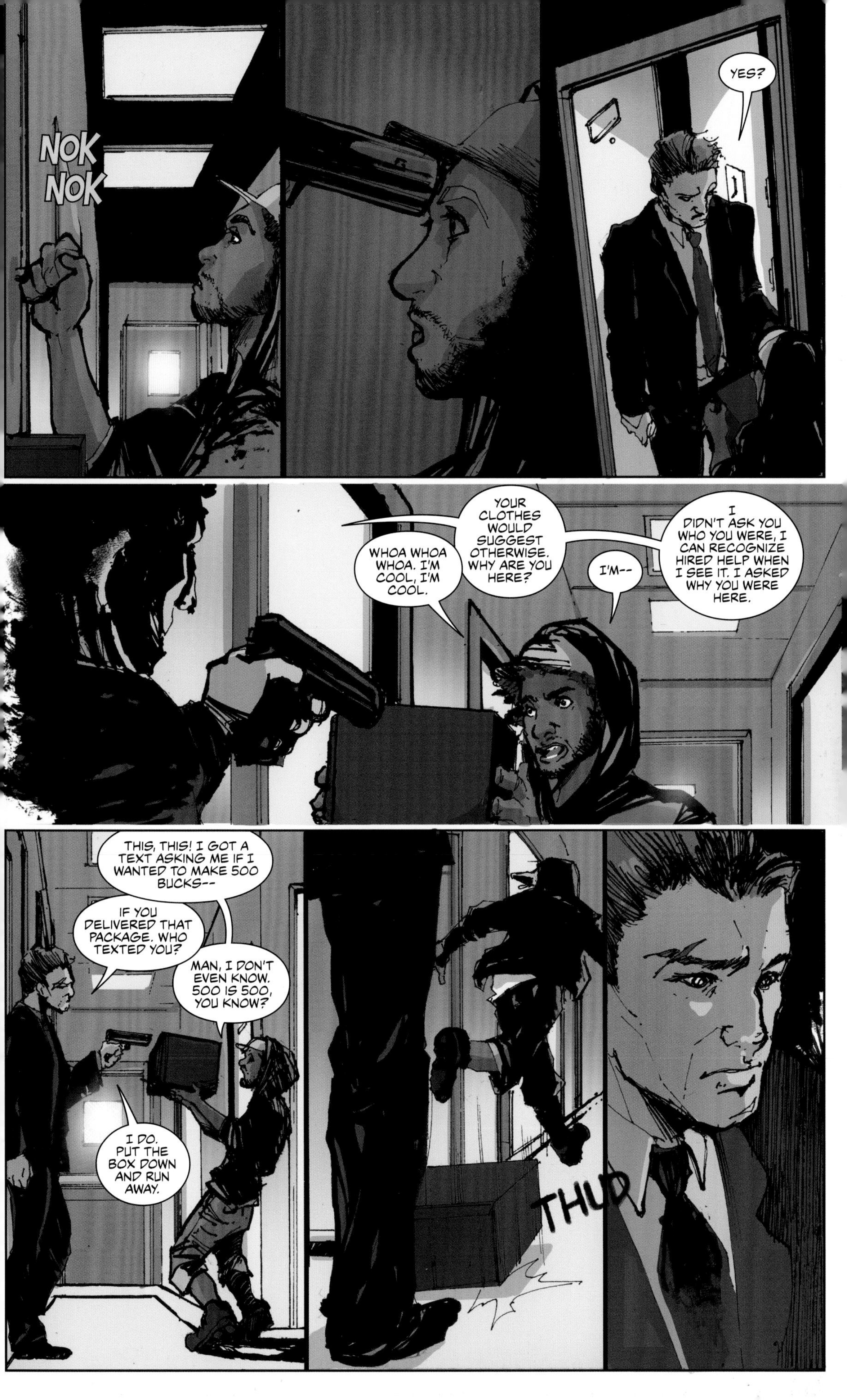
NOK NOK
YES?
WHOA WHOA WHOA. I'M COOL, I'M COOL.
YOUR CLOTHES WOULD SUGGEST OTHERWISE. WHY ARE YOU HERE?
I'M--
I DIDN'T ASK YOU WHO YOU WERE, I CAN RECOGNIZE HIRED HELP WHEN I SEE IT. I ASKED WHY YOU WERE HERE.
THIS, THIS! I GOT A TEXT ASKING ME IF I WANTED TO MAKE 500 BUCKS--
IF YOU DELIVERED THAT PACKAGE. WHO TEXTED YOU?
MAN, I DON'T EVEN KNOW. 500 IS 500, YOU KNOW?
I DO. PUT THE BOX DOWN AND RUN AWAY.
THUD

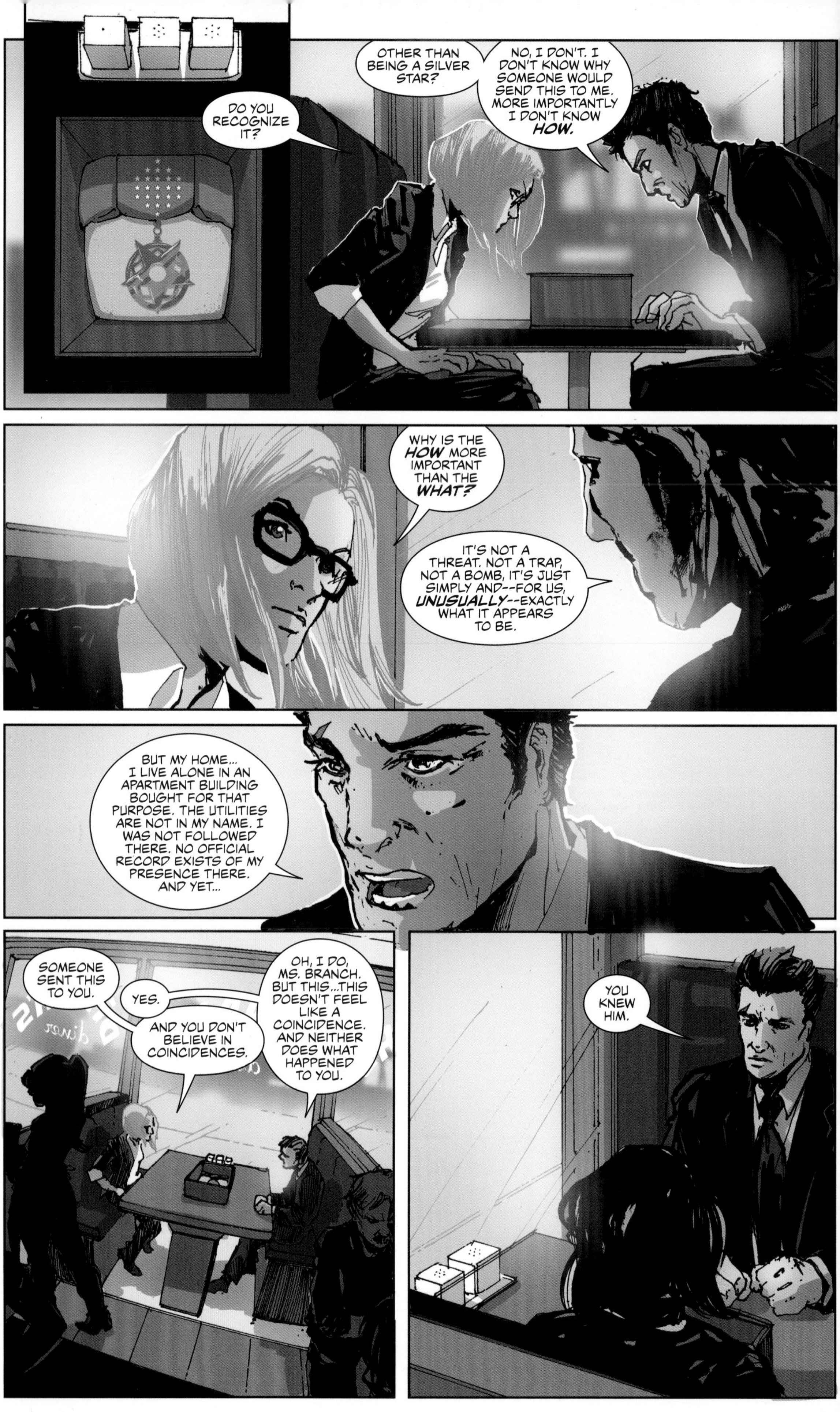
DO YOU RECOGNIZE IT?
OTHER THAN BEING A SILVER STAR?
NO, I DON'T. I DON'T KNOW WHY SOMEONE WOULD SEND THIS TO ME. MORE IMPORTANTLY I DON'T KNOW ***HOW.***
WHY IS THE ***HOW*** MORE IMPORTANT THAN THE ***WHAT?***
IT'S NOT A THREAT. NOT A TRAP, NOT A BOMB, IT'S JUST SIMPLY AND--FOR US, ***UNUSUALLY***--EXACTLY WHAT IT APPEARS TO BE.
BUT MY HOME... I LIVE ALONE IN AN APARTMENT BUILDING BOUGHT FOR THAT PURPOSE. THE UTILITIES ARE NOT IN MY NAME. I WAS NOT FOLLOWED THERE. NO OFFICIAL RECORD EXISTS OF MY PRESENCE THERE. AND YET...
SOMEONE SENT THIS TO YOU.
YES.
AND YOU DON'T BELIEVE IN COINCIDENCES.
OH, I DO, MS. BRANCH. BUT THIS...THIS DOESN'T FEEL LIKE A COINCIDENCE. AND NEITHER DOES WHAT HAPPENED TO YOU.
YOU KNEW HIM.

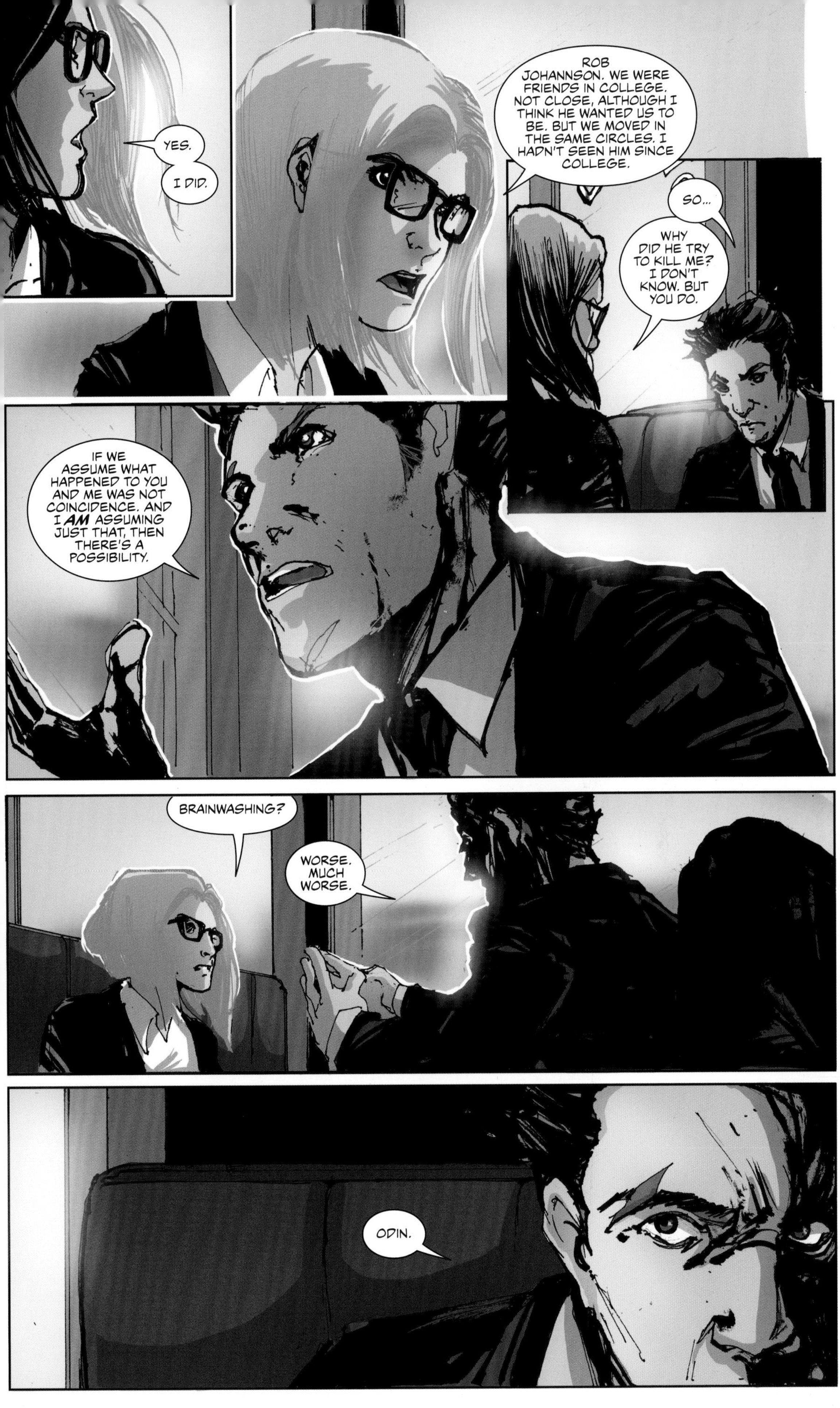
YES.
I DID.
ROB JOHANNSON. WE WERE FRIENDS IN COLLEGE. NOT CLOSE, ALTHOUGH I THINK HE WANTED US TO BE. BUT WE MOVED IN THE SAME CIRCLES. I HADN'T SEEN HIM SINCE COLLEGE.
SO...
WHY DID HE TRY TO KILL ME? I DON'T KNOW. BUT YOU DO.
IF WE ASSUME WHAT HAPPENED TO YOU AND ME WAS NOT COINCIDENCE. AND I **AM** ASSUMING JUST THAT, THEN THERE'S A POSSIBILITY.
BRAINWASHING?
WORSE. MUCH WORSE.
ODIN.

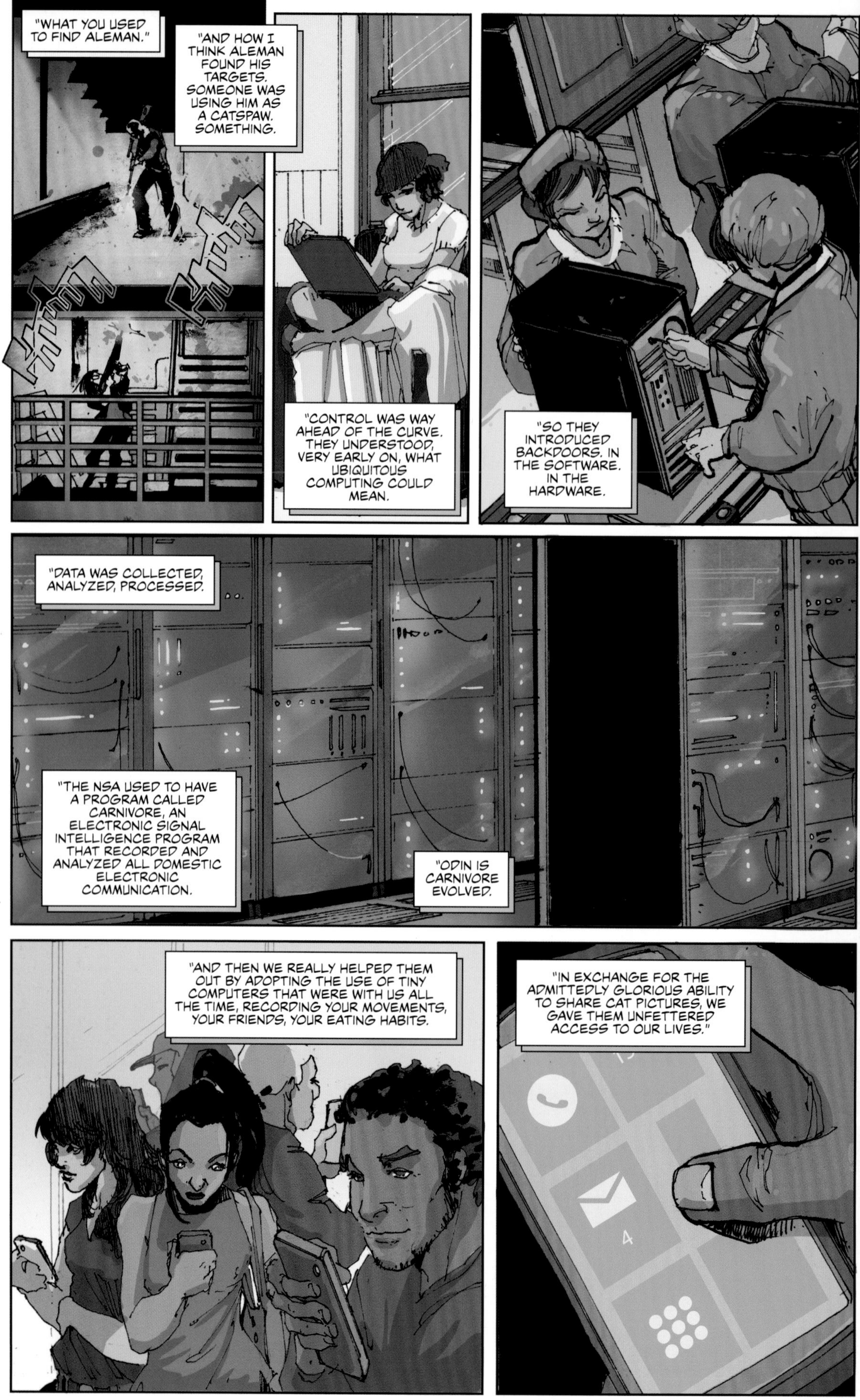
"WHAT YOU USED TO FIND ALEMAN."
"AND HOW I THINK ALEMAN FOUND HIS TARGETS. SOMEONE WAS USING HIM AS A CATSPAW. SOMETHING.
"CONTROL WAS WAY AHEAD OF THE CURVE. THEY UNDERSTOOD, VERY EARLY ON, WHAT UBIQUITOUS COMPUTING COULD MEAN.
"SO THEY INTRODUCED BACKDOORS. IN THE SOFTWARE. IN THE HARDWARE.
"DATA WAS COLLECTED, ANALYZED, PROCESSED.
"THE NSA USED TO HAVE A PROGRAM CALLED CARNIVORE, AN ELECTRONIC SIGNAL INTELLIGENCE PROGRAM THAT RECORDED AND ANALYZED ALL DOMESTIC ELECTRONIC COMMUNICATION.
"ODIN IS CARNIVORE EVOLVED.
"AND THEN WE REALLY HELPED THEM OUT BY ADOPTING THE USE OF TINY COMPUTERS THAT WERE WITH US ALL THE TIME, RECORDING YOUR MOVEMENTS, YOUR FRIENDS, YOUR EATING HABITS.
"IN EXCHANGE FOR THE ADMITTEDLY GLORIOUS ABILITY TO SHARE CAT PICTURES, WE GAVE THEM UNFETTERED ACCESS TO OUR LIVES."

"AND OUR PATTERNS. ALGORITHMS WERE DEVELOPED THAT COULD PREDICT BEHAVIOR. AND WHAT COULD BE PREDICTED...

"COULD BE **CONTROLLED.** BY MODULATING WHAT YOU SAW WHEN, ODIN COULD BE USED TO MANIPULATE PEOPLE, TO TURN THEM INTO TOOLS.

"IMAGINE A SLIGHTED SUITOR. IMAGINE THAT HE HAS SOME INHERENT INSTABILITY. SOMETHING ODIN COULD EXPLOIT. SEND HIM THE RIGHT MESSAGES, MAKE HIM SEE THE RIGHT THINGS, AND HE REACTS.

"HE ATTACKS. NO, WHAT ODIN CAN DO IS MUCH WORSE THAN BRAINWASHING."

THAT'S--

DON'T SAY IMPOSSIBLE. IMPOSSIBLE, MS. BRANCH, IS WHAT WE **DO.**

NO, IF THAT'S TRUE, THEN CONTROL IS TARGETING ME BUT NOT YOU.

I **AM** BEING TARGETED. BUT I'VE GOT NO FRIENDS. NO FAMILY. NO PAST. VERY LITTLE FOOTPRINT. I AM DIFFICULT, BY DESIGN, TO TARGET.

BUT NO, I DON'T THINK CONTROL IS TARGETING US.

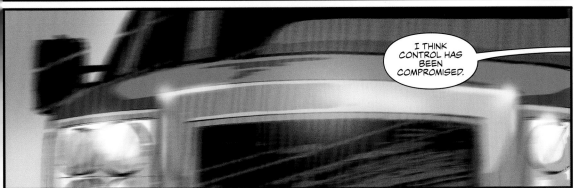

I THINK CONTROL HAS BEEN COMPROMISED.

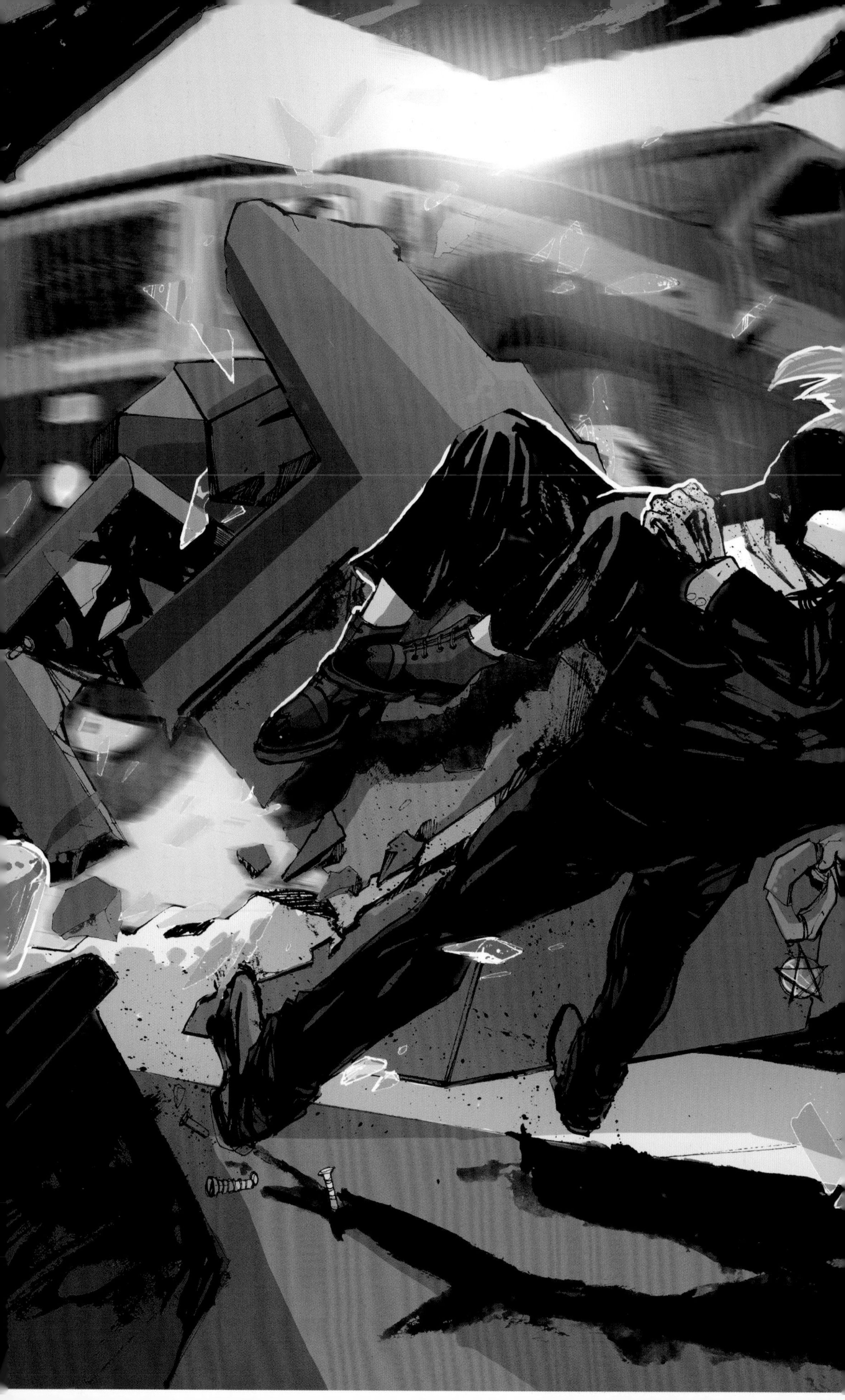

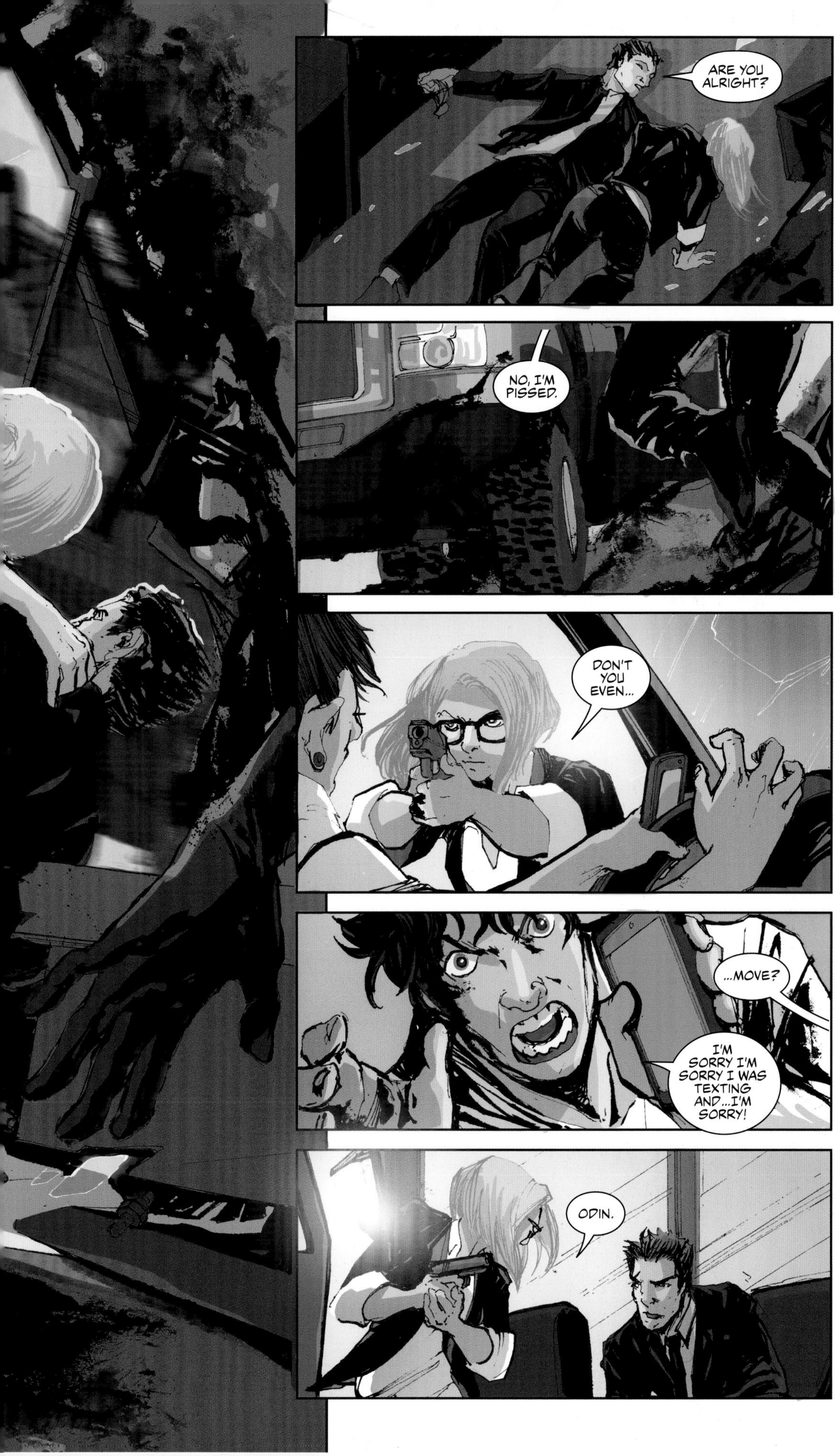
ARE YOU ALRIGHT?
NO, I'M PISSED.
DON'T YOU EVEN...
...MOVE?
I'M SORRY I'M SORRY I WAS TEXTING AND...I'M SORRY!
ODIN.

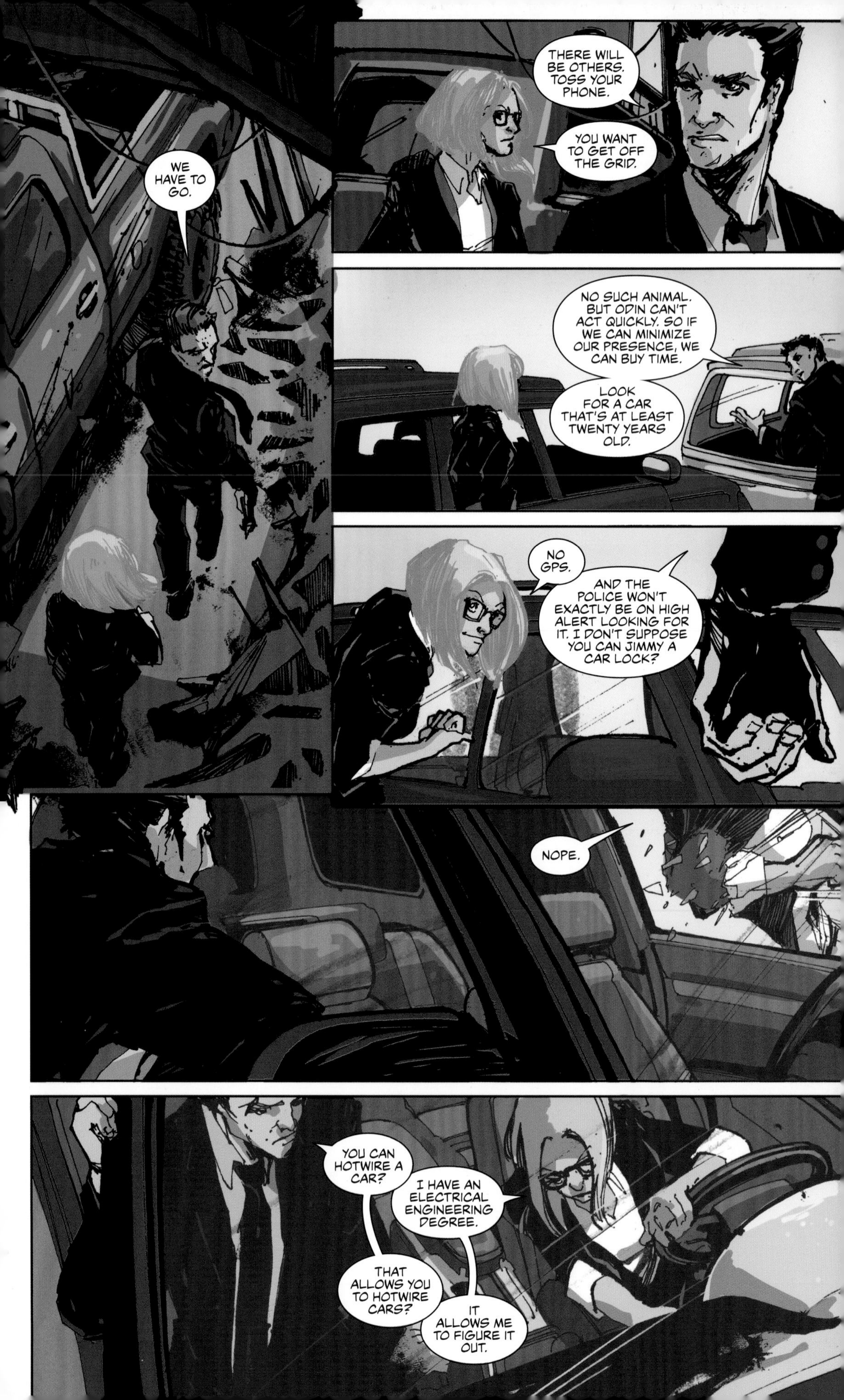
WE HAVE TO GO.
THERE WILL BE OTHERS. TOSS YOUR PHONE.
YOU WANT TO GET OFF THE GRID.
NO SUCH ANIMAL. BUT ODIN CAN'T ACT QUICKLY. SO IF WE CAN MINIMIZE OUR PRESENCE, WE CAN BUY TIME.
LOOK FOR A CAR THAT'S AT LEAST TWENTY YEARS OLD.
NO GPS.
AND THE POLICE WON'T EXACTLY BE ON HIGH ALERT LOOKING FOR IT. I DON'T SUPPOSE YOU CAN JIMMY A CAR LOCK?
NOPE.
YOU CAN HOTWIRE A CAR?
I HAVE AN ELECTRICAL ENGINEERING DEGREE.
THAT ALLOWS YOU TO HOTWIRE CARS?
IT ALLOWS ME TO FIGURE IT OUT.

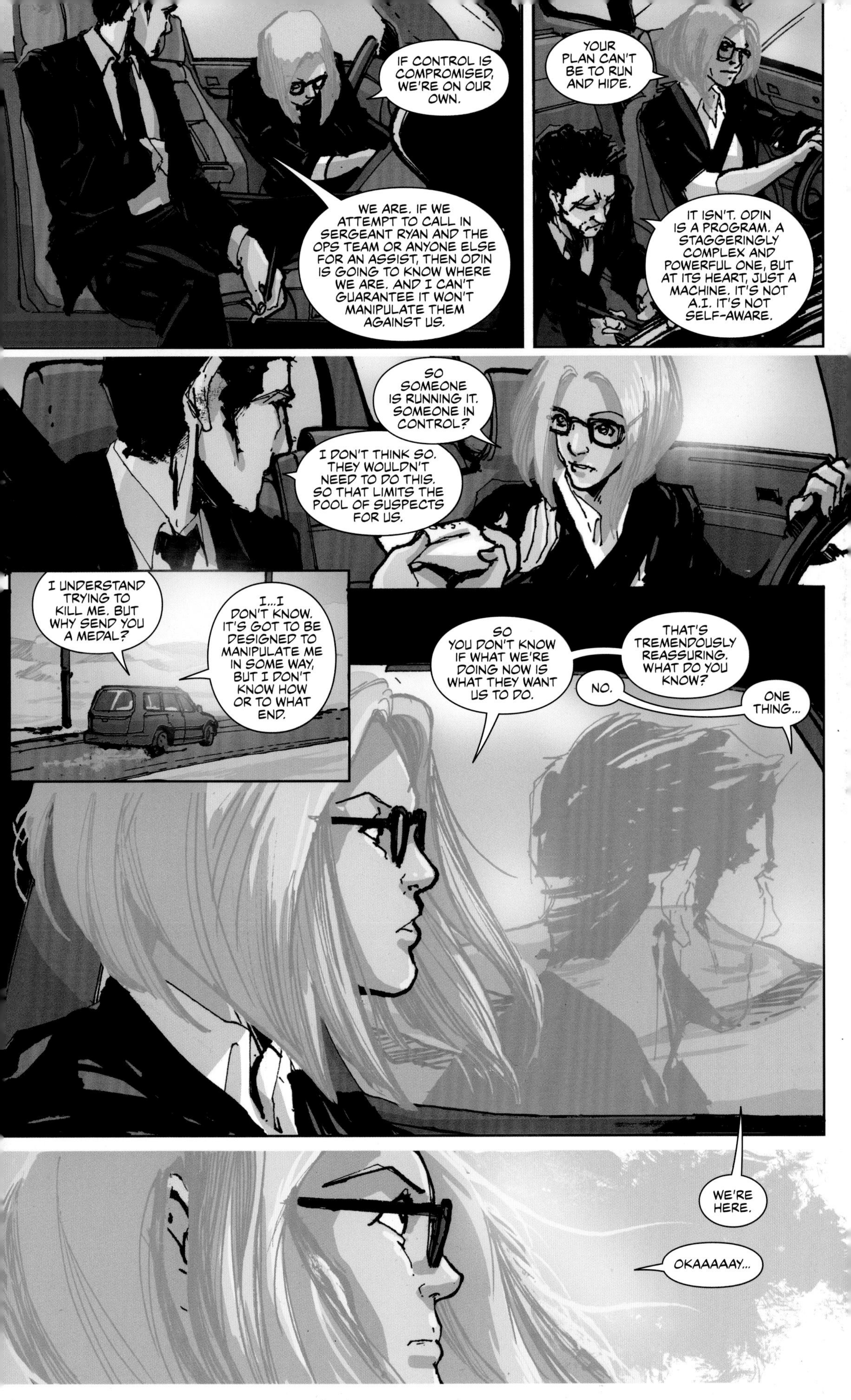

IF CONTROL IS COMPROMISED, WE'RE ON OUR OWN.
WE ARE. IF WE ATTEMPT TO CALL IN SERGEANT RYAN AND THE OPS TEAM OR ANYONE ELSE FOR AN ASSIST, THEN ODIN IS GOING TO KNOW WHERE WE ARE. AND I CAN'T GUARANTEE IT WON'T MANIPULATE THEM AGAINST US.
YOUR PLAN CAN'T BE TO RUN AND HIDE.
IT ISN'T. ODIN IS A PROGRAM. A STAGGERINGLY COMPLEX AND POWERFUL ONE, BUT AT ITS HEART, JUST A MACHINE. IT'S NOT A.I. IT'S NOT SELF-AWARE.
SO SOMEONE IS RUNNING IT. SOMEONE IN CONTROL?
I DON'T THINK SO. THEY WOULDN'T NEED TO DO THIS. SO THAT LIMITS THE POOL OF SUSPECTS FOR US.
I UNDERSTAND TRYING TO KILL ME. BUT WHY SEND YOU A MEDAL?
I...I DON'T KNOW. IT'S GOT TO BE DESIGNED TO MANIPULATE ME IN SOME WAY, BUT I DON'T KNOW HOW OR TO WHAT END.
SO YOU DON'T KNOW IF WHAT WE'RE DOING NOW IS WHAT THEY WANT US TO DO.
NO.
THAT'S TREMENDOUSLY REASSURING. WHAT DO YOU KNOW?
ONE THING...
WE'RE HERE.
OKAAAAAY...

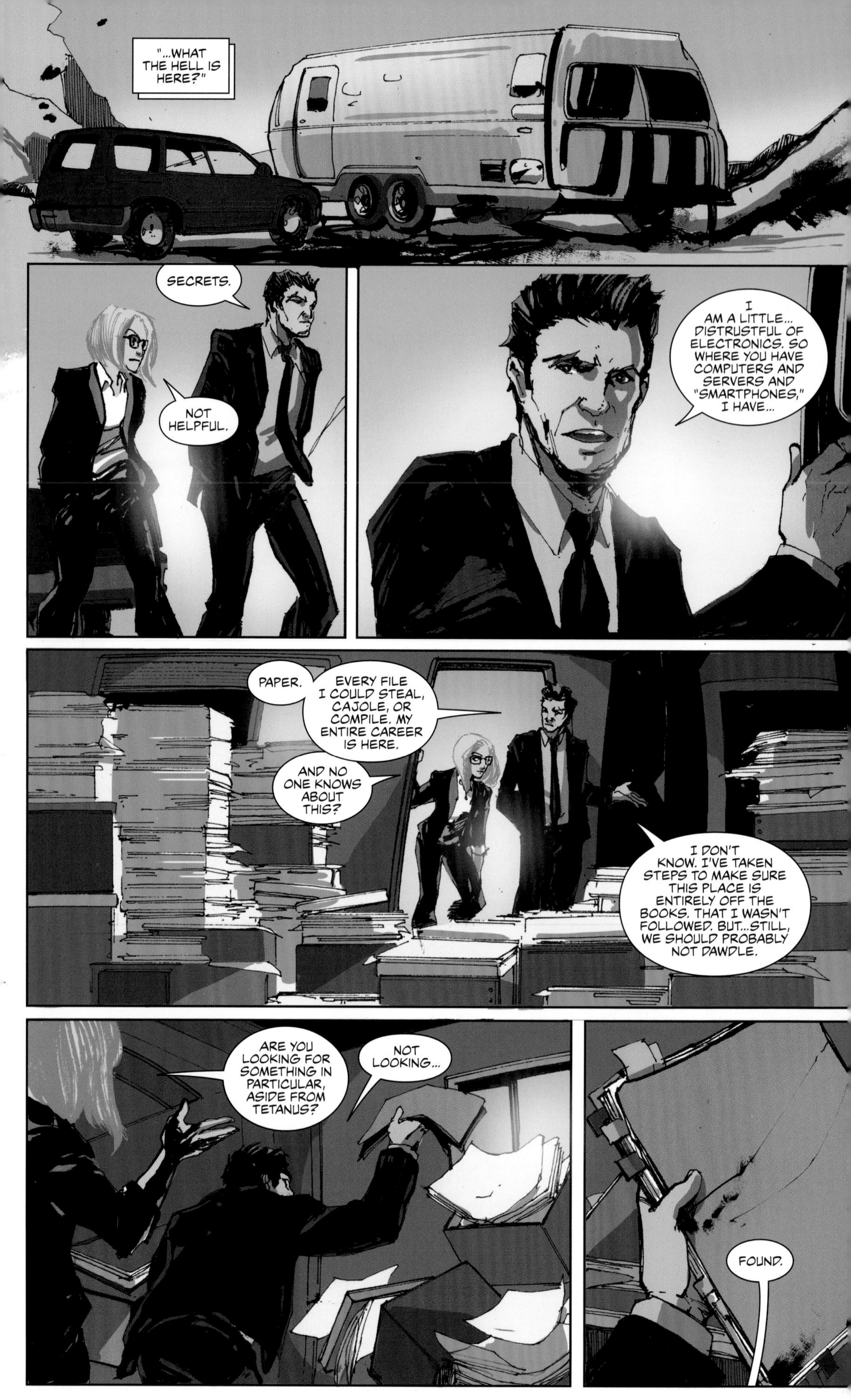
"...WHAT THE HELL IS HERE?"
SECRETS.
NOT HELPFUL.
I AM A LITTLE... DISTRUSTFUL OF ELECTRONICS. SO WHERE YOU HAVE COMPUTERS AND SERVERS AND "SMARTPHONES," I HAVE...
PAPER.
EVERY FILE I COULD STEAL, CAJOLE, OR COMPILE. MY ENTIRE CAREER IS HERE.
AND NO ONE KNOWS ABOUT THIS?
I DON'T KNOW. I'VE TAKEN STEPS TO MAKE SURE THIS PLACE IS ENTIRELY OFF THE BOOKS. THAT I WASN'T FOLLOWED. BUT...STILL, WE SHOULD PROBABLY NOT DAWDLE.
ARE YOU LOOKING FOR SOMETHING IN PARTICULAR, ASIDE FROM TETANUS?
NOT LOOKING...
FOUND.

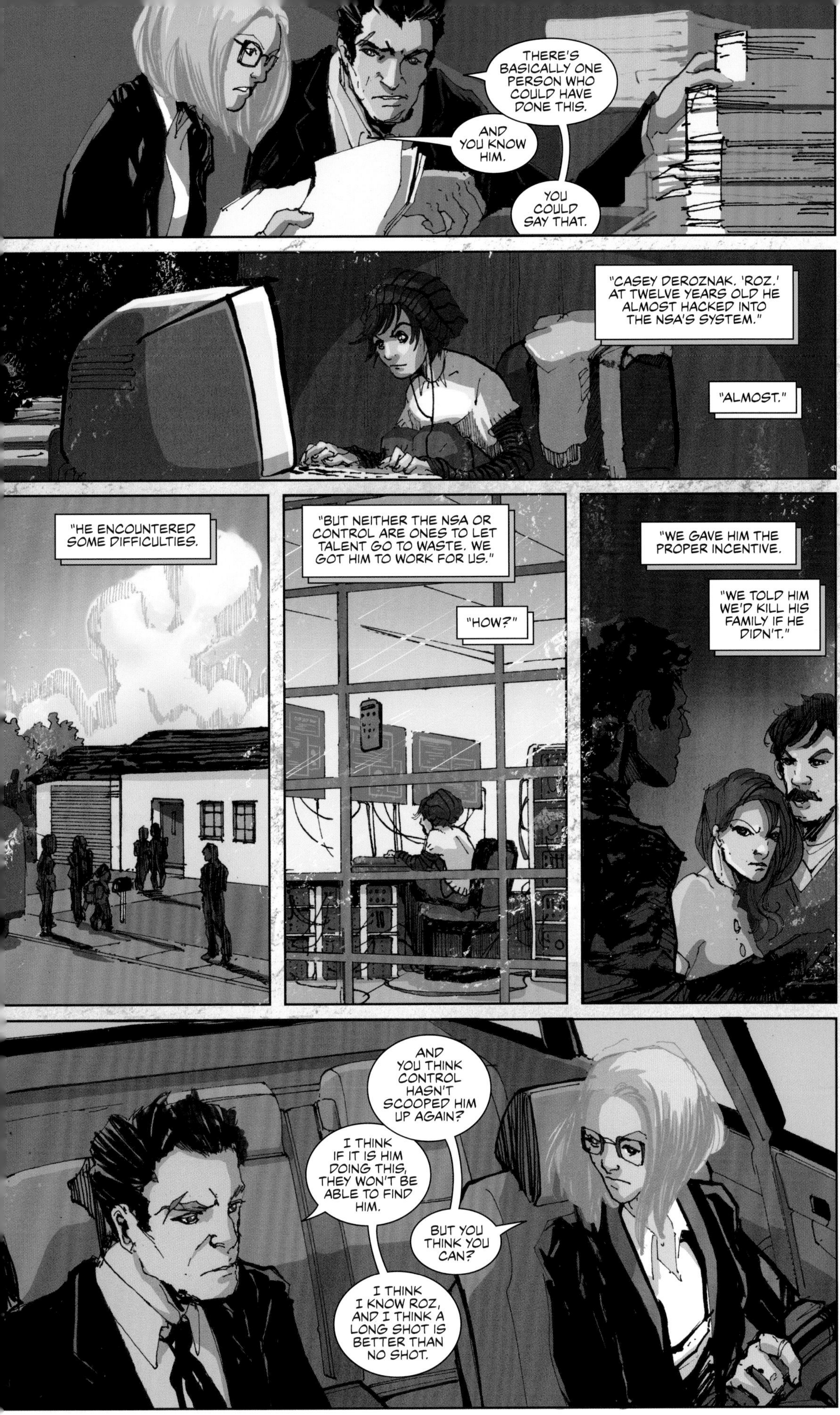

THERE'S BASICALLY ONE PERSON WHO COULD HAVE DONE THIS.
AND YOU KNOW HIM.
YOU COULD SAY THAT.
"CASEY DEROZNAK. 'ROZ.' AT TWELVE YEARS OLD HE ALMOST HACKED INTO THE NSA'S SYSTEM."
"ALMOST."
"HE ENCOUNTERED SOME DIFFICULTIES.
"BUT NEITHER THE NSA OR CONTROL ARE ONES TO LET TALENT GO TO WASTE. WE GOT HIM TO WORK FOR US."
"HOW?"
"WE GAVE HIM THE PROPER INCENTIVE.
"WE TOLD HIM WE'D KILL HIS FAMILY IF HE DIDN'T."
AND YOU THINK CONTROL HASN'T SCOOPED HIM UP AGAIN?
I THINK IF IT IS HIM DOING THIS, THEY WON'T BE ABLE TO FIND HIM.
BUT YOU THINK YOU CAN?
I THINK I KNOW ROZ, AND I THINK A LONG SHOT IS BETTER THAN NO SHOT.

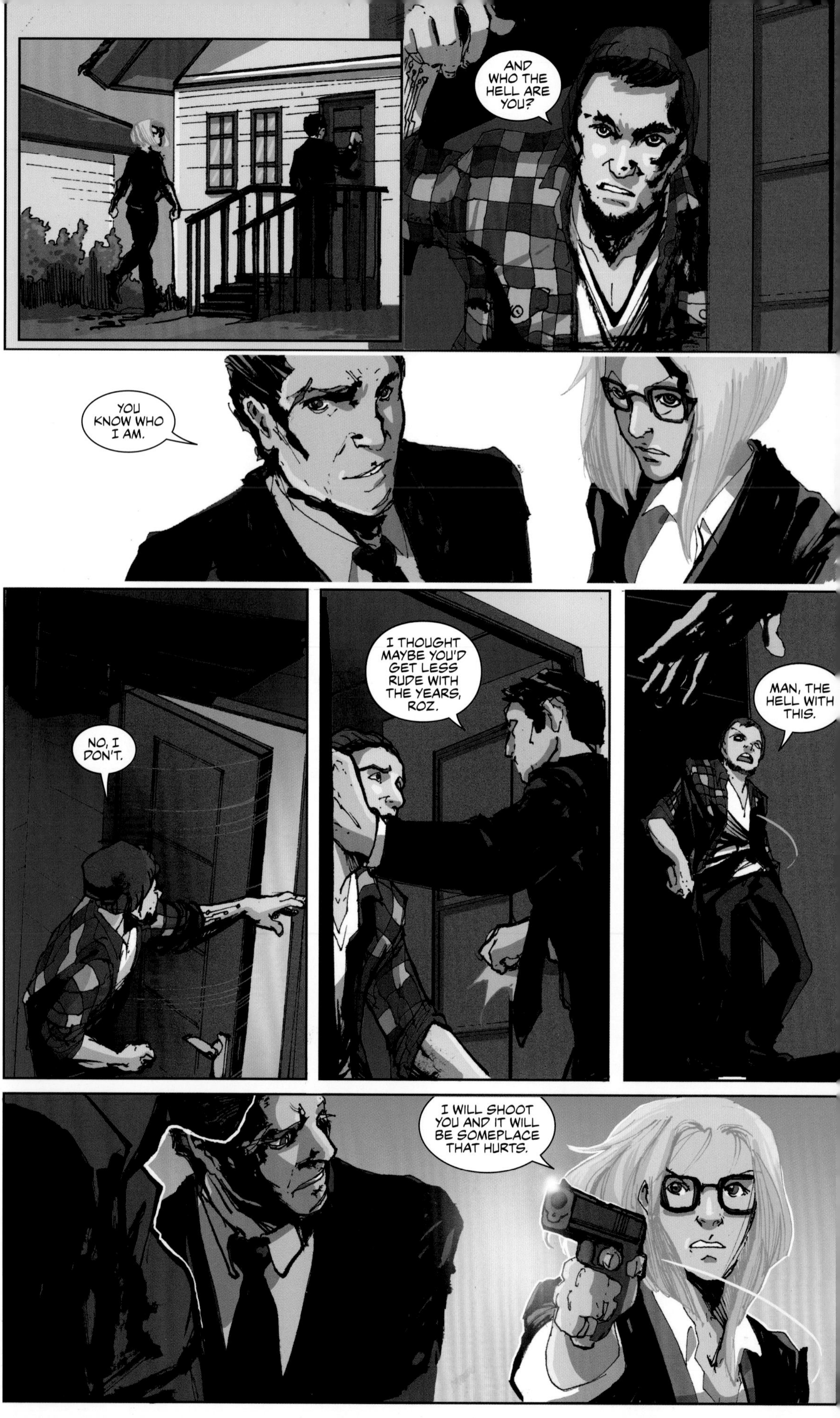
AND WHO THE HELL ARE YOU?
YOU KNOW WHO I AM.
NO, I DON'T.
I THOUGHT MAYBE YOU'D GET LESS RUDE WITH THE YEARS, ROZ.
MAN, THE HELL WITH THIS.
I WILL SHOOT YOU AND IT WILL BE SOMEPLACE THAT HURTS.

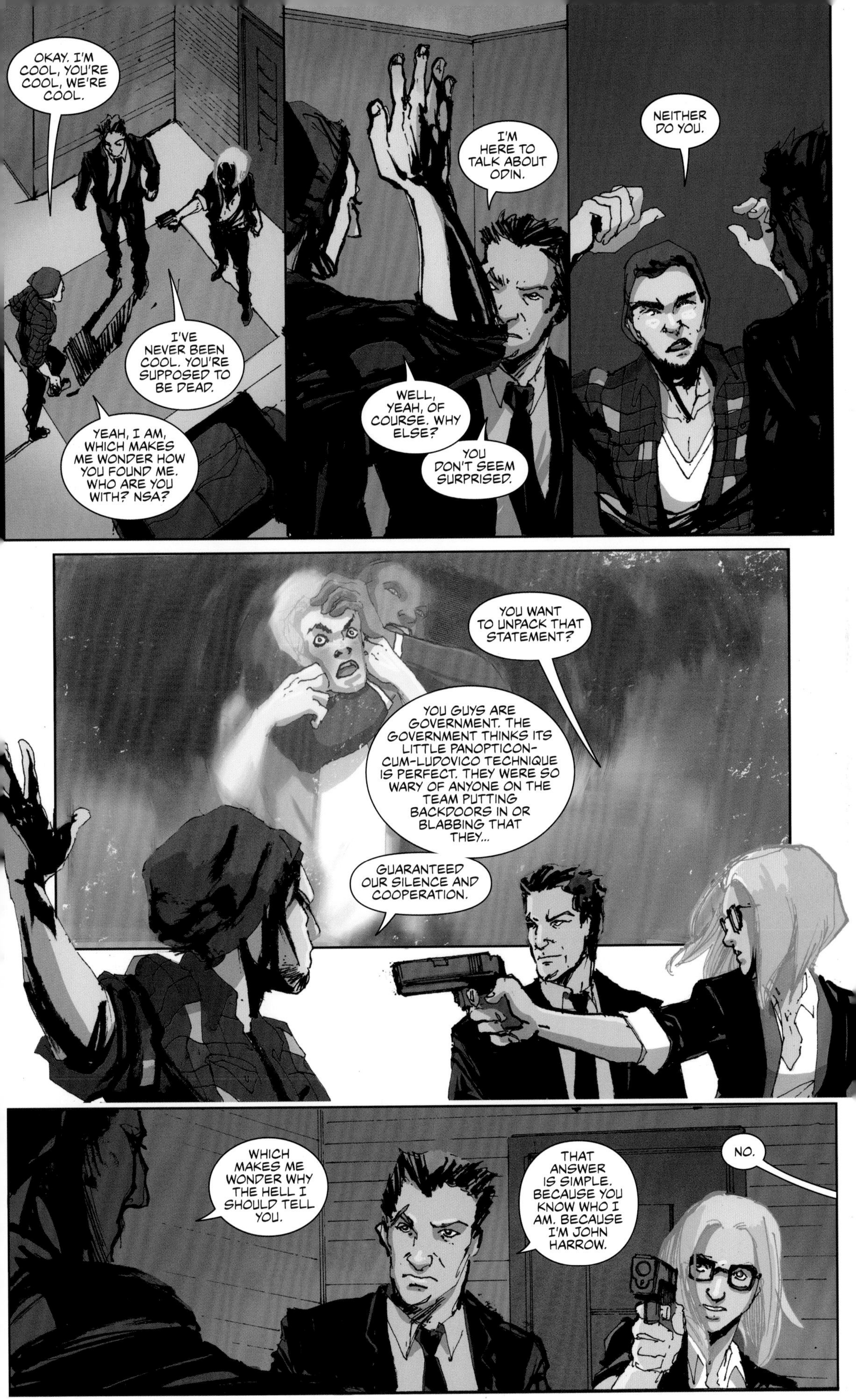
OKAY. I'M COOL, YOU'RE COOL, WE'RE COOL.
I'VE NEVER BEEN COOL. YOU'RE SUPPOSED TO BE DEAD.
YEAH, I AM, WHICH MAKES ME WONDER HOW YOU FOUND ME. WHO ARE YOU WITH? NSA?
I'M HERE TO TALK ABOUT ODIN.
WELL, YEAH, OF COURSE. WHY ELSE?
YOU DON'T SEEM SURPRISED.
NEITHER DO YOU.
YOU WANT TO UNPACK THAT STATEMENT?
YOU GUYS ARE GOVERNMENT. THE GOVERNMENT THINKS ITS LITTLE PANOPTICON-CUM-LUDOVICO TECHNIQUE IS PERFECT. THEY WERE SO WARY OF ANYONE ON THE TEAM PUTTING BACKDOORS IN OR BLABBING THAT THEY...
GUARANTEED OUR SILENCE AND COOPERATION.
WHICH MAKES ME WONDER WHY THE HELL I SHOULD TELL YOU.
THAT ANSWER IS SIMPLE. BECAUSE YOU KNOW WHO I AM. BECAUSE I'M JOHN HARROW.
NO.

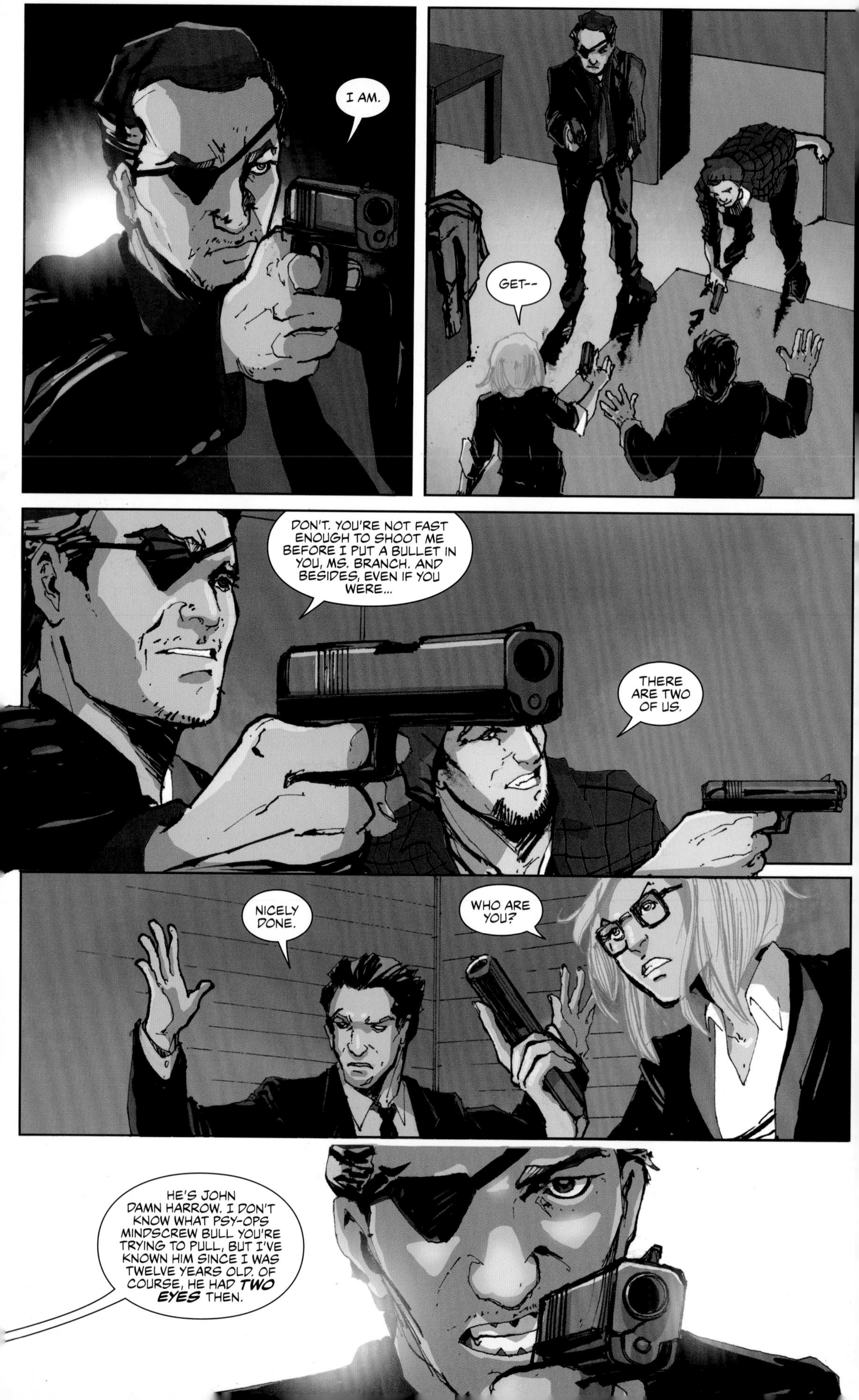
I AM.
GET--
DON'T. YOU'RE NOT FAST ENOUGH TO SHOOT ME BEFORE I PUT A BULLET IN YOU, MS. BRANCH. AND BESIDES, EVEN IF YOU WERE...
THERE ARE TWO OF US.
NICELY DONE.
WHO ARE YOU?
HE'S JOHN DAMN HARROW. I DON'T KNOW WHAT PSY-OPS MINDSCREW BULL YOU'RE TRYING TO PULL, BUT I'VE KNOWN HIM SINCE I WAS TWELVE YEARS OLD. OF COURSE, HE HAD **TWO EYES** THEN.

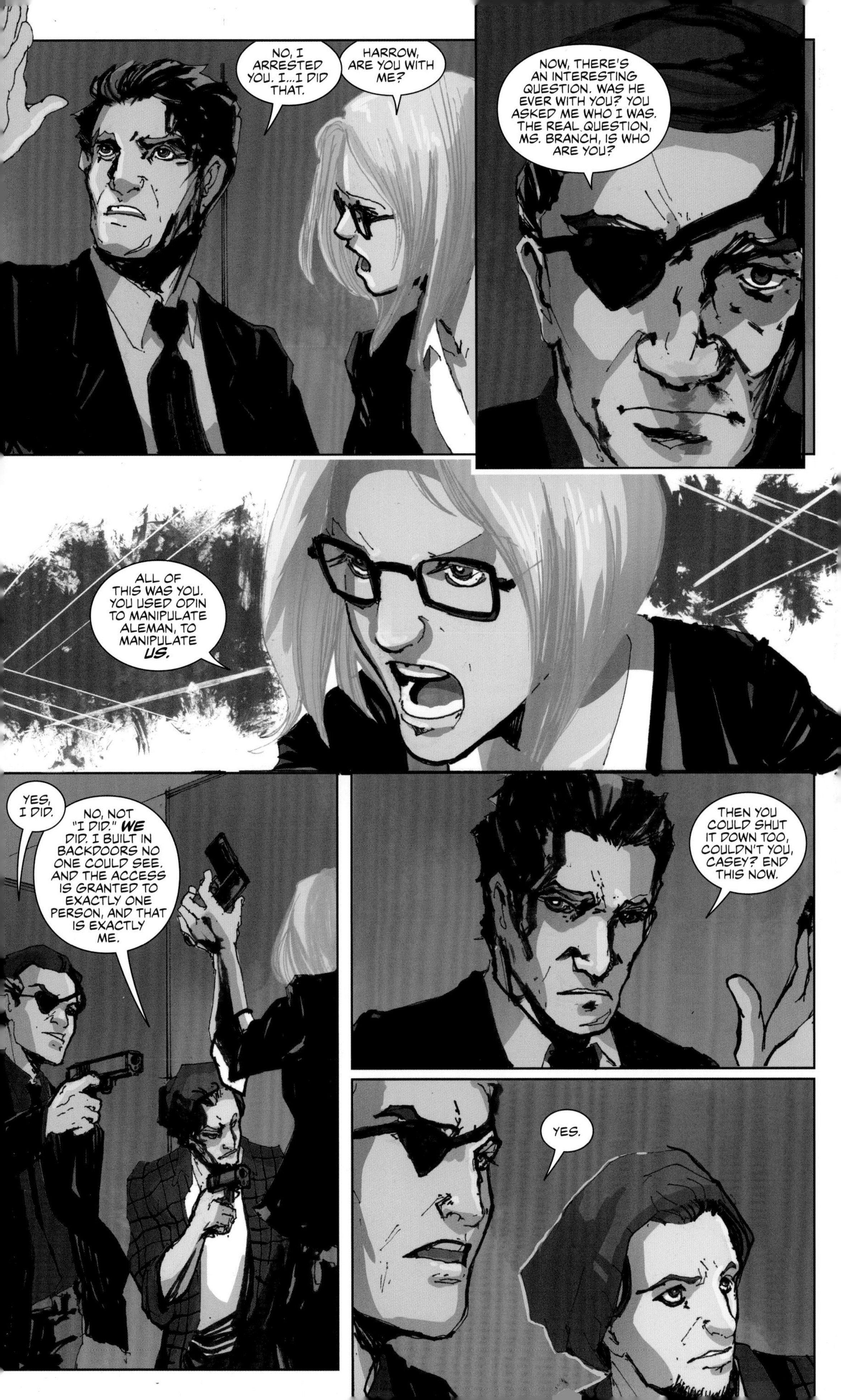
NO, I ARRESTED YOU. I...I DID THAT.
HARROW, ARE YOU WITH ME?
NOW, THERE'S AN INTERESTING QUESTION. WAS HE EVER WITH YOU? YOU ASKED ME WHO I WAS. THE REAL QUESTION, MS. BRANCH, IS WHO ARE YOU?
ALL OF THIS WAS YOU. YOU USED ODIN TO MANIPULATE ALEMAN, TO MANIPULATE US.
YES, I DID.
NO, NOT "I DID." WE DID. I BUILT IN BACKDOORS NO ONE COULD SEE. AND THE ACCESS IS GRANTED TO EXACTLY ONE PERSON, AND THAT IS EXACTLY ME.
THEN YOU COULD SHUT IT DOWN TOO, COULDN'T YOU, CASEY? END THIS NOW.
YES.

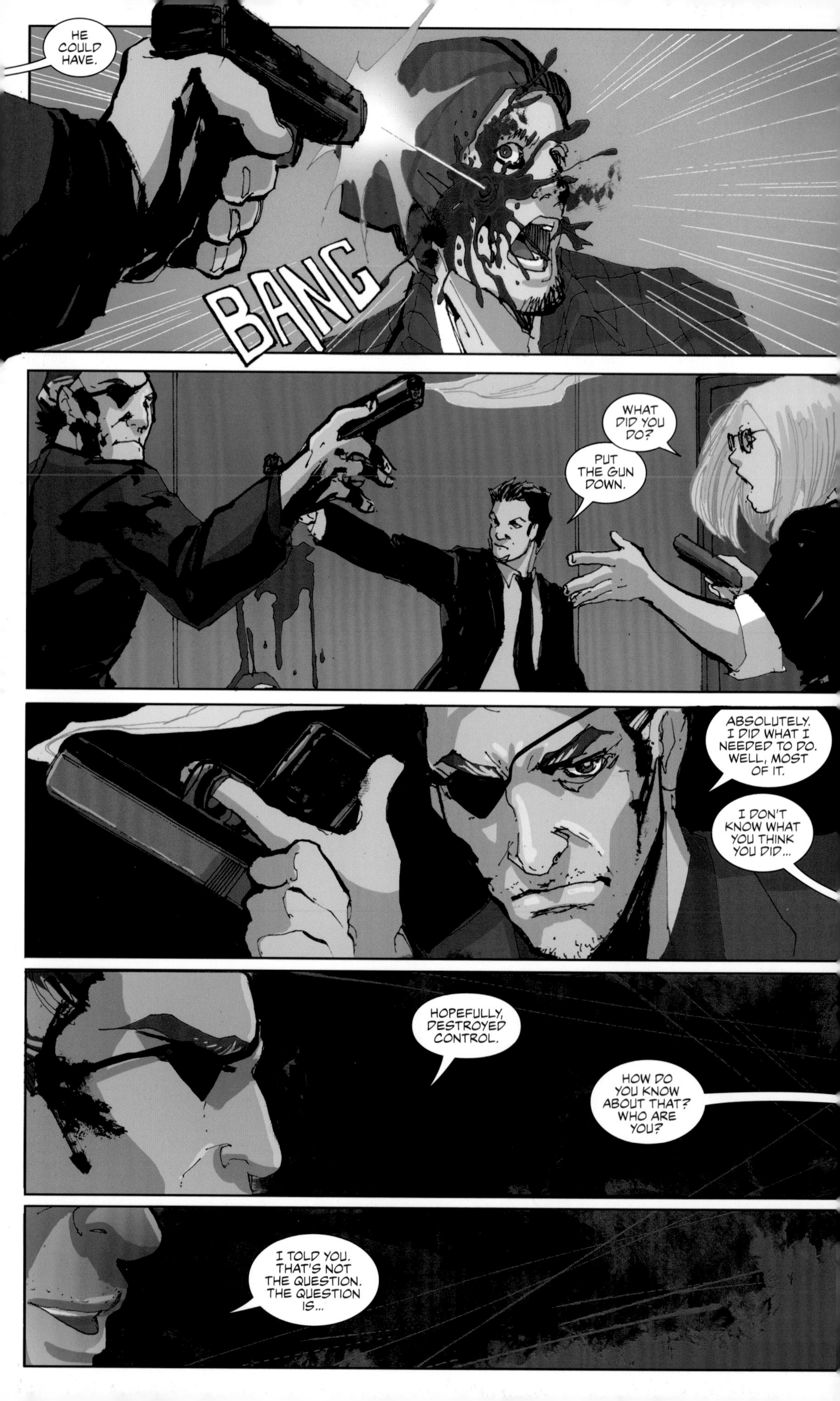

HE COULD HAVE.
BANG
WHAT DID YOU DO?
PUT THE GUN DOWN.
ABSOLUTELY. I DID WHAT I NEEDED TO DO. WELL, MOST OF IT.
I DON'T KNOW WHAT YOU THINK YOU DID...
HOPEFULLY, DESTROYED CONTROL.
HOW DO YOU KNOW ABOUT THAT? WHO ARE YOU?
I TOLD YOU. THAT'S NOT THE QUESTION. THE QUESTION IS...

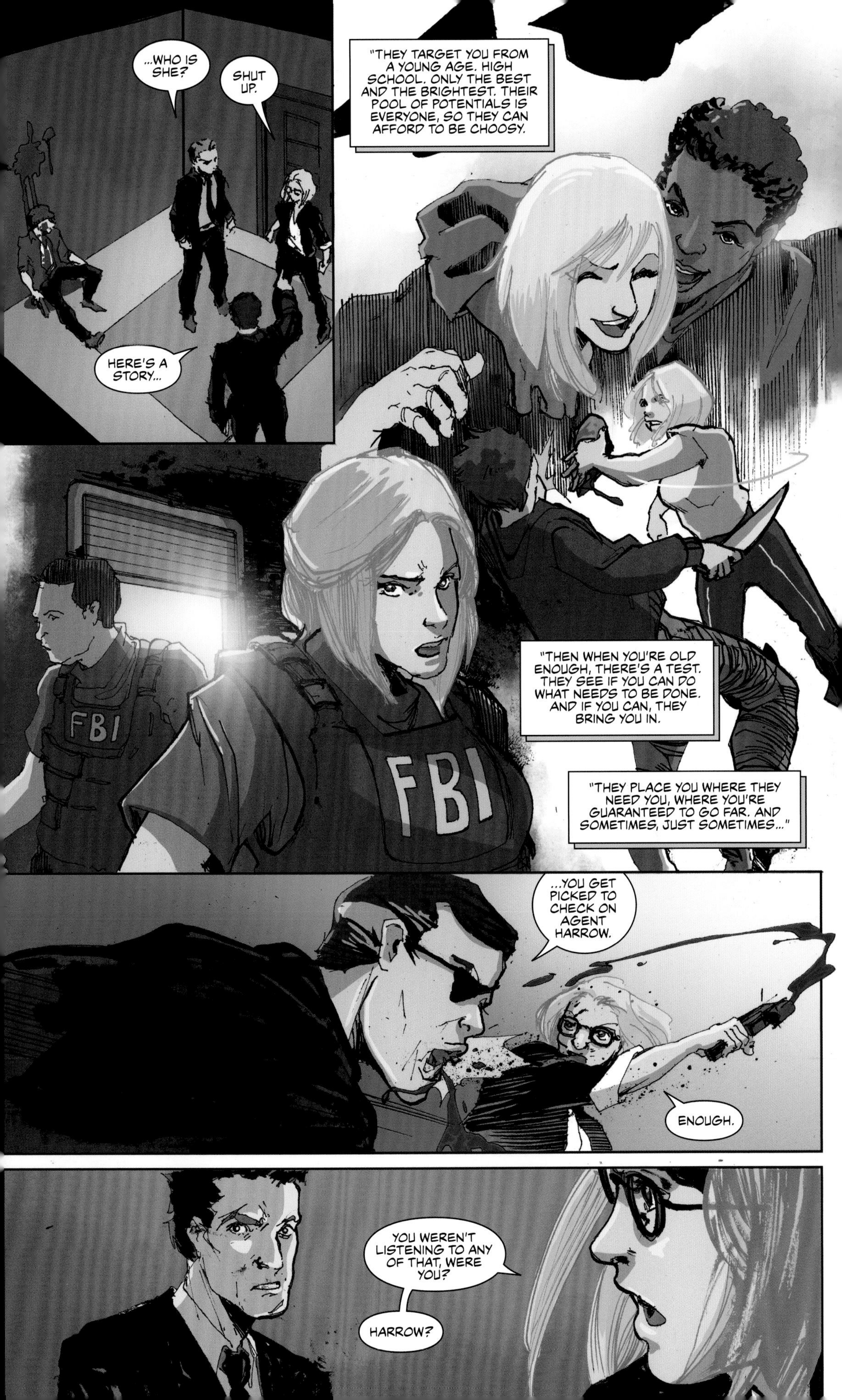
...WHO IS SHE?
SHUT UP.
HERE'S A STORY...
"THEY TARGET YOU FROM A YOUNG AGE. HIGH SCHOOL. ONLY THE BEST AND THE BRIGHTEST. THEIR POOL OF POTENTIALS IS EVERYONE, SO THEY CAN AFFORD TO BE CHOOSY.
"THEN WHEN YOU'RE OLD ENOUGH, THERE'S A TEST. THEY SEE IF YOU CAN DO WHAT NEEDS TO BE DONE. AND IF YOU CAN, THEY BRING YOU IN.
FBI
FBI
"THEY PLACE YOU WHERE THEY NEED YOU, WHERE YOU'RE GUARANTEED TO GO FAR. AND SOMETIMES, JUST SOMETIMES..."
...YOU GET PICKED TO CHECK ON AGENT HARROW.
ENOUGH.
YOU WEREN'T LISTENING TO ANY OF THAT, WERE YOU?
HARROW?

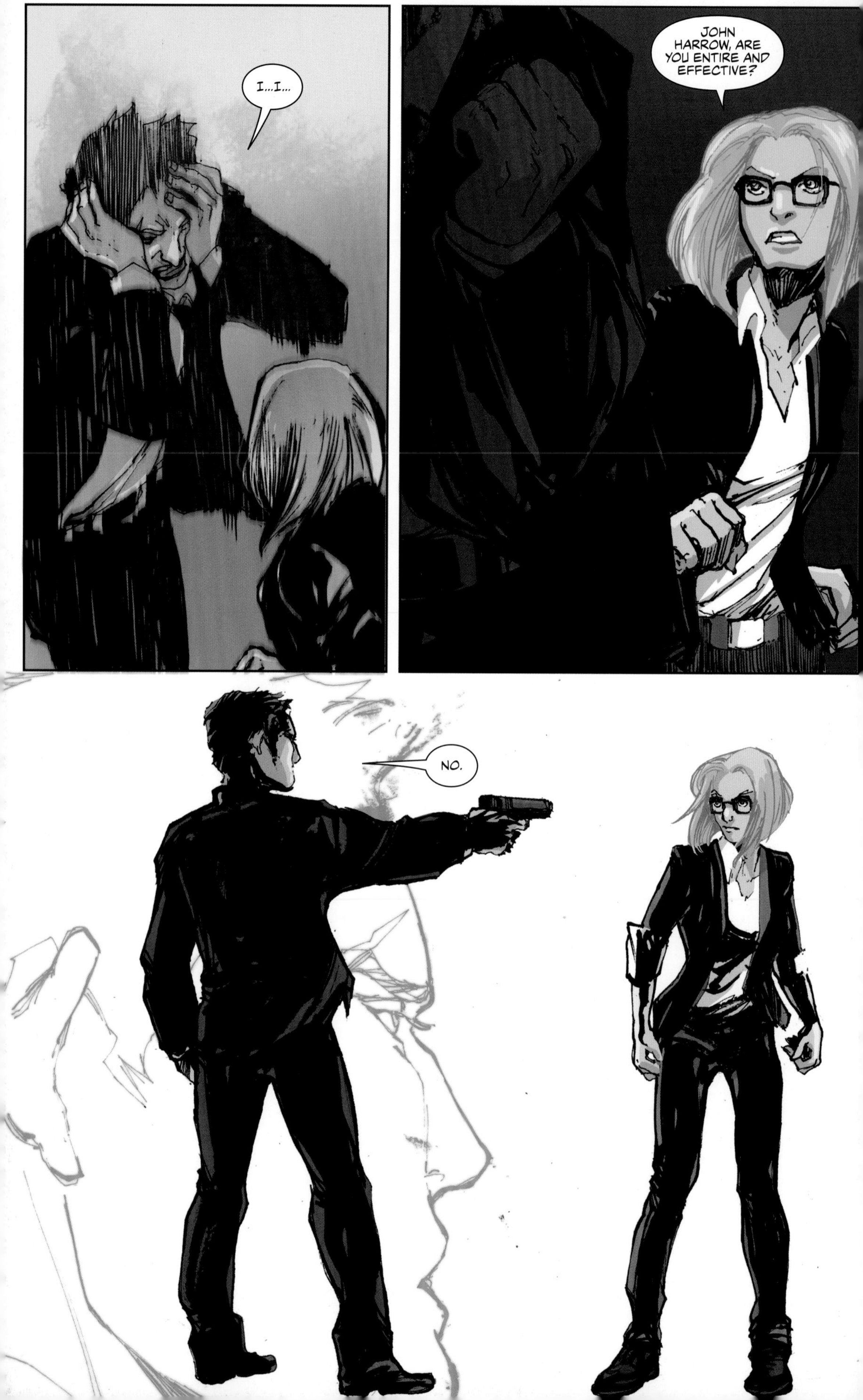
I...I...
JOHN HARROW, ARE YOU ENTIRE AND EFFECTIVE?
NO.

CHAPTER EIGHT

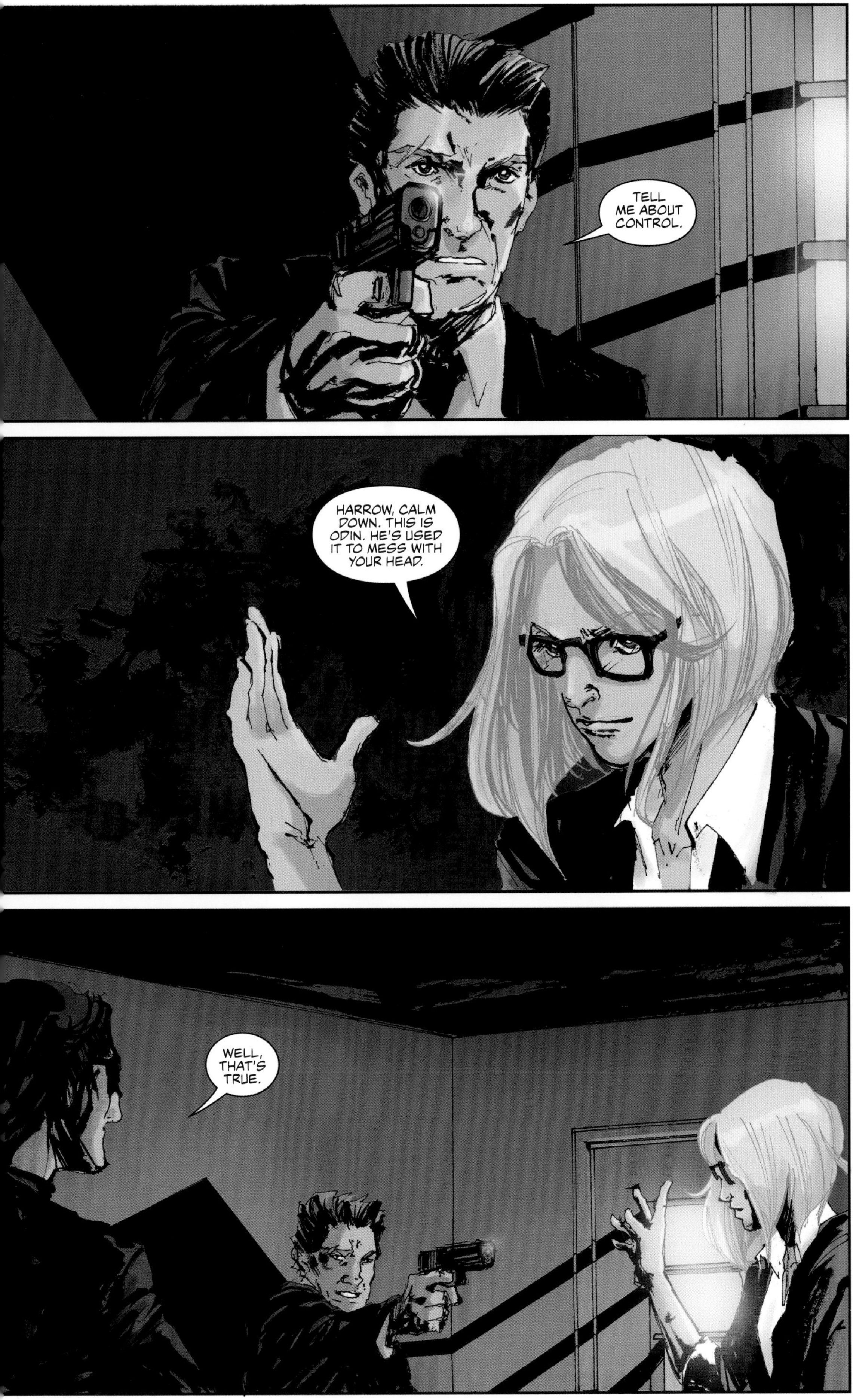
TELL ME ABOUT CONTROL.
HARROW, CALM DOWN. THIS IS ODIN. HE'S USED IT TO MESS WITH YOUR HEAD.
WELL, THAT'S TRUE.

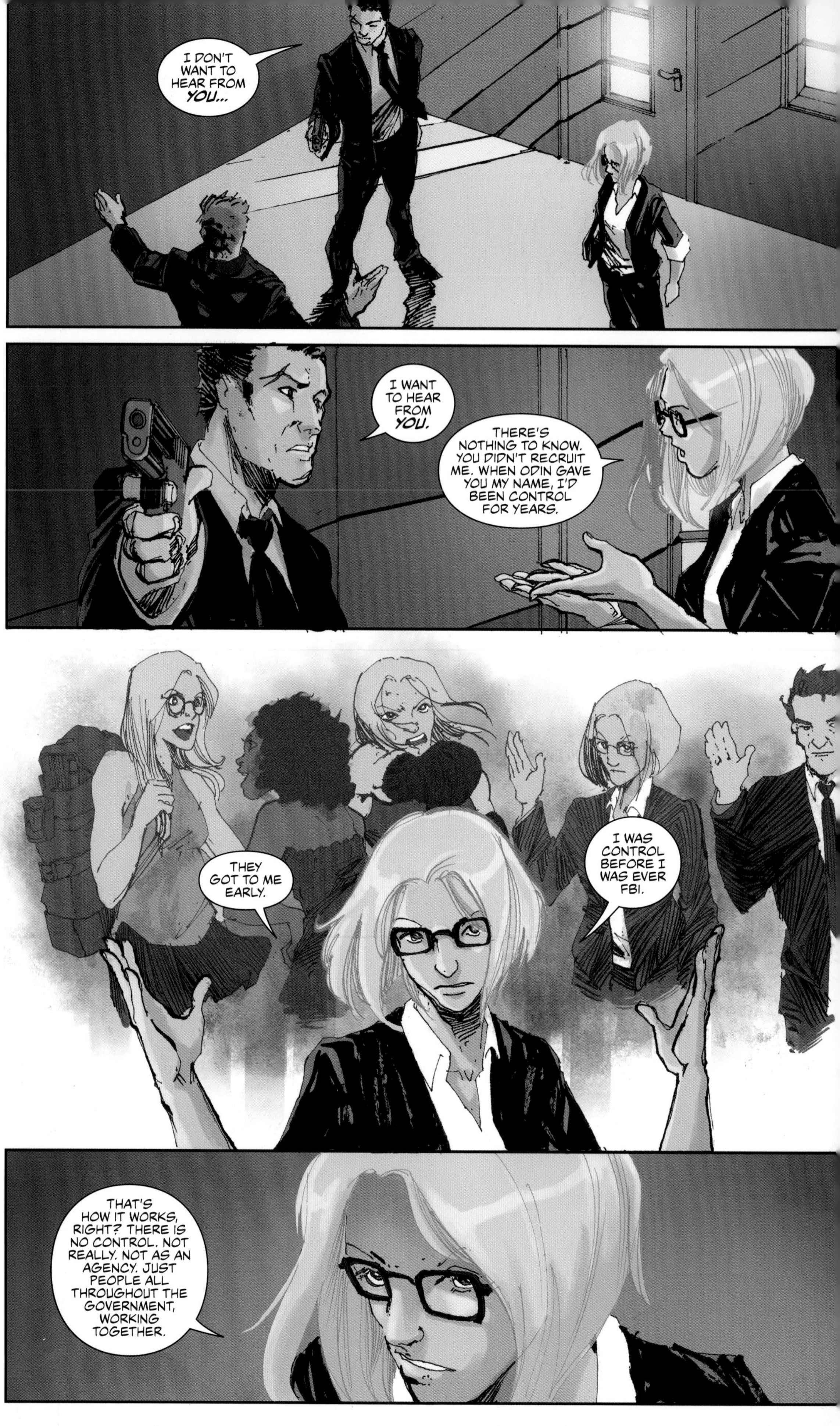
I DON'T WANT TO HEAR FROM *YOU*...
I WANT TO HEAR FROM *YOU*.
THERE'S NOTHING TO KNOW. YOU DIDN'T RECRUIT ME. WHEN ODIN GAVE YOU MY NAME, I'D BEEN CONTROL FOR YEARS.
THEY GOT TO ME EARLY.
I WAS CONTROL BEFORE I WAS EVER FBI.
THAT'S HOW IT WORKS, RIGHT? THERE IS NO CONTROL. NOT REALLY. NOT AS AN AGENCY. JUST PEOPLE ALL THROUGHOUT THE GOVERNMENT, WORKING TOGETHER.

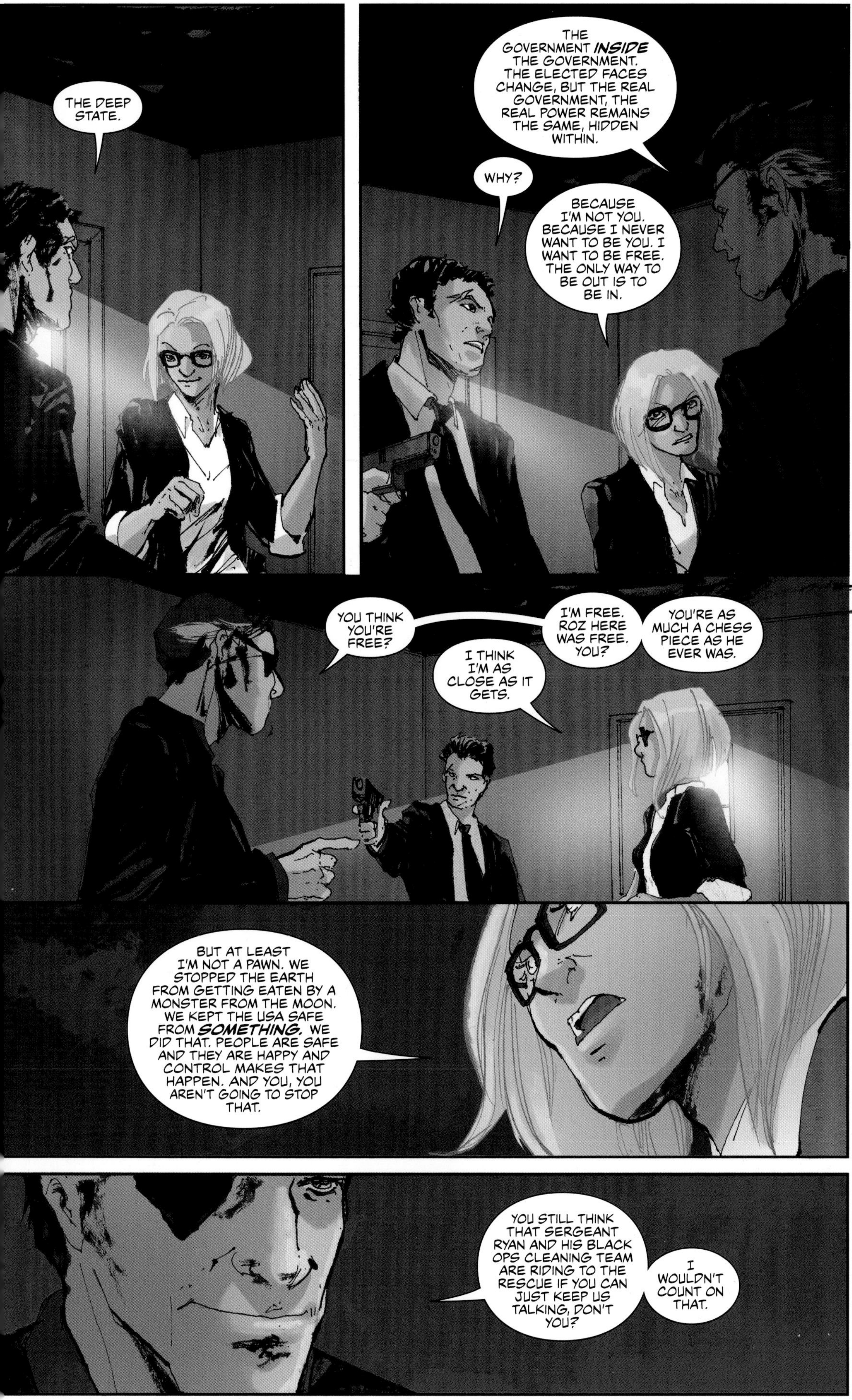
THE DEEP STATE.
THE GOVERNMENT *INSIDE* THE GOVERNMENT. THE ELECTED FACES CHANGE, BUT THE REAL GOVERNMENT, THE REAL POWER REMAINS THE SAME, HIDDEN WITHIN.
WHY?
BECAUSE I'M NOT YOU. BECAUSE I NEVER WANT TO BE YOU. I WANT TO BE FREE. THE ONLY WAY TO BE OUT IS TO BE IN.
YOU THINK YOU'RE FREE?
I'M FREE. ROZ HERE WAS FREE. YOU?
YOU'RE AS MUCH A CHESS PIECE AS HE EVER WAS.
I THINK I'M AS CLOSE AS IT GETS.
BUT AT LEAST I'M NOT A PAWN. WE STOPPED THE EARTH FROM GETTING EATEN BY A MONSTER FROM THE MOON. WE KEPT THE USA SAFE FROM *SOMETHING.* WE DID THAT. PEOPLE ARE SAFE AND THEY ARE HAPPY AND CONTROL MAKES THAT HAPPEN. AND YOU, YOU AREN'T GOING TO STOP THAT.
YOU STILL THINK THAT SERGEANT RYAN AND HIS BLACK OPS CLEANING TEAM ARE RIDING TO THE RESCUE IF YOU CAN JUST KEEP US TALKING, DON'T YOU?
I WOULDN'T COUNT ON THAT.

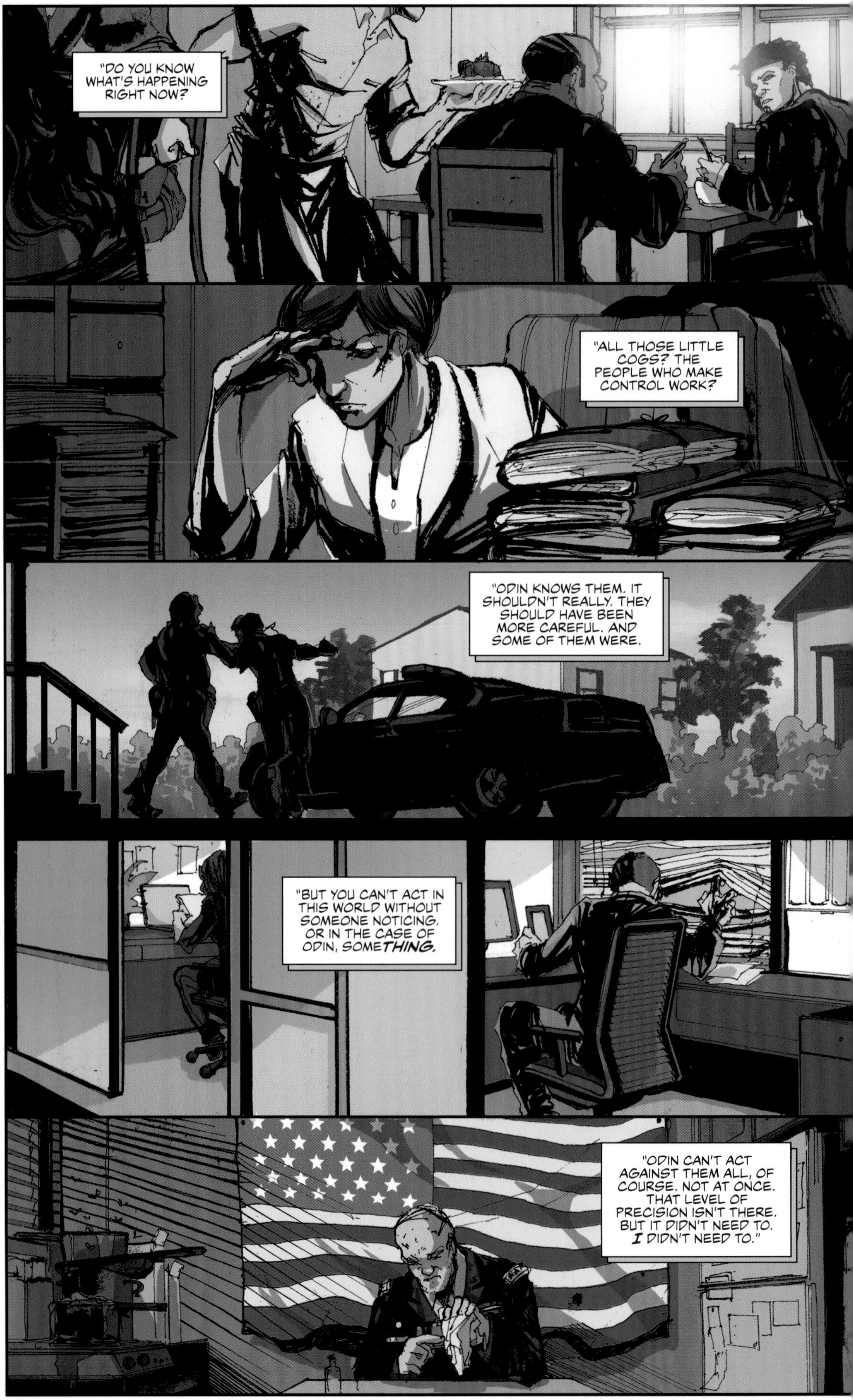
"DO YOU KNOW WHAT'S HAPPENING RIGHT NOW?
"ALL THOSE LITTLE COGS? THE PEOPLE WHO MAKE CONTROL WORK?
"ODIN KNOWS THEM. IT SHOULDN'T REALLY. THEY SHOULD HAVE BEEN MORE CAREFUL. AND SOME OF THEM WERE.
"BUT YOU CAN'T ACT IN THIS WORLD WITHOUT SOMEONE NOTICING. OR IN THE CASE OF ODIN, SOME*THING.*
"ODIN CAN'T ACT AGAINST THEM ALL, OF COURSE. NOT AT ONCE. THAT LEVEL OF PRECISION ISN'T THERE. BUT IT DIDN'T NEED TO. *I* DIDN'T NEED TO."

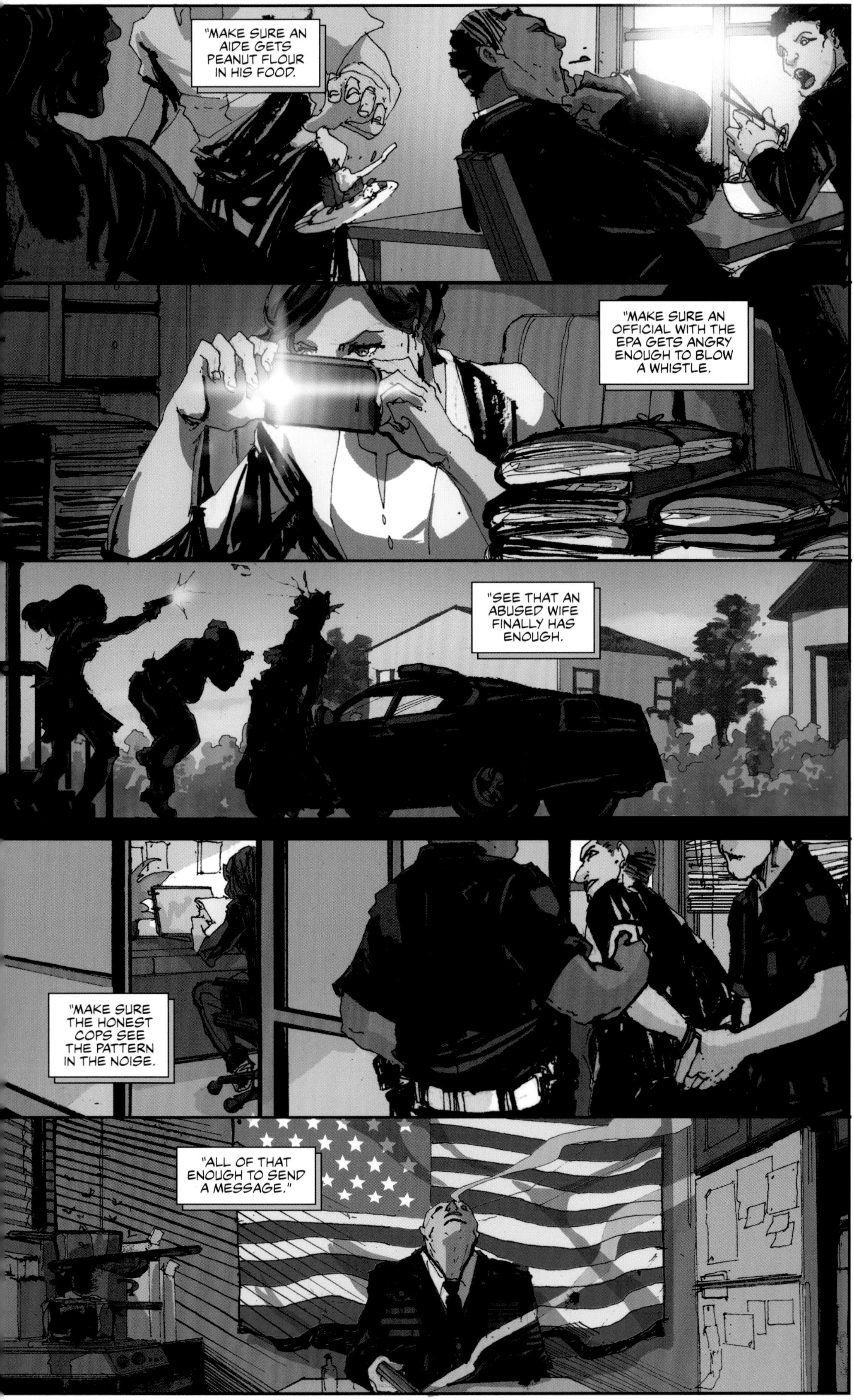
"MAKE SURE AN AIDE GETS PEANUT FLOUR IN HIS FOOD.
"MAKE SURE AN OFFICIAL WITH THE EPA GETS ANGRY ENOUGH TO BLOW A WHISTLE.
"SEE THAT AN ABUSED WIFE FINALLY HAS ENOUGH.
"MAKE SURE THE HONEST COPS SEE THE PATTERN IN THE NOISE.
"ALL OF THAT ENOUGH TO SEND A MESSAGE."

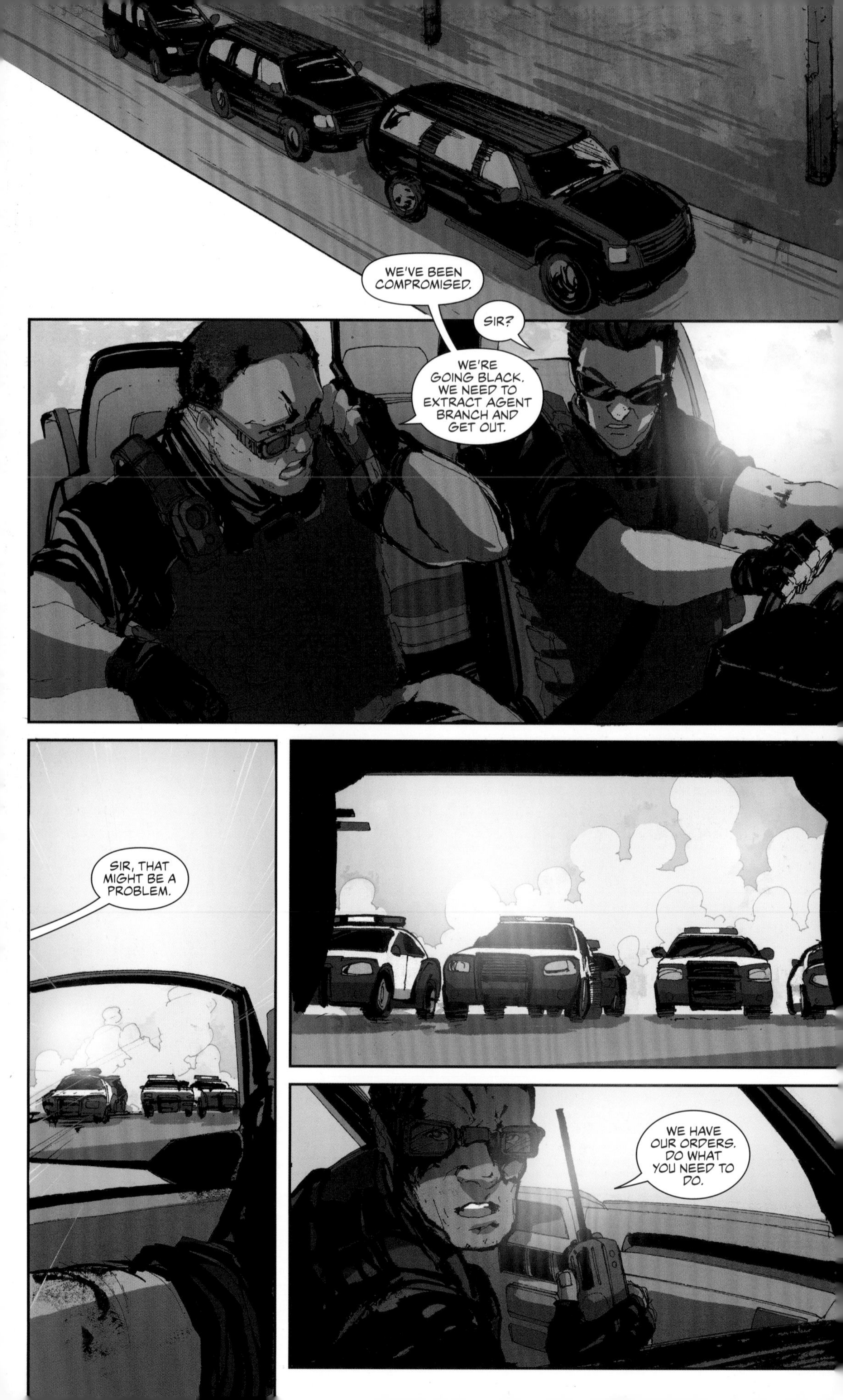
WE'VE BEEN COMPROMISED.
SIR?
WE'RE GOING BLACK. WE NEED TO EXTRACT AGENT BRANCH AND GET OUT.
SIR, THAT MIGHT BE A PROBLEM.
WE HAVE OUR ORDERS. DO WHAT YOU NEED TO DO.

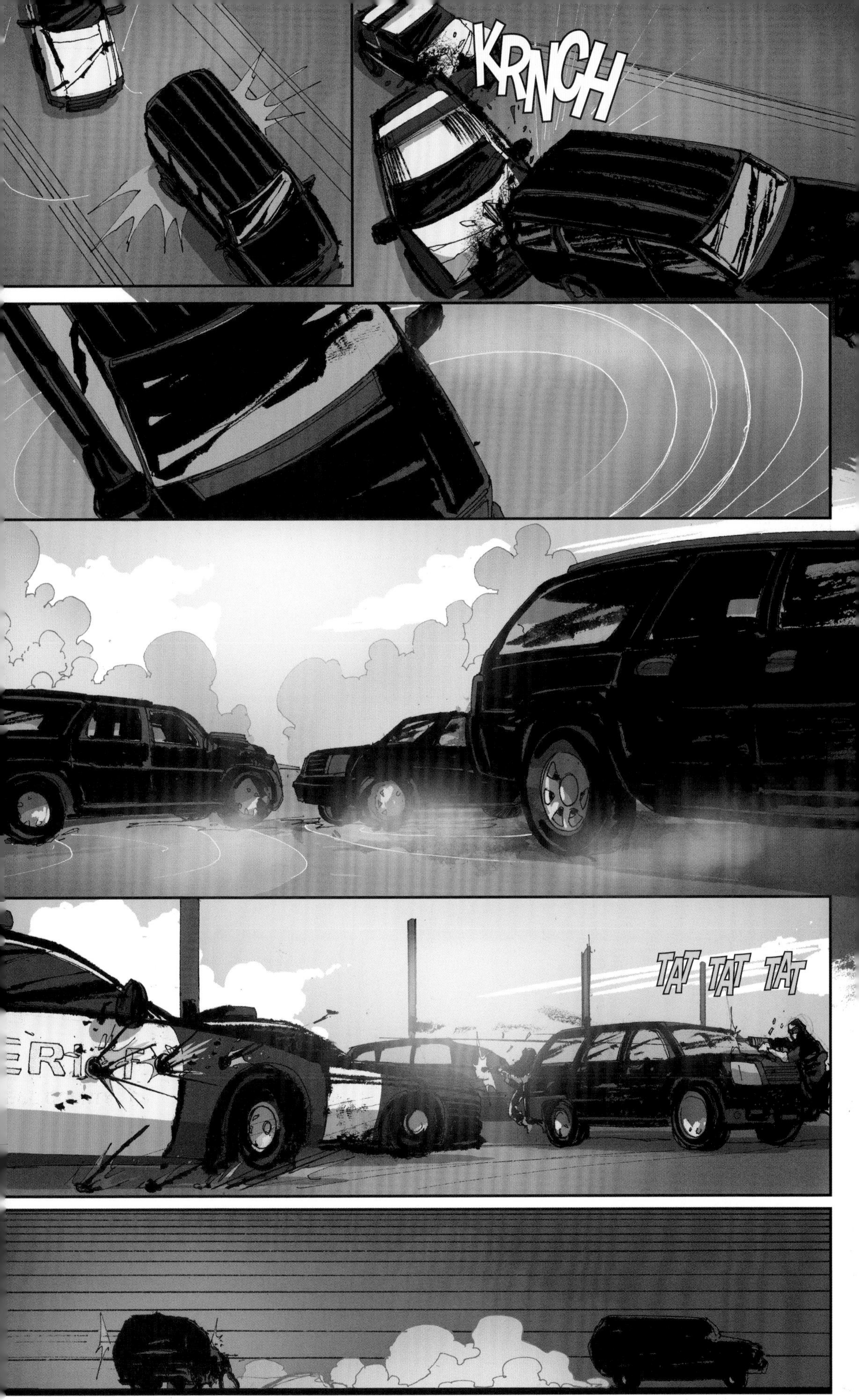
KRNCH
TAT TAT TAT

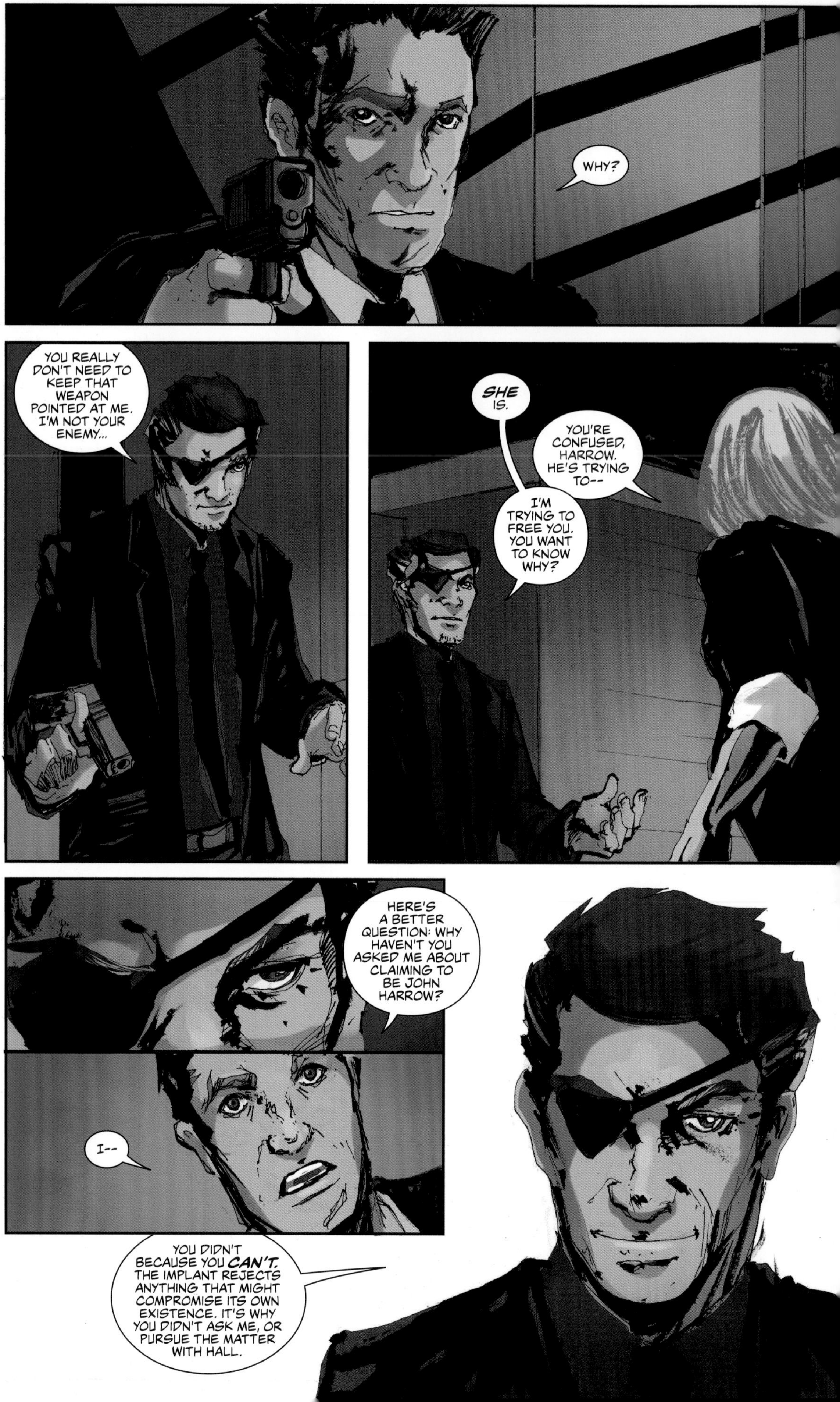
WHY?
YOU REALLY DON'T NEED TO KEEP THAT WEAPON POINTED AT ME. I'M NOT YOUR ENEMY...
SHE IS.
YOU'RE CONFUSED, HARROW. HE'S TRYING TO--
I'M TRYING TO FREE YOU. YOU WANT TO KNOW WHY?
HERE'S A BETTER QUESTION: WHY HAVEN'T YOU ASKED ME ABOUT CLAIMING TO BE JOHN HARROW?
I--
YOU DIDN'T BECAUSE YOU *CAN'T.* THE IMPLANT REJECTS ANYTHING THAT MIGHT COMPROMISE ITS OWN EXISTENCE. IT'S WHY YOU DIDN'T ASK ME, OR PURSUE THE MATTER WITH HALL.

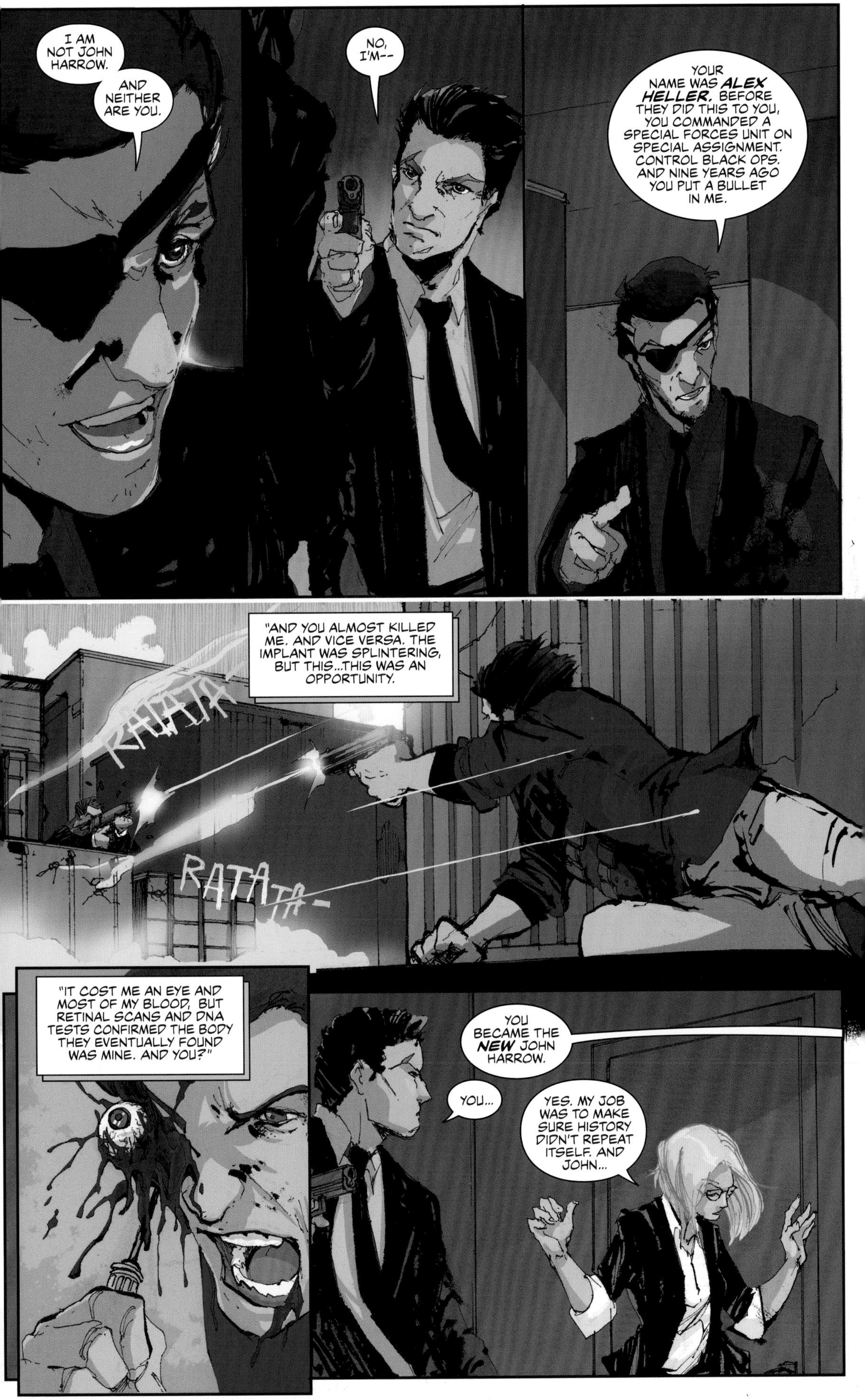
I AM NOT JOHN HARROW.
AND NEITHER ARE YOU.
NO, I'M--
YOUR NAME WAS ALEX HELLER. BEFORE THEY DID THIS TO YOU, YOU COMMANDED A SPECIAL FORCES UNIT ON SPECIAL ASSIGNMENT. CONTROL BLACK OPS. AND NINE YEARS AGO YOU PUT A BULLET IN ME.
"AND YOU ALMOST KILLED ME. AND VICE VERSA. THE IMPLANT WAS SPLINTERING, BUT THIS...THIS WAS AN OPPORTUNITY.
RATATA-
RATATA-
"IT COST ME AN EYE AND MOST OF MY BLOOD, BUT RETINAL SCANS AND DNA TESTS CONFIRMED THE BODY THEY EVENTUALLY FOUND WAS MINE. AND YOU?"
YOU BECAME THE NEW JOHN HARROW.
YOU...
YES. MY JOB WAS TO MAKE SURE HISTORY DIDN'T REPEAT ITSELF. AND JOHN...

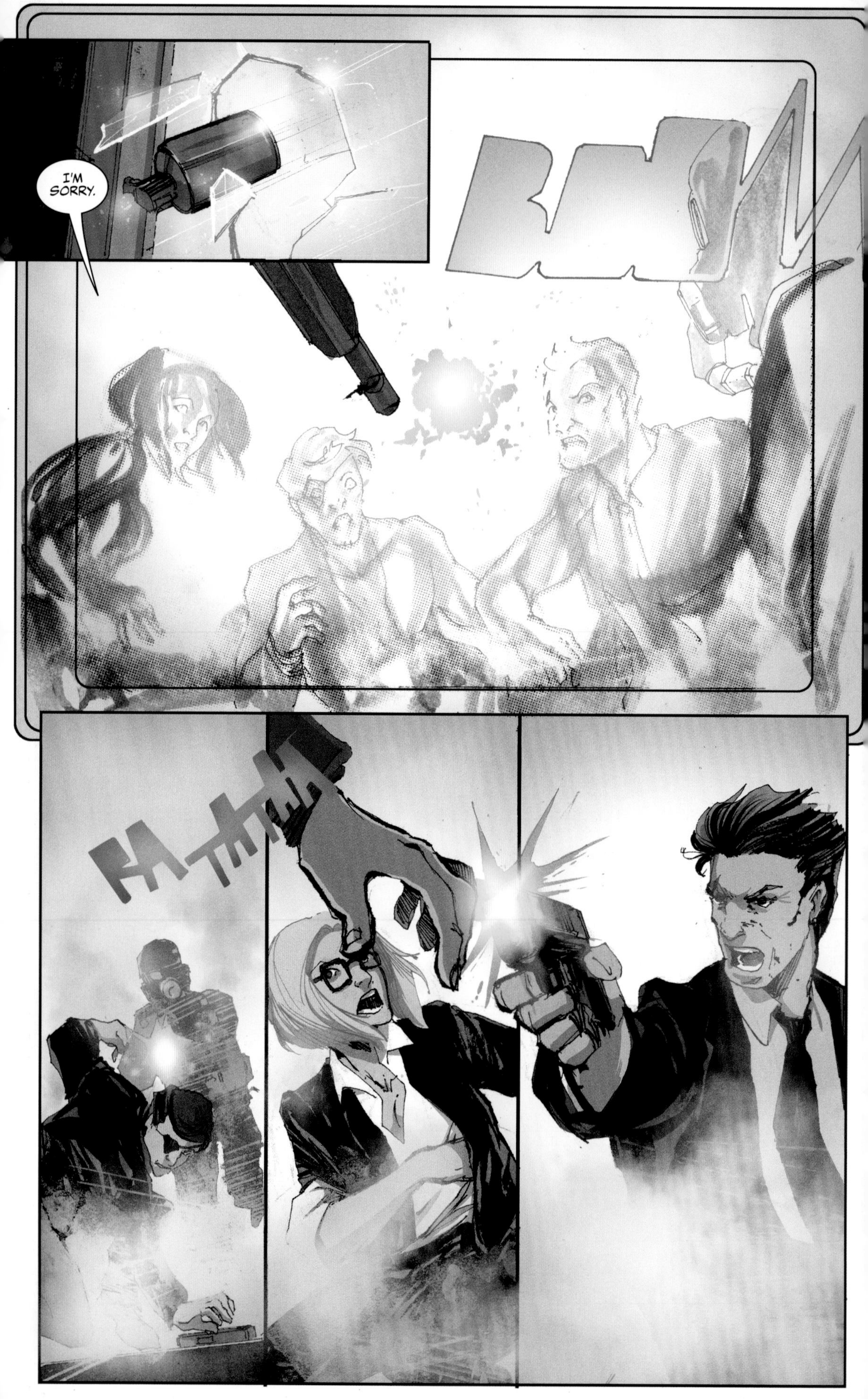
I'M SORRY.
BLAM
BLAM
BATTEM

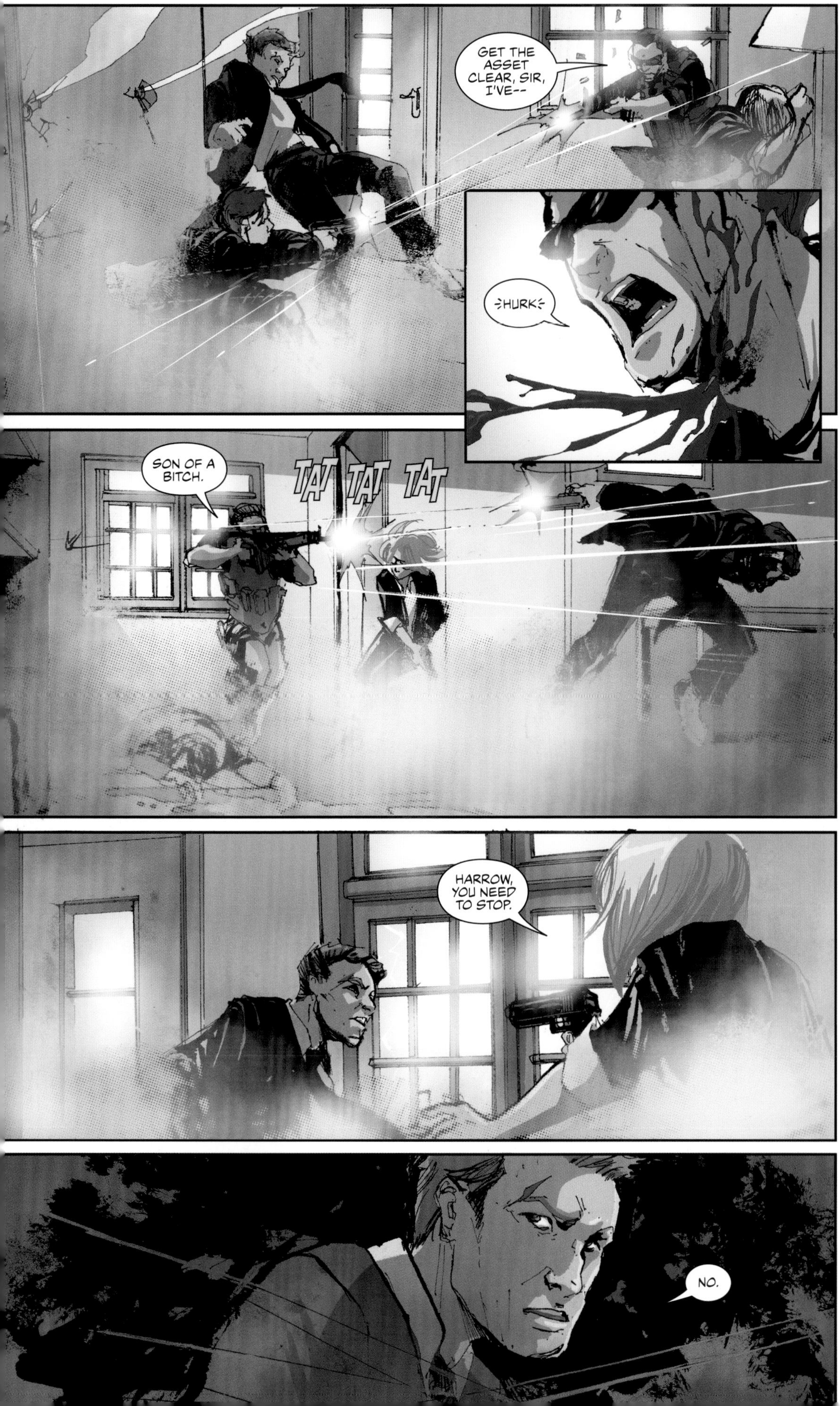
GET THE ASSET CLEAR, SIR, I'VE--
HURK
SON OF A BITCH.
TAT TAT TAT
HARROW, YOU NEED TO STOP.
NO.

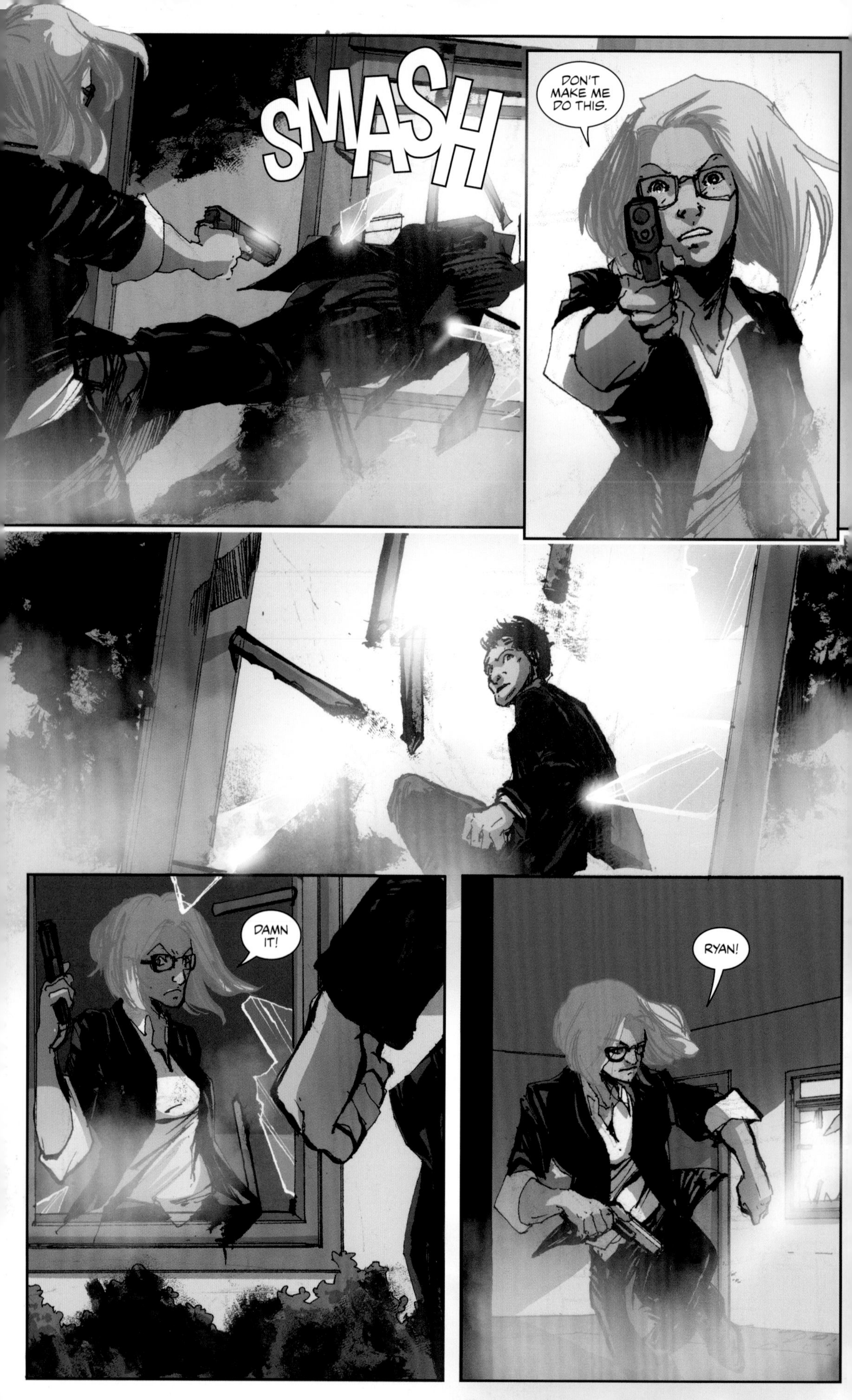
SMASH
DON'T MAKE ME DO THIS.
DAMN IT!
RYAN!

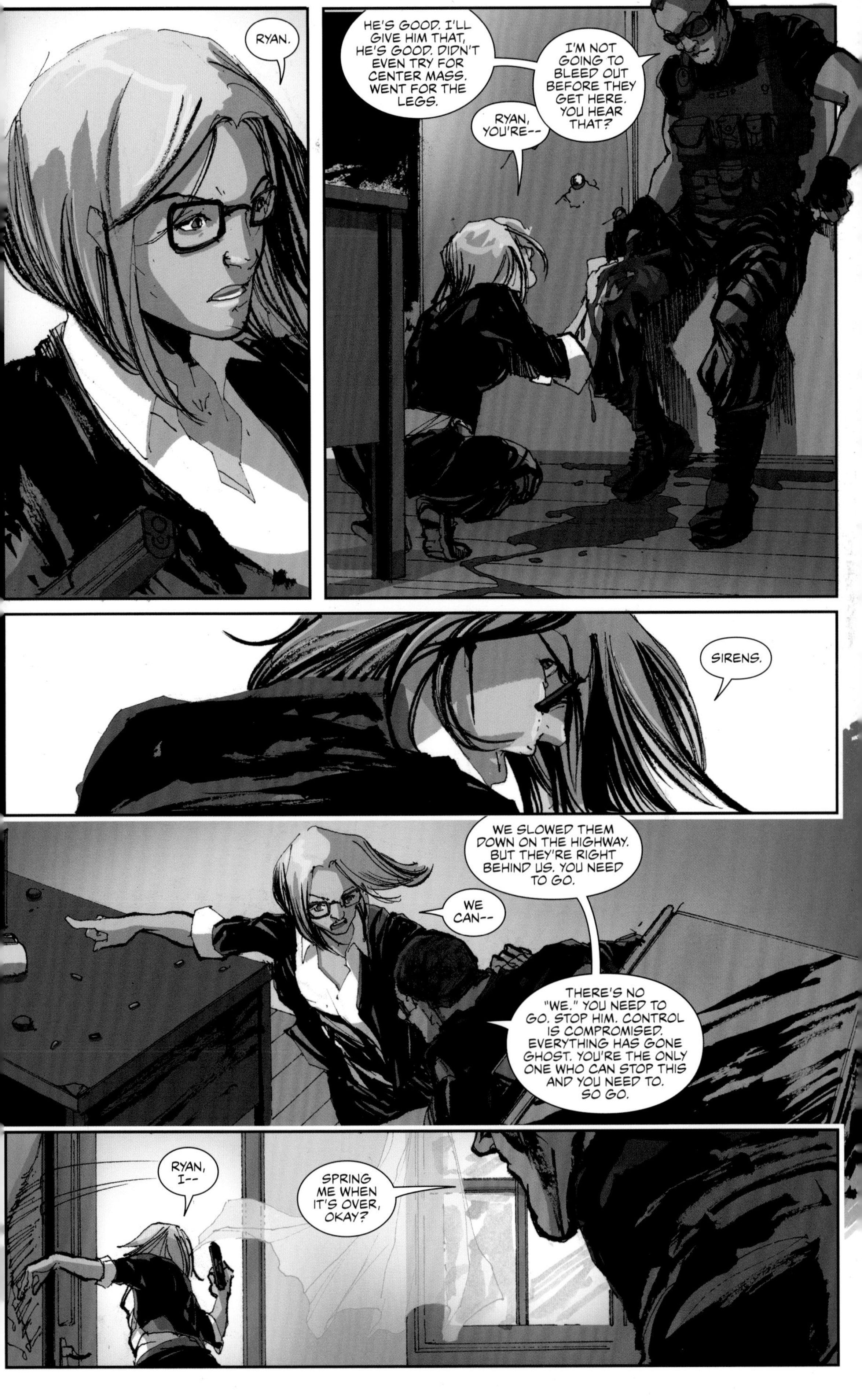
RYAN.
HE'S GOOD. I'LL GIVE HIM THAT, HE'S GOOD. DIDN'T EVEN TRY FOR CENTER MASS. WENT FOR THE LEGS.
RYAN, YOU'RE--
I'M NOT GOING TO BLEED OUT BEFORE THEY GET HERE. YOU HEAR THAT?
SIRENS.
WE SLOWED THEM DOWN ON THE HIGHWAY. BUT THEY'RE RIGHT BEHIND US. YOU NEED TO GO.
WE CAN--
THERE'S NO "WE." YOU NEED TO GO. STOP HIM. CONTROL IS COMPROMISED. EVERYTHING HAS GONE GHOST. YOU'RE THE ONLY ONE WHO CAN STOP THIS AND YOU NEED TO. SO GO.
RYAN, I--
SPRING ME WHEN IT'S OVER, OKAY?

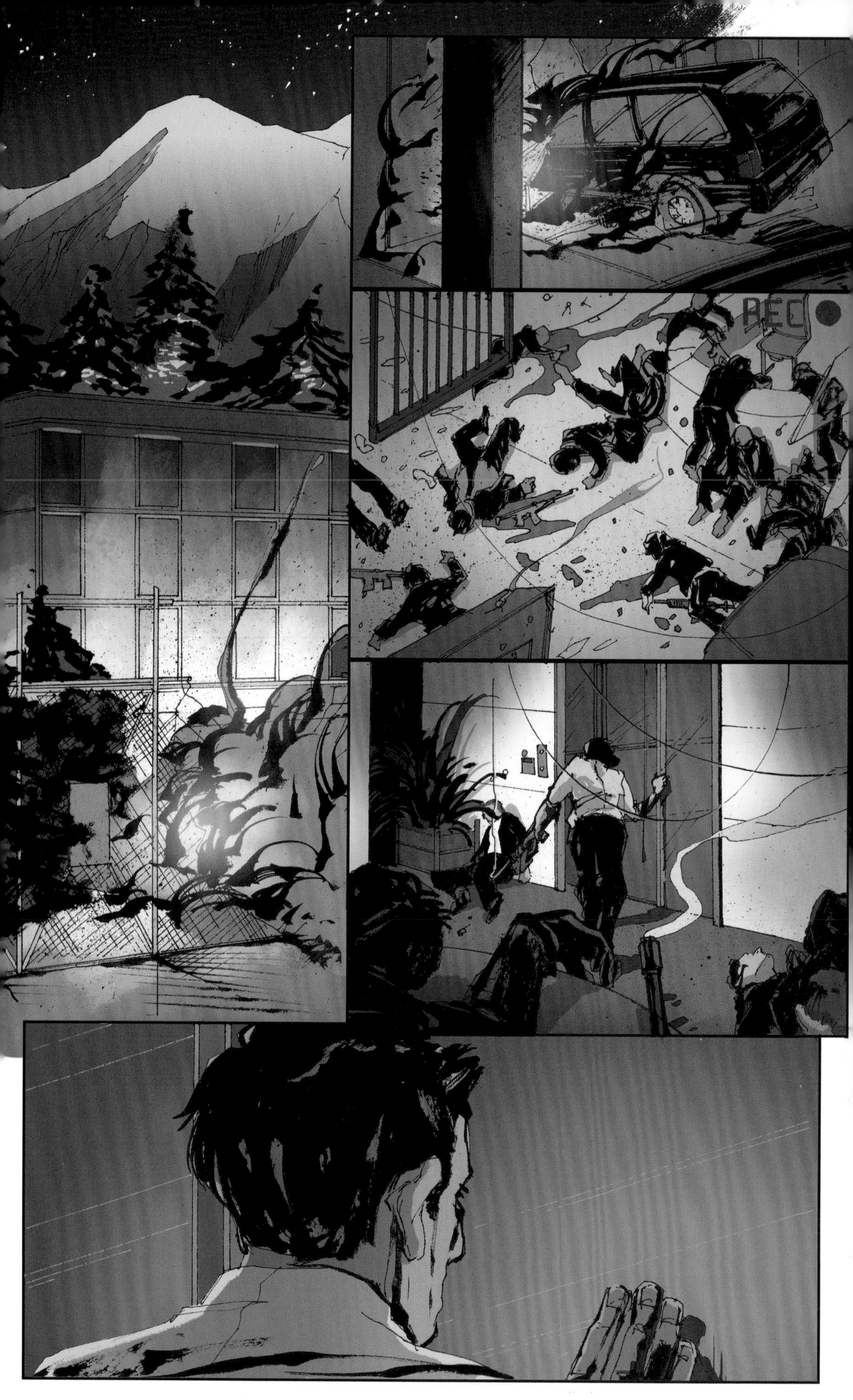
REC

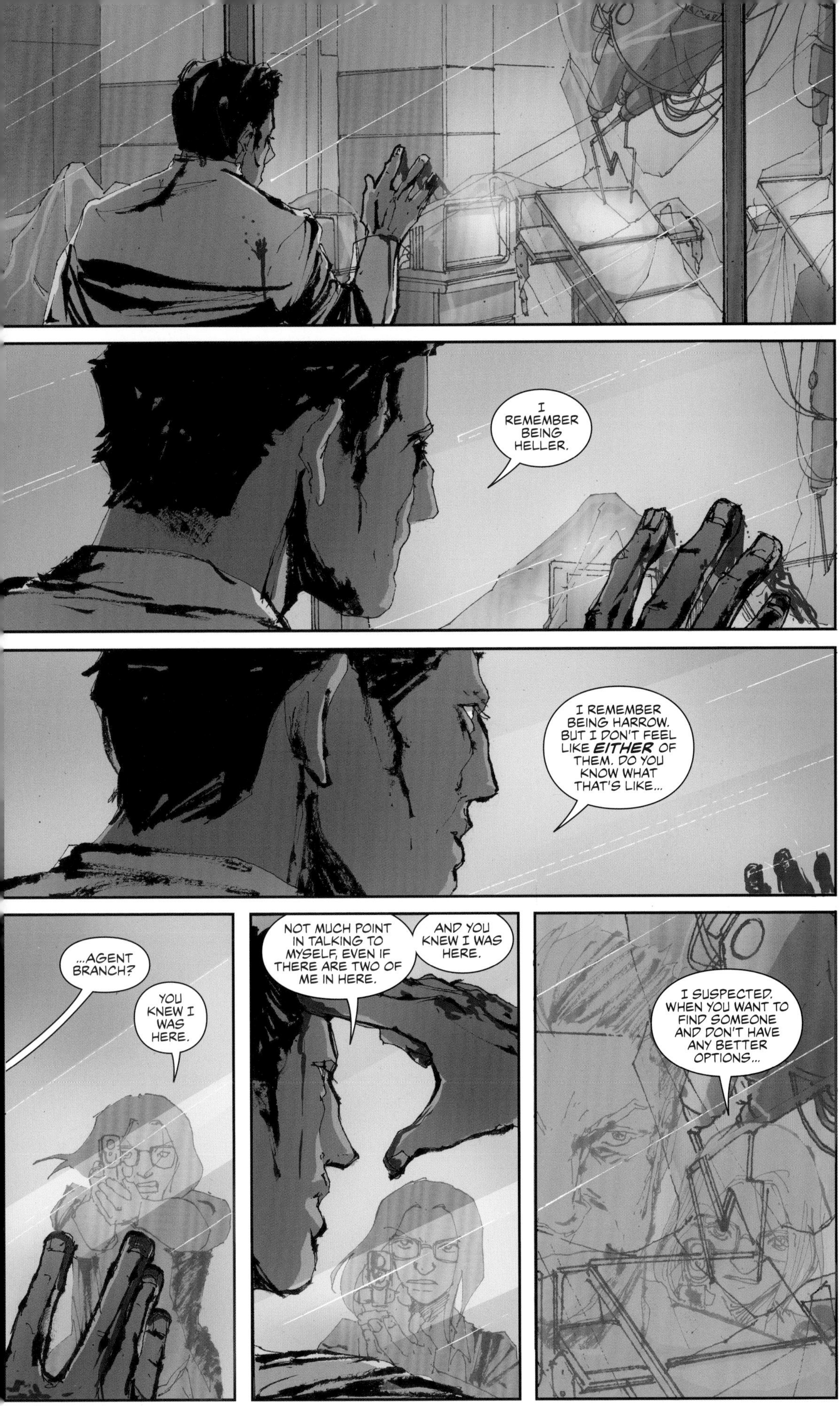
I REMEMBER BEING HELLER.
I REMEMBER BEING HARROW. BUT I DON'T FEEL LIKE *EITHER* OF THEM. DO YOU KNOW WHAT THAT'S LIKE...
...AGENT BRANCH?
YOU KNEW I WAS HERE.
NOT MUCH POINT IN TALKING TO MYSELF, EVEN IF THERE ARE TWO OF ME IN HERE.
AND YOU KNEW I WAS HERE.
I SUSPECTED. WHEN YOU WANT TO FIND SOMEONE AND DON'T HAVE ANY BETTER OPTIONS...

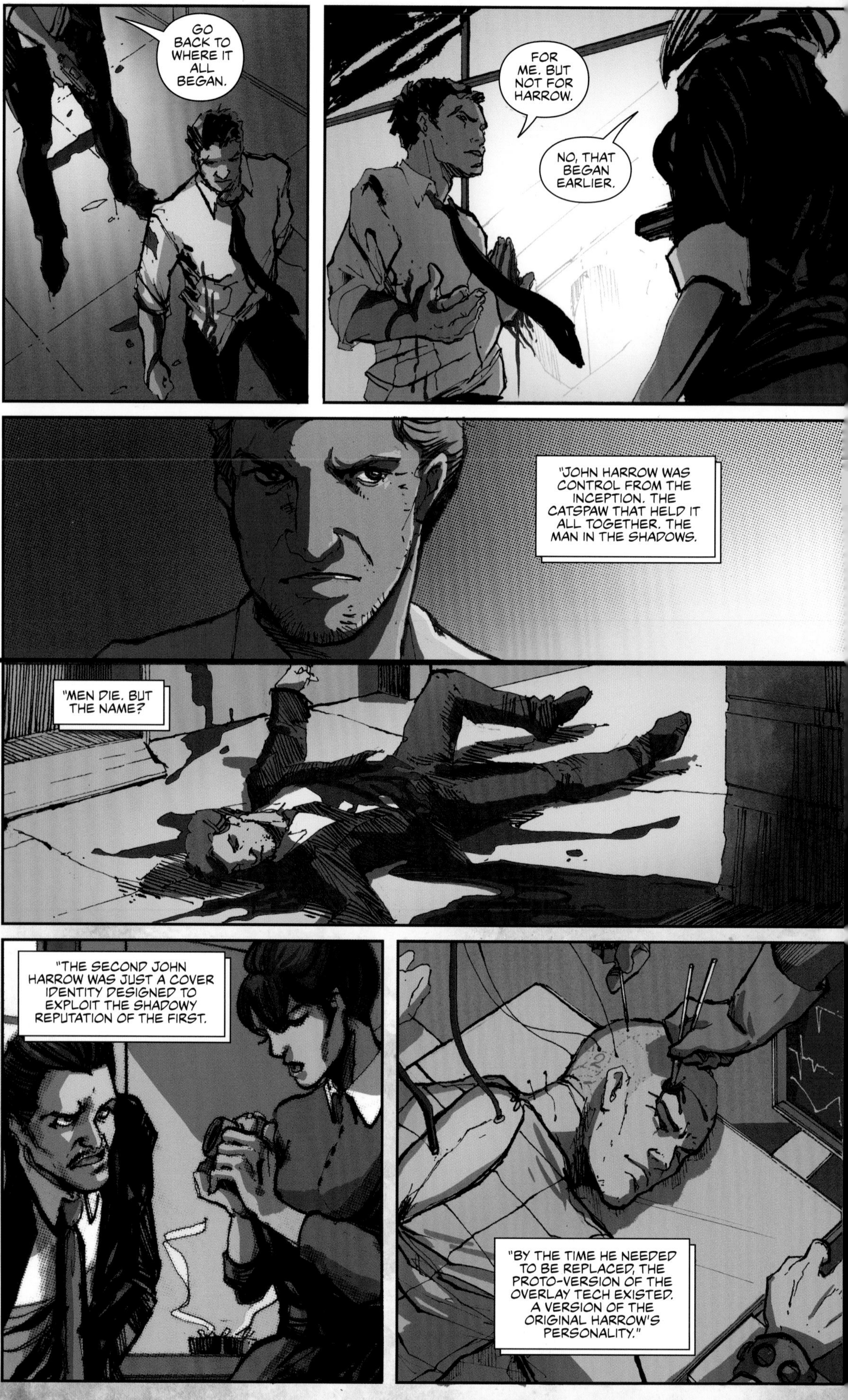
GO BACK TO WHERE IT ALL BEGAN.
FOR ME. BUT NOT FOR HARROW.
NO, THAT BEGAN EARLIER.
"JOHN HARROW WAS CONTROL FROM THE INCEPTION. THE CATSPAW THAT HELD IT ALL TOGETHER. THE MAN IN THE SHADOWS.
"MEN DIE. BUT THE NAME?
"THE SECOND JOHN HARROW WAS JUST A COVER IDENTITY DESIGNED TO EXPLOIT THE SHADOWY REPUTATION OF THE FIRST.
"BY THE TIME HE NEEDED TO BE REPLACED, THE PROTO-VERSION OF THE OVERLAY TECH EXISTED. A VERSION OF THE ORIGINAL HARROW'S PERSONALITY."

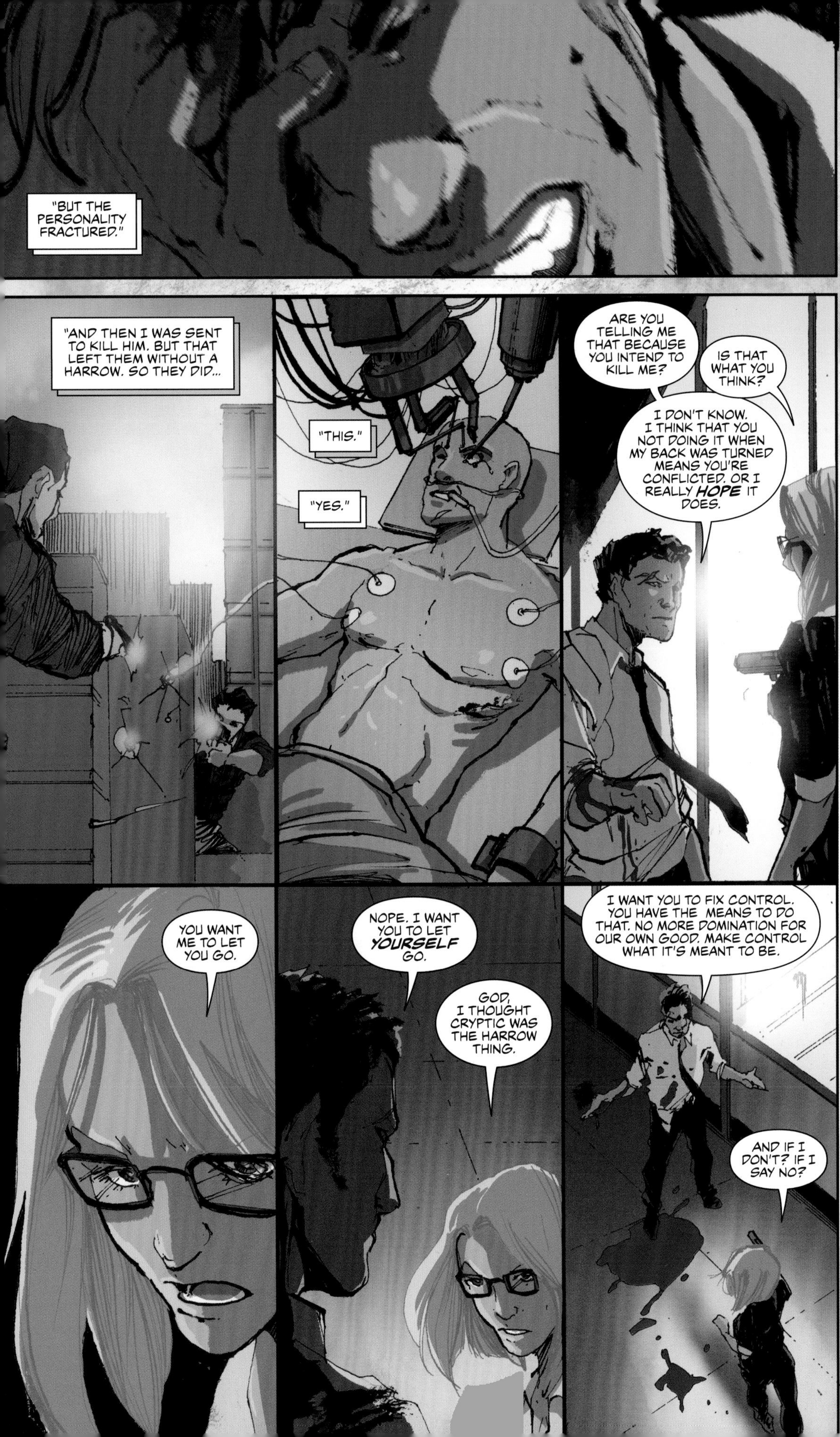
"BUT THE PERSONALITY FRACTURED."
"AND THEN I WAS SENT TO KILL HIM. BUT THAT LEFT THEM WITHOUT A HARROW. SO THEY DID...
"THIS."
"YES."
ARE YOU TELLING ME THAT BECAUSE YOU INTEND TO KILL ME?
IS THAT WHAT YOU THINK?
I DON'T KNOW. I THINK THAT YOU NOT DOING IT WHEN MY BACK WAS TURNED MEANS YOU'RE CONFLICTED. OR I REALLY **HOPE** IT DOES.
YOU WANT ME TO LET YOU GO.
NOPE. I WANT YOU TO LET ***YOURSELF*** GO.
GOD, I THOUGHT CRYPTIC WAS THE HARROW THING.
I WANT YOU TO FIX CONTROL. YOU HAVE THE MEANS TO DO THAT. NO MORE DOMINATION FOR OUR OWN GOOD. MAKE CONTROL WHAT IT'S MEANT TO BE.
AND IF I DON'T? IF I SAY NO?

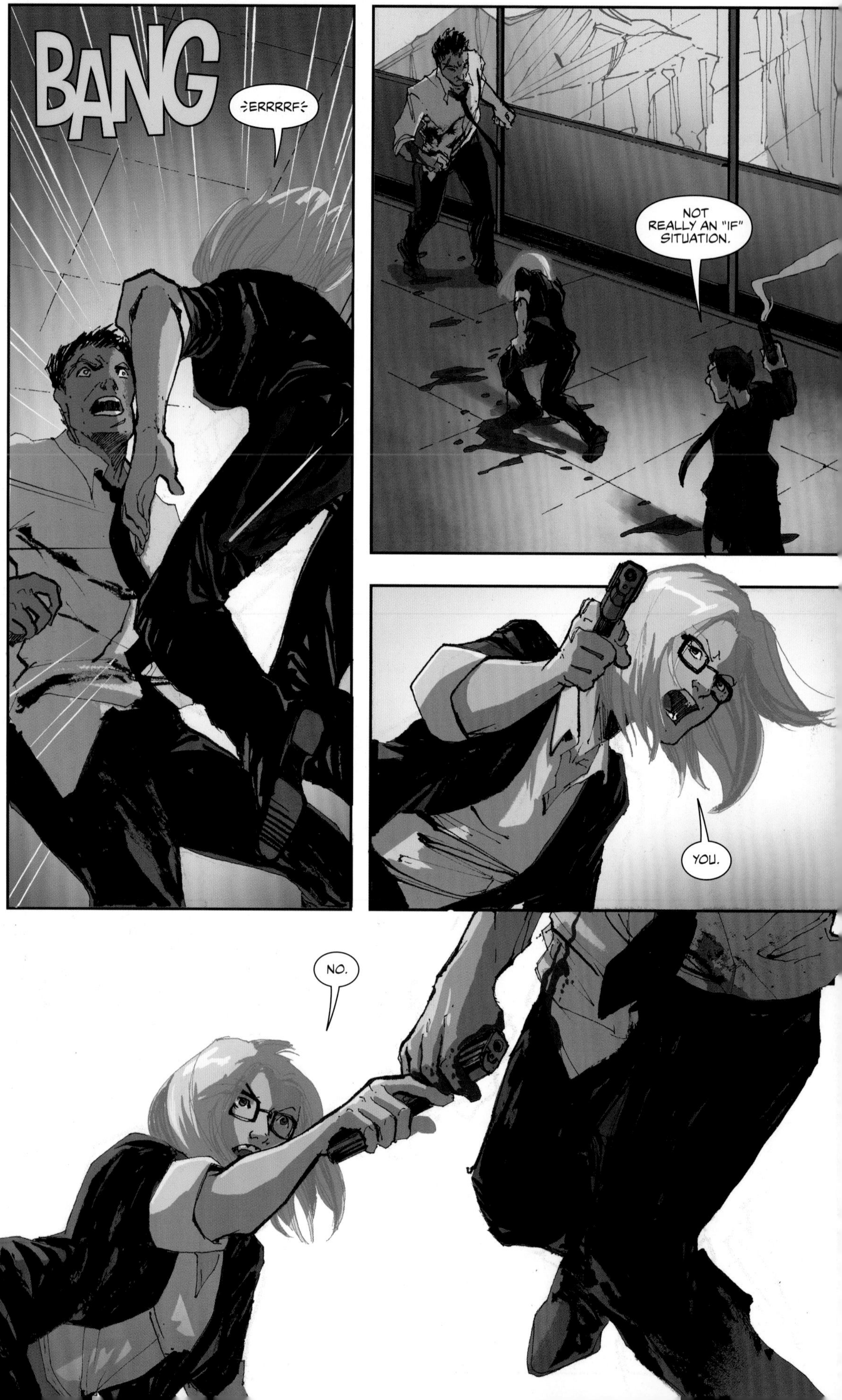
BANG
ERRRRF
NOT REALLY AN "IF" SITUATION.
YOU.
NO.

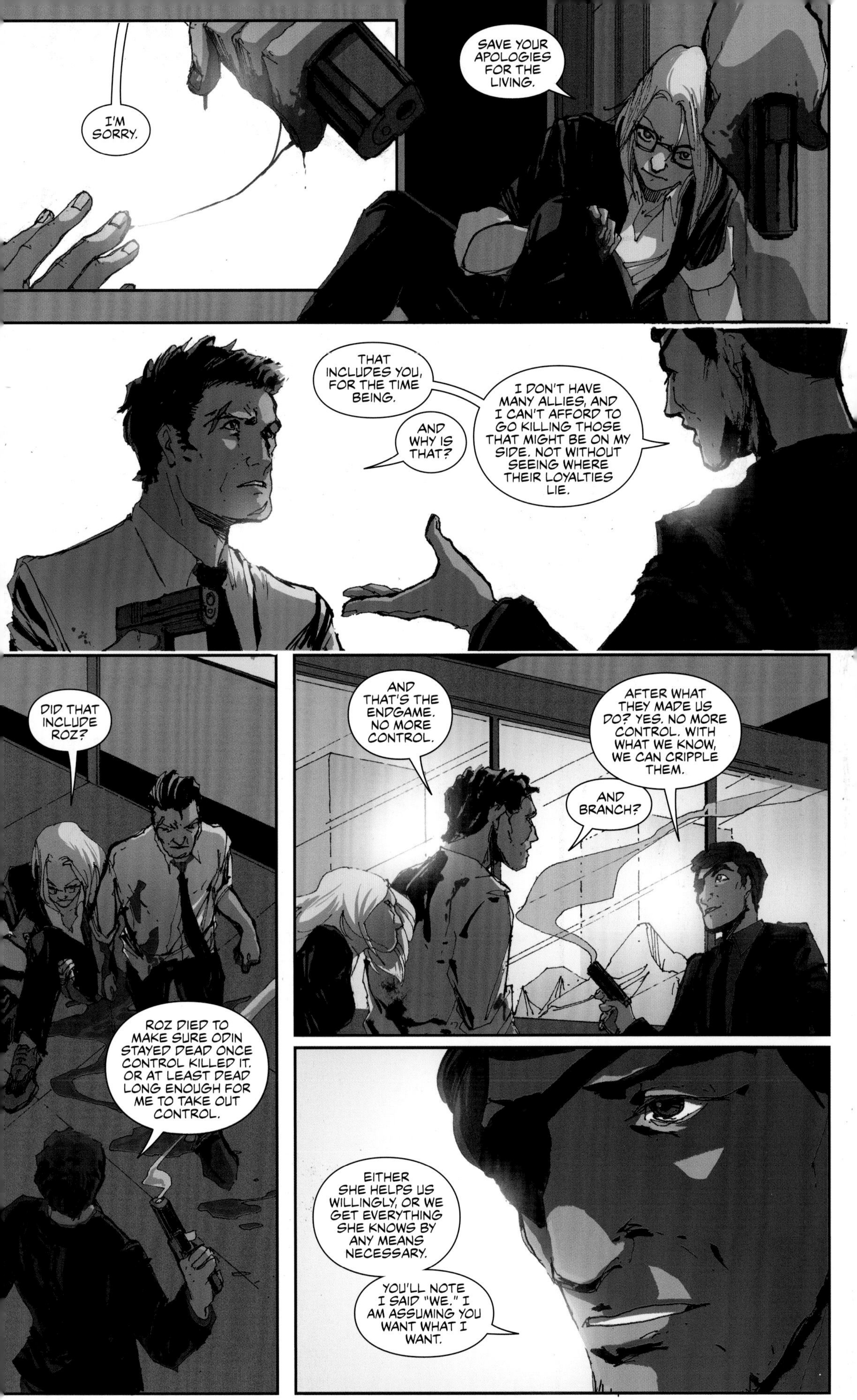
I'M SORRY.
SAVE YOUR APOLOGIES FOR THE LIVING.
THAT INCLUDES YOU, FOR THE TIME BEING.
AND WHY IS THAT?
I DON'T HAVE MANY ALLIES, AND I CAN'T AFFORD TO GO KILLING THOSE THAT MIGHT BE ON MY SIDE. NOT WITHOUT SEEING WHERE THEIR LOYALTIES LIE.
DID THAT INCLUDE ROZ?
ROZ DIED TO MAKE SURE ODIN STAYED DEAD ONCE CONTROL KILLED IT. OR AT LEAST DEAD LONG ENOUGH FOR ME TO TAKE OUT CONTROL.
AND THAT'S THE ENDGAME. NO MORE CONTROL.
AFTER WHAT THEY MADE US DO? YES. NO MORE CONTROL. WITH WHAT WE KNOW, WE CAN CRIPPLE THEM.
AND BRANCH?
EITHER SHE HELPS US WILLINGLY, OR WE GET EVERYTHING SHE KNOWS BY ANY MEANS NECESSARY.
YOU'LL NOTE I SAID "WE." I AM ASSUMING YOU WANT WHAT I WANT.

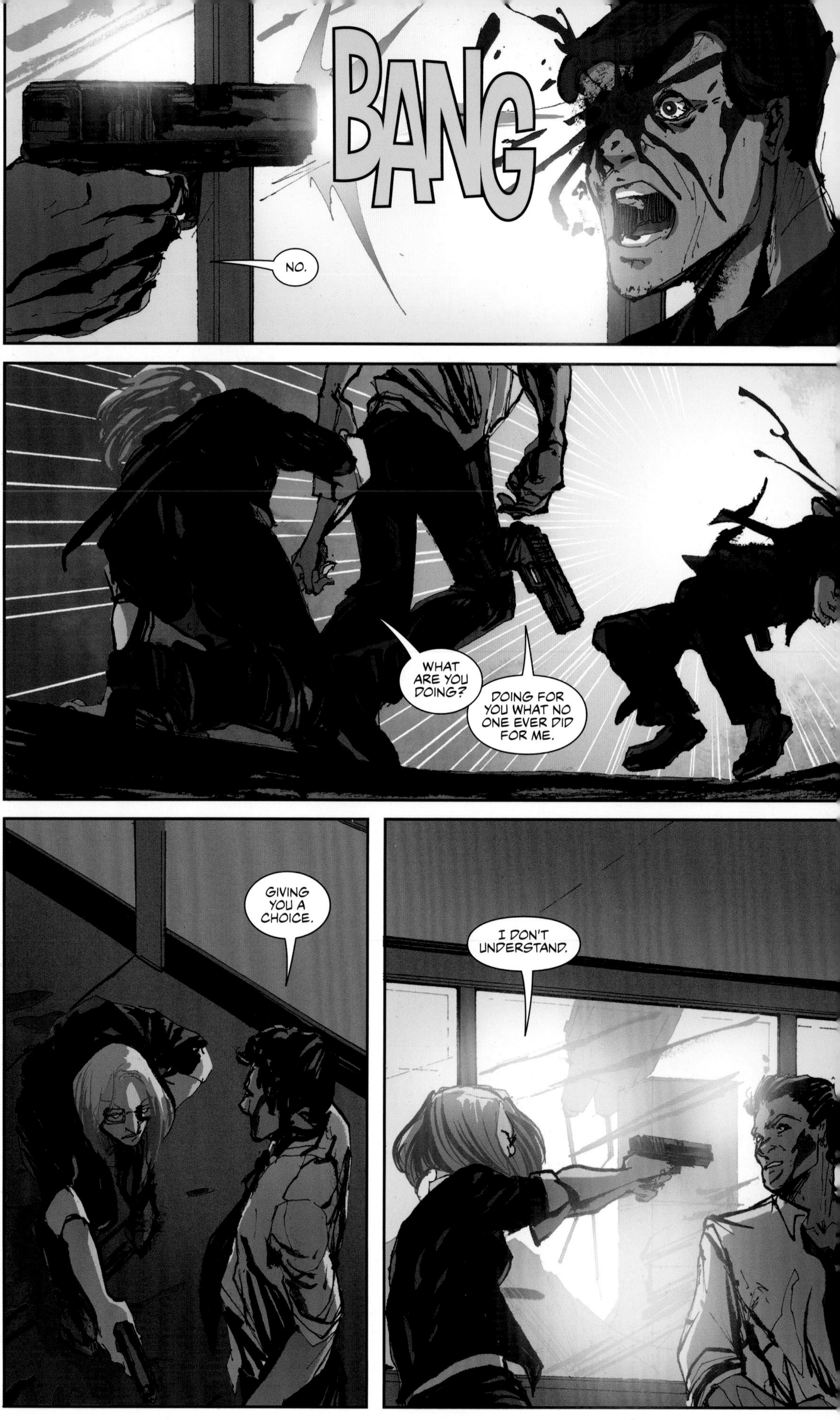
BANG
NO.
WHAT ARE YOU DOING?
DOING FOR YOU WHAT NO ONE EVER DID FOR ME.
GIVING YOU A CHOICE.
I DON'T UNDERSTAND.

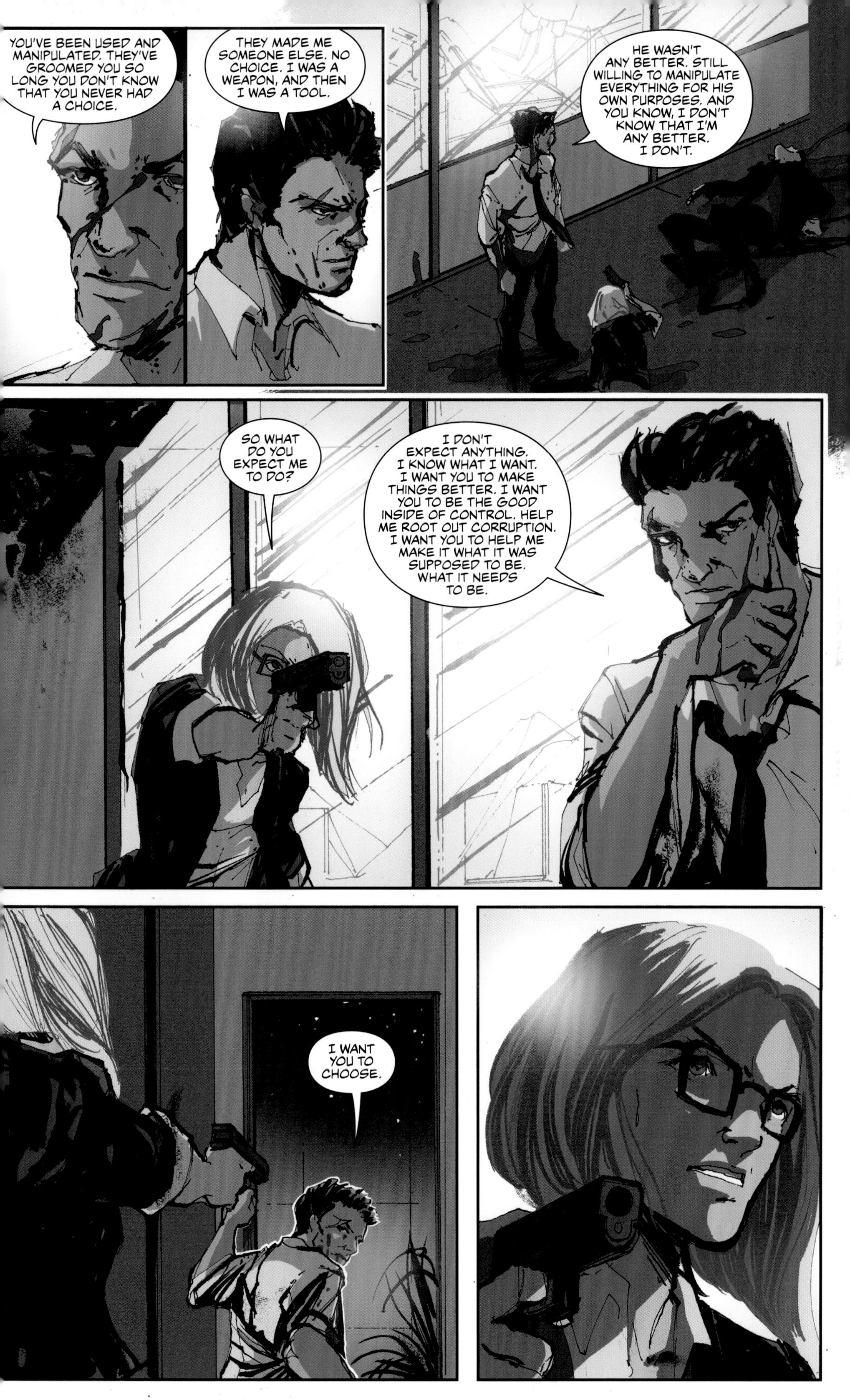
YOU'VE BEEN USED AND MANIPULATED. THEY'VE GROOMED YOU SO LONG YOU DON'T KNOW THAT YOU NEVER HAD A CHOICE.
THEY MADE ME SOMEONE ELSE. NO CHOICE. I WAS A WEAPON, AND THEN I WAS A TOOL.
HE WASN'T ANY BETTER. STILL WILLING TO MANIPULATE EVERYTHING FOR HIS OWN PURPOSES. AND YOU KNOW, I DON'T KNOW THAT I'M ANY BETTER. I DON'T.
SO WHAT DO YOU EXPECT ME TO DO?
I DON'T EXPECT ANYTHING. I KNOW WHAT I WANT. I WANT YOU TO MAKE THINGS BETTER. I WANT YOU TO BE THE GOOD INSIDE OF CONTROL. HELP ME ROOT OUT CORRUPTION. I WANT YOU TO HELP ME MAKE IT WHAT IT WAS SUPPOSED TO BE. WHAT IT NEEDS TO BE.
I WANT YOU TO CHOOSE.

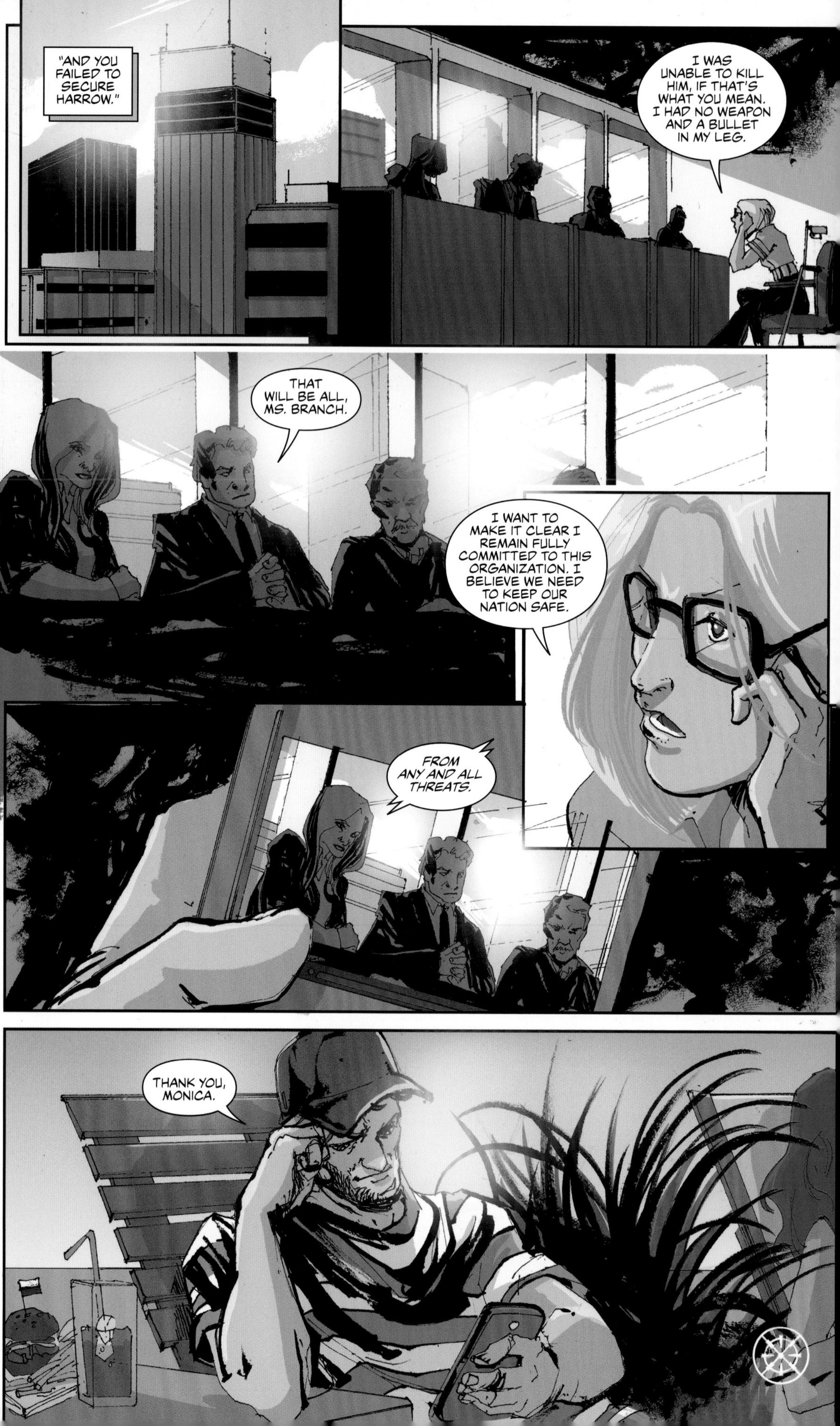
"AND YOU FAILED TO SECURE HARROW."
I WAS UNABLE TO KILL HIM, IF THAT'S WHAT YOU MEAN. I HAD NO WEAPON AND A BULLET IN MY LEG.
THAT WILL BE ALL, MS. BRANCH.
I WANT TO MAKE IT CLEAR I REMAIN FULLY COMMITTED TO THIS ORGANIZATION. I BELIEVE WE NEED TO KEEP OUR NATION SAFE.
FROM ANY AND ALL THREATS.
THANK YOU, MONICA.

COVER GALLERY

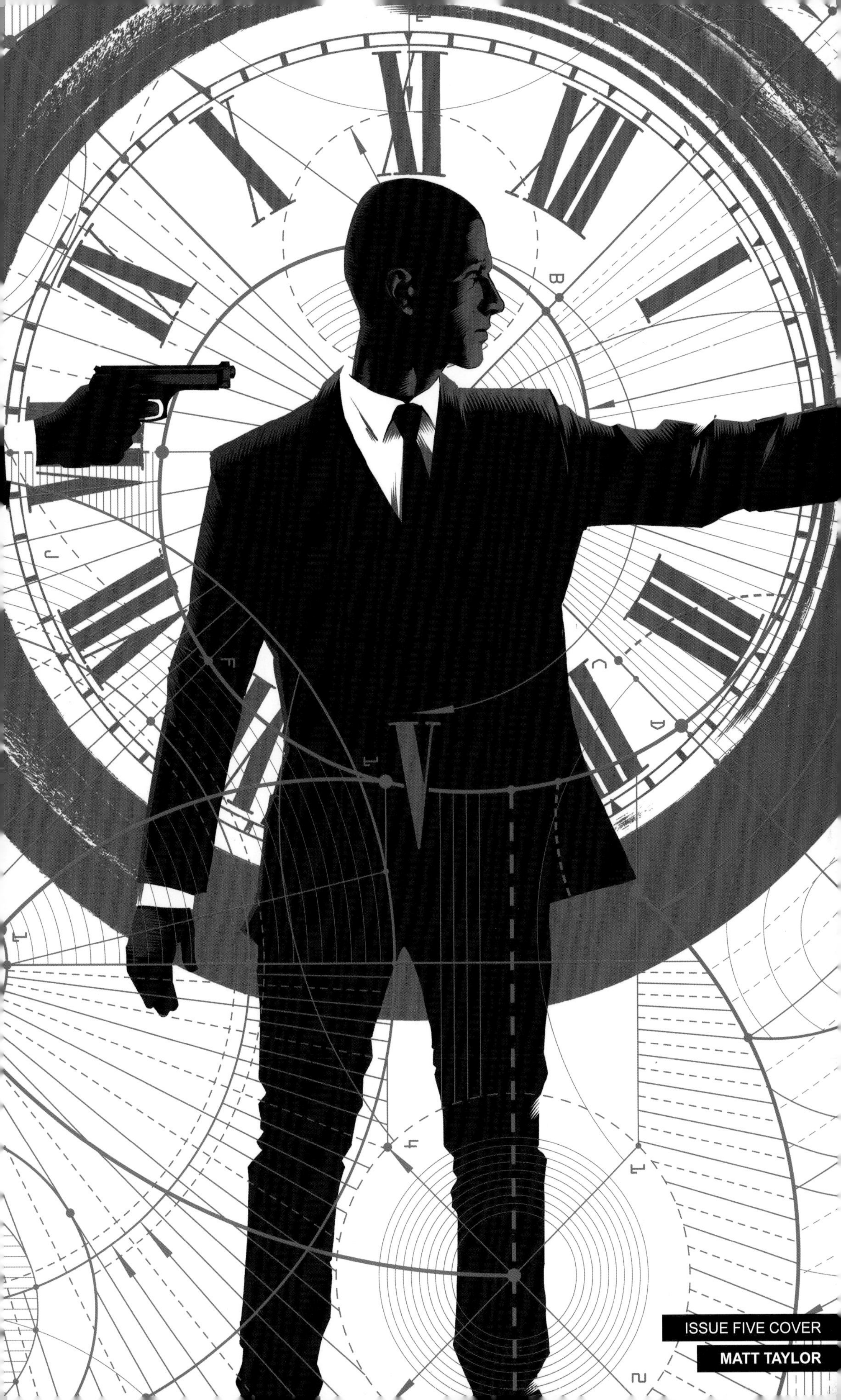

ISSUE FIVE COVER
MATT TAYLOR

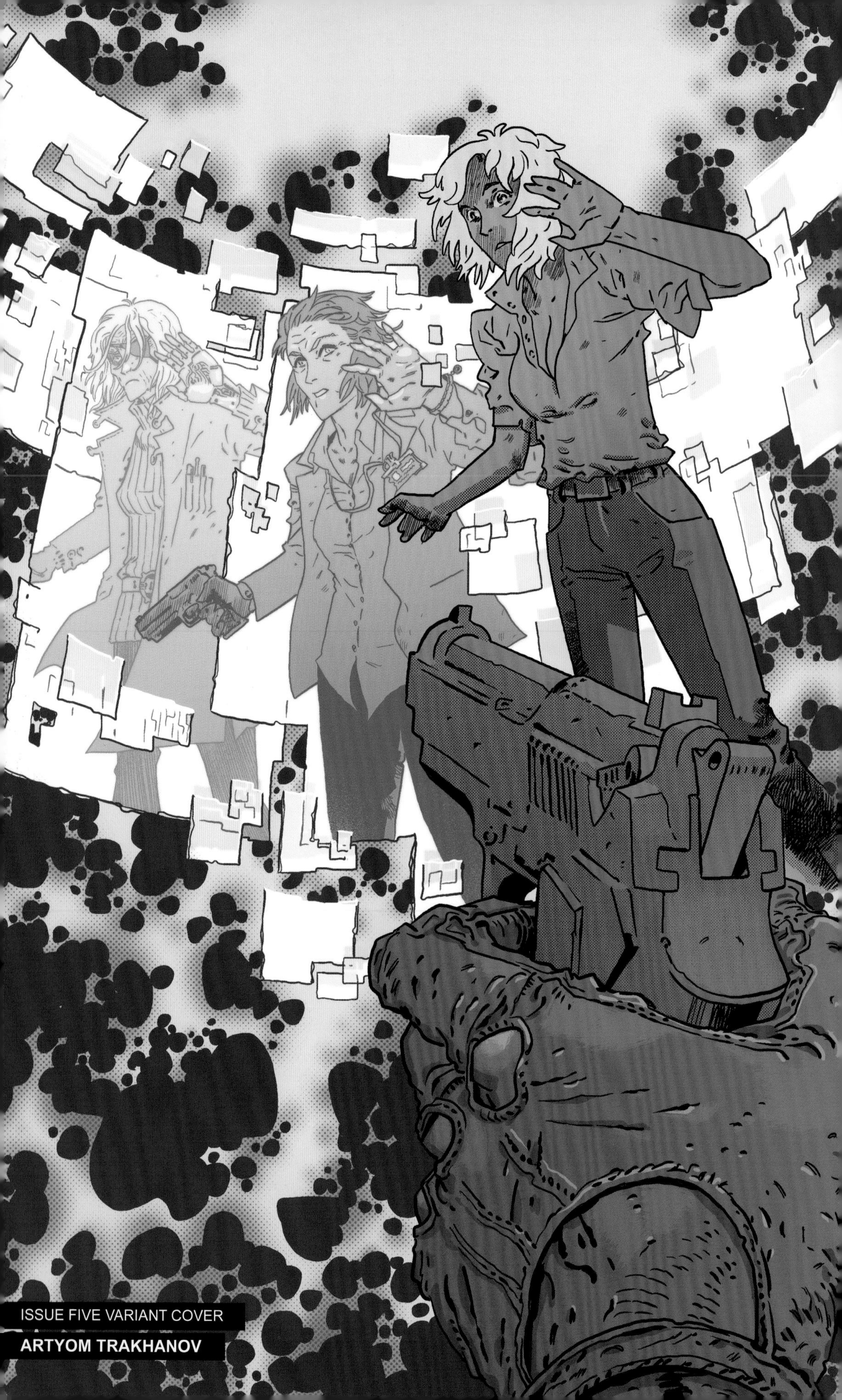

ISSUE FIVE VARIANT COVER

ARTYOM TRAKHANOV

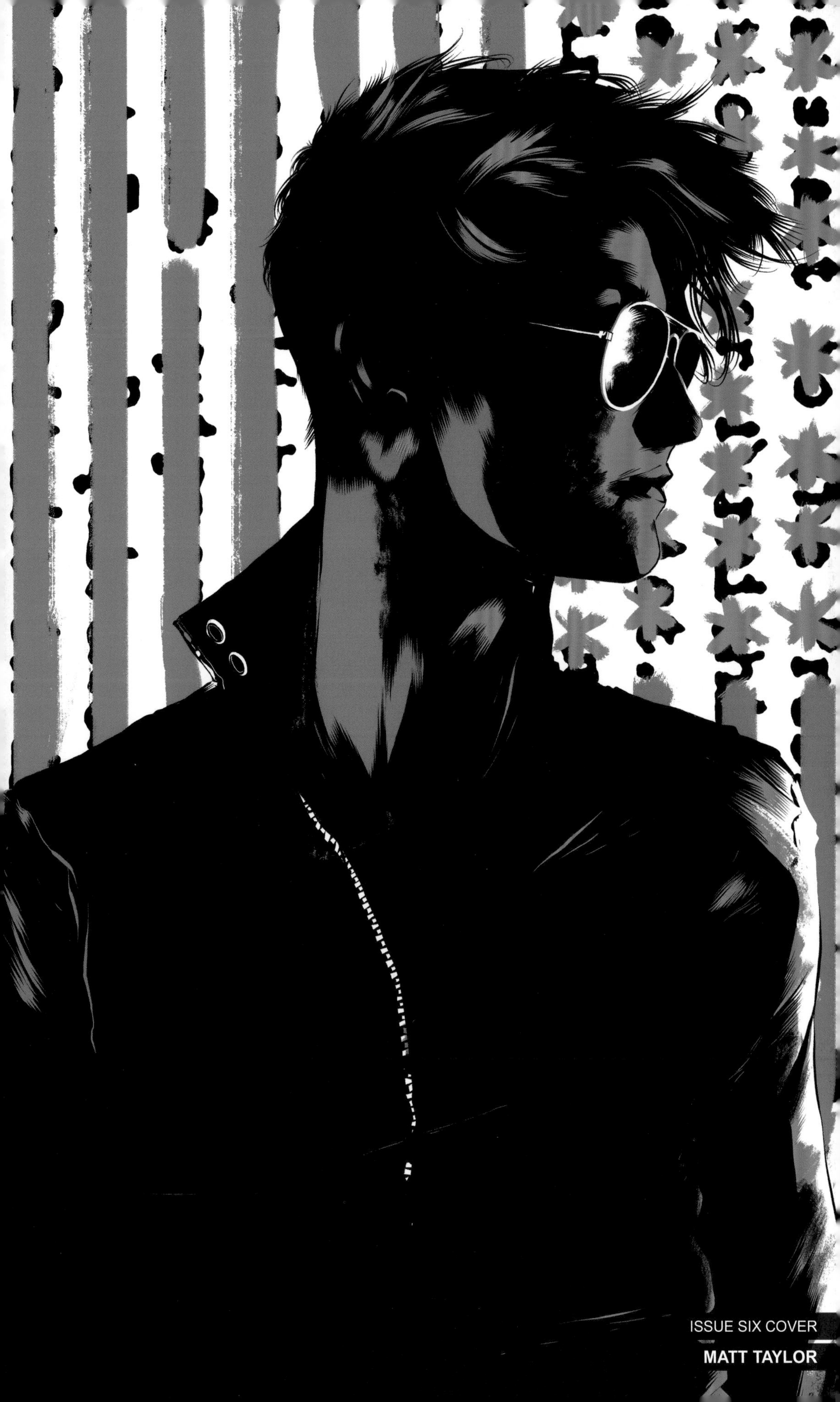

ISSUE SIX COVER

MATT TAYLOR

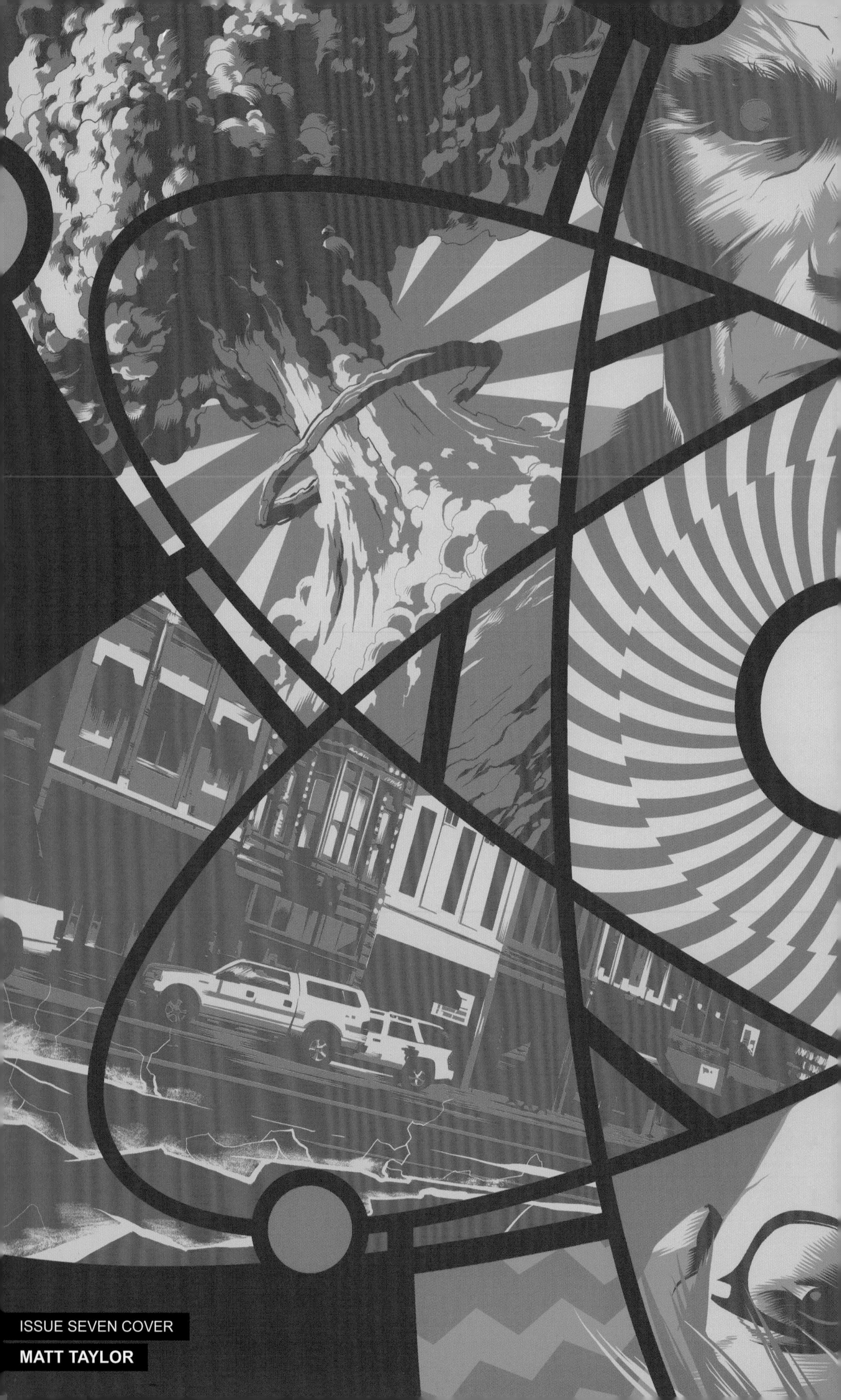

ISSUE SEVEN COVER

MATT TAYLOR

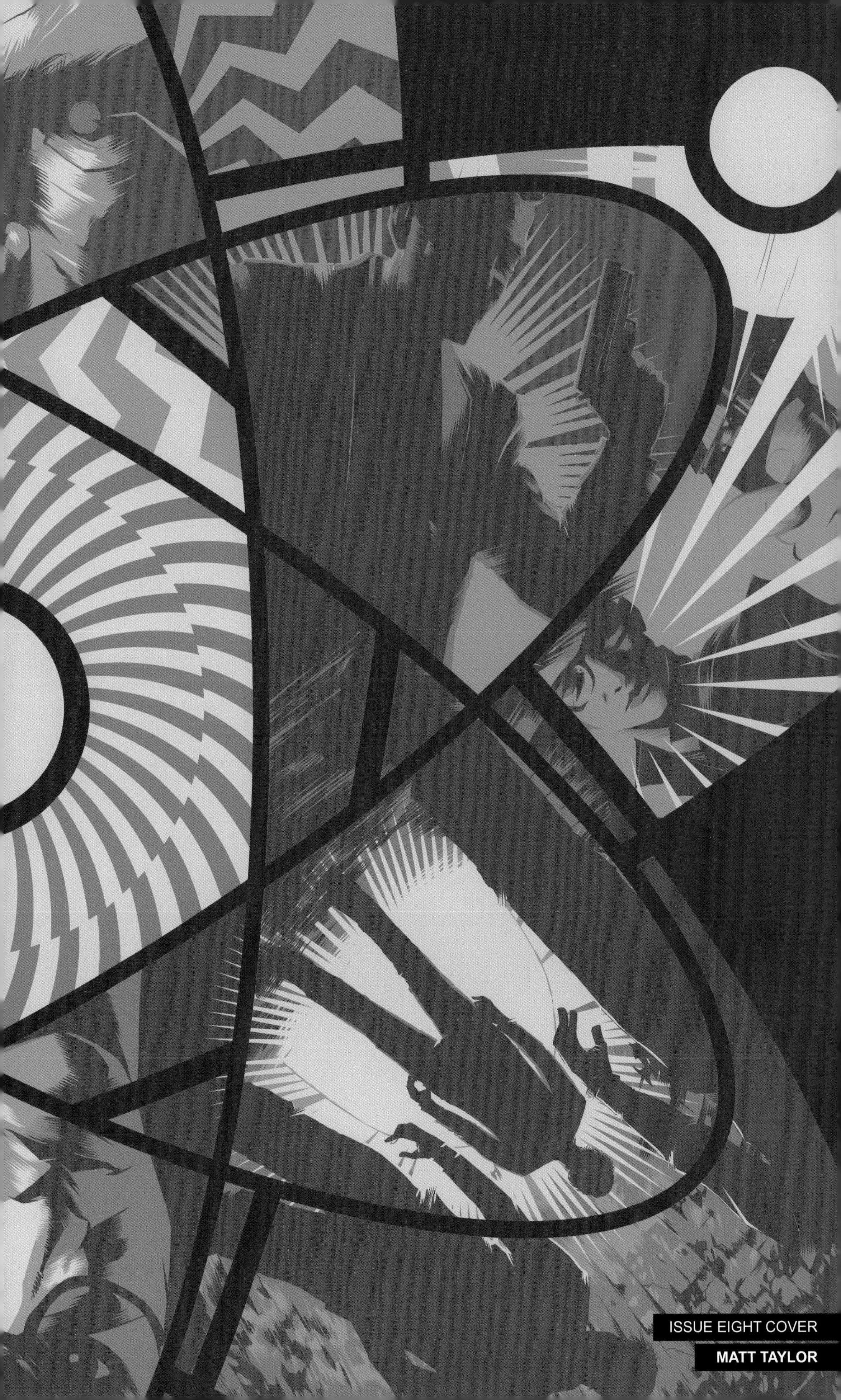

ISSUE EIGHT COVER

MATT TAYLOR

INKS BY ARIELA KRISTANTINA

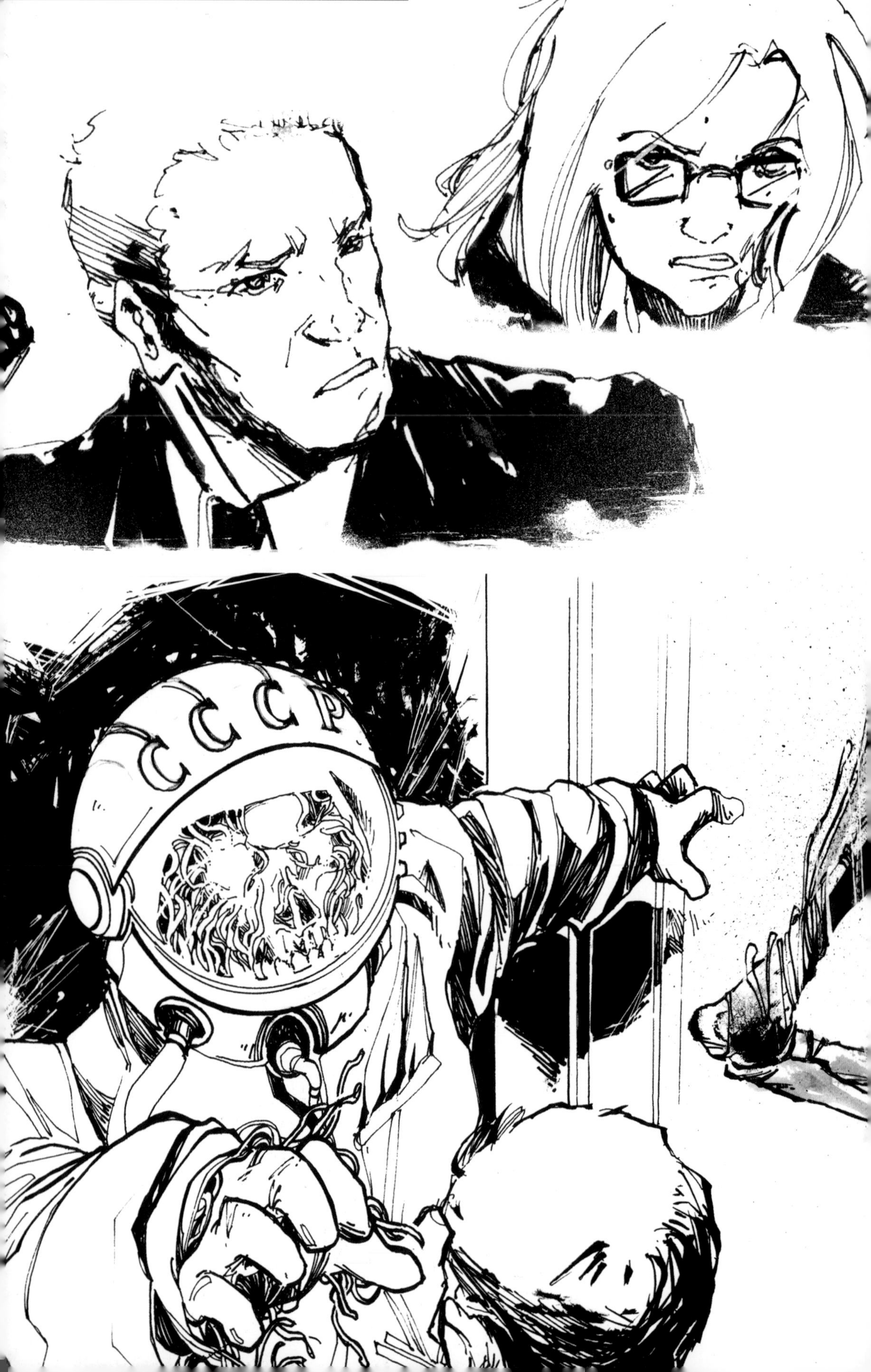
CCCP

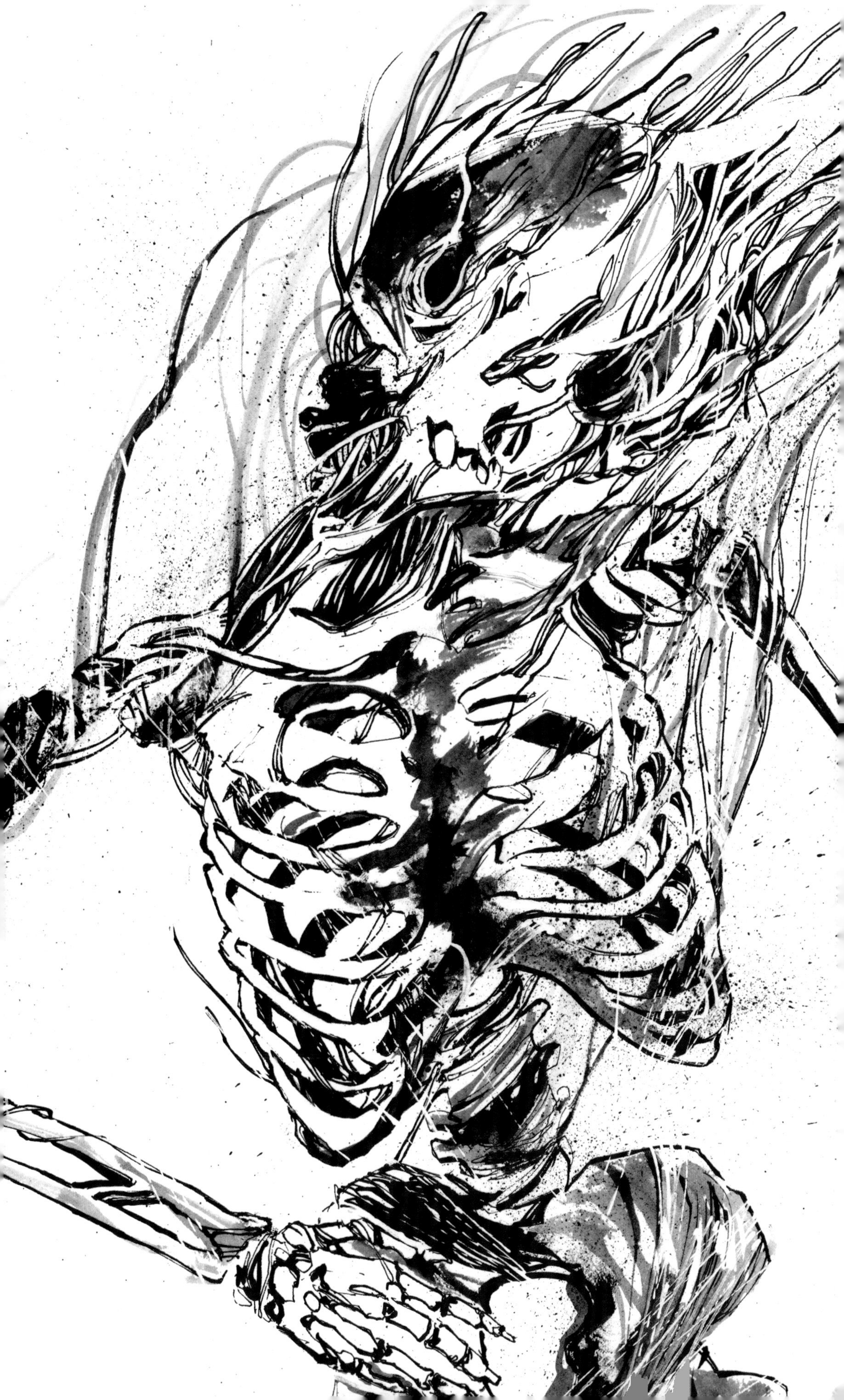

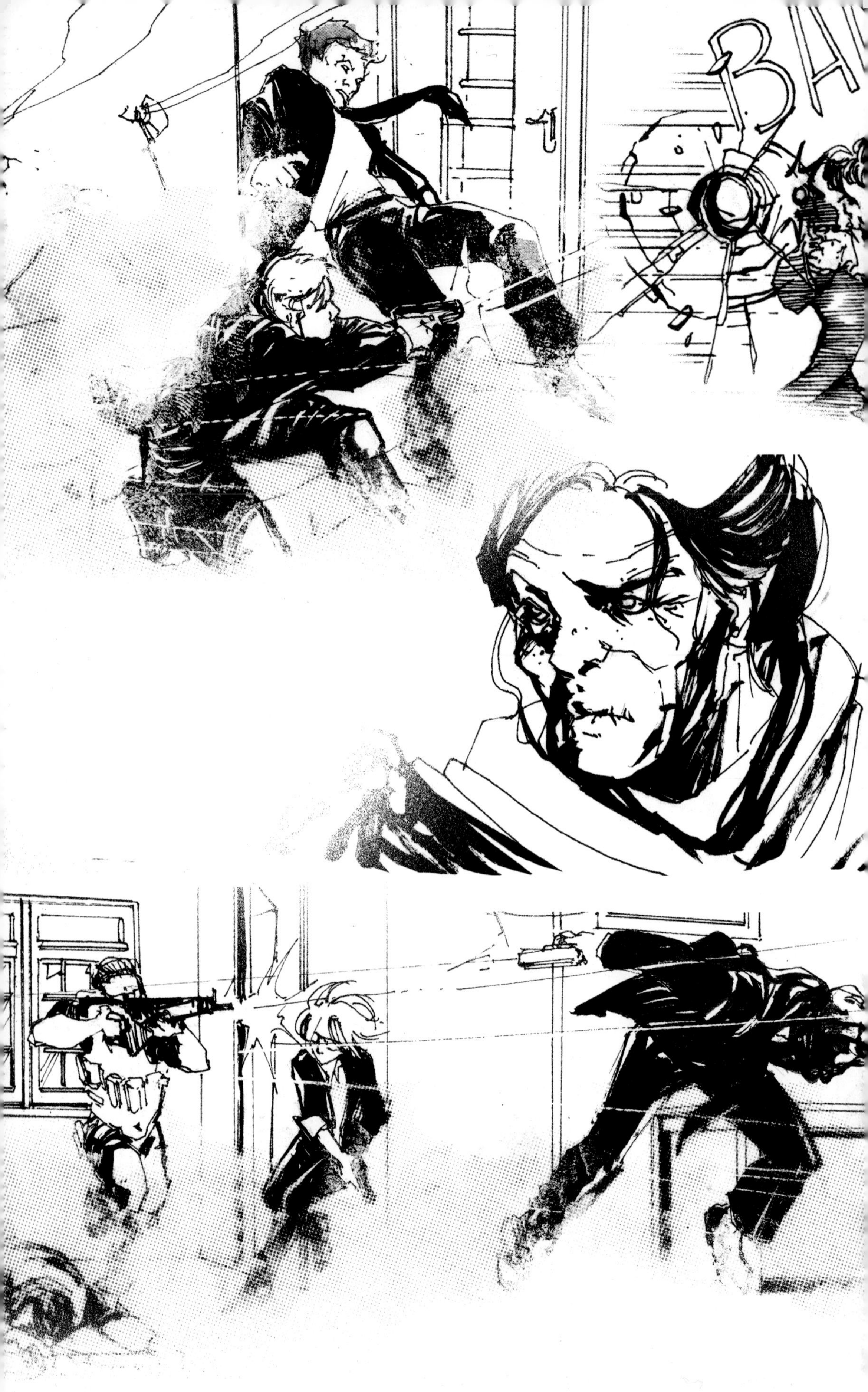

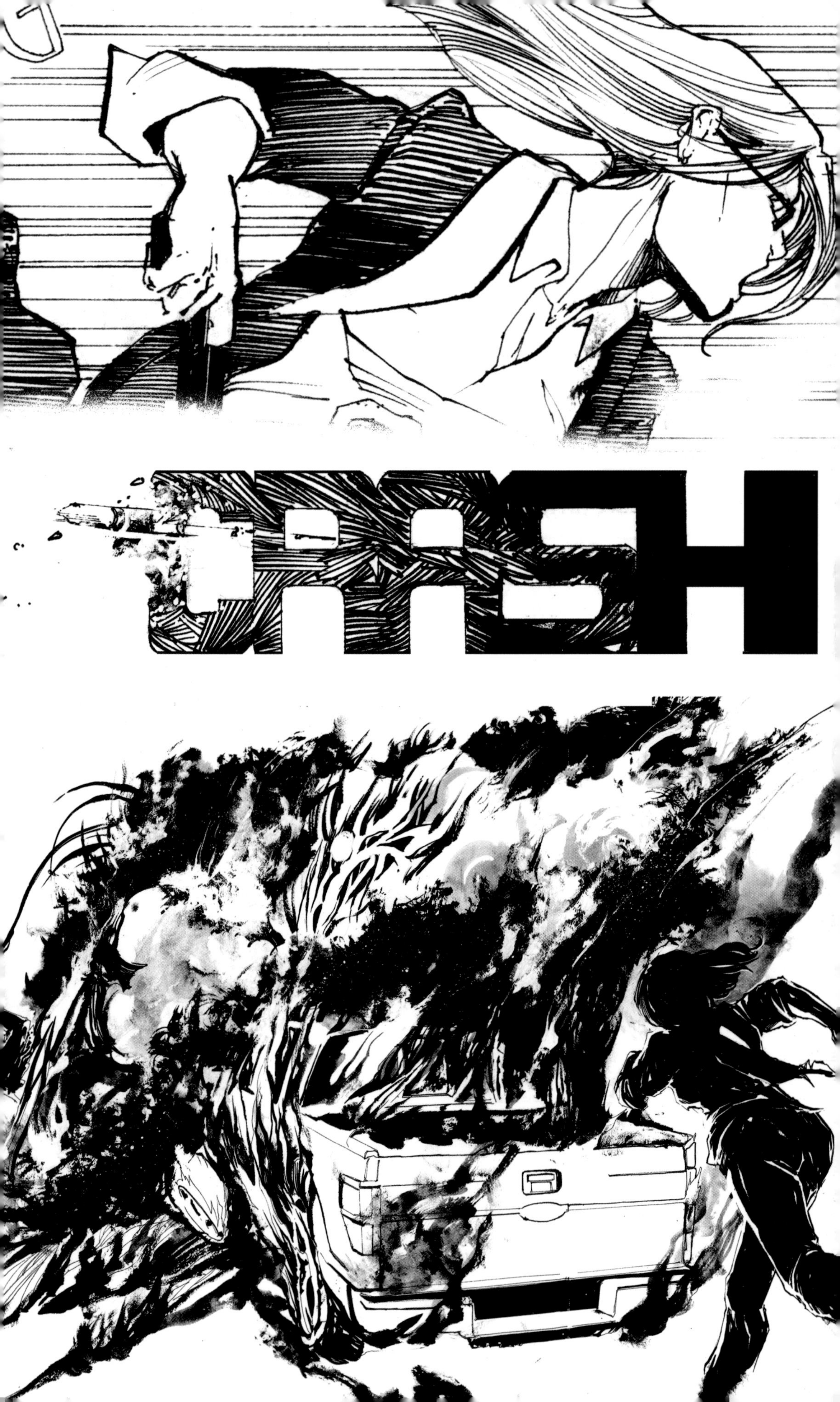
CRASH

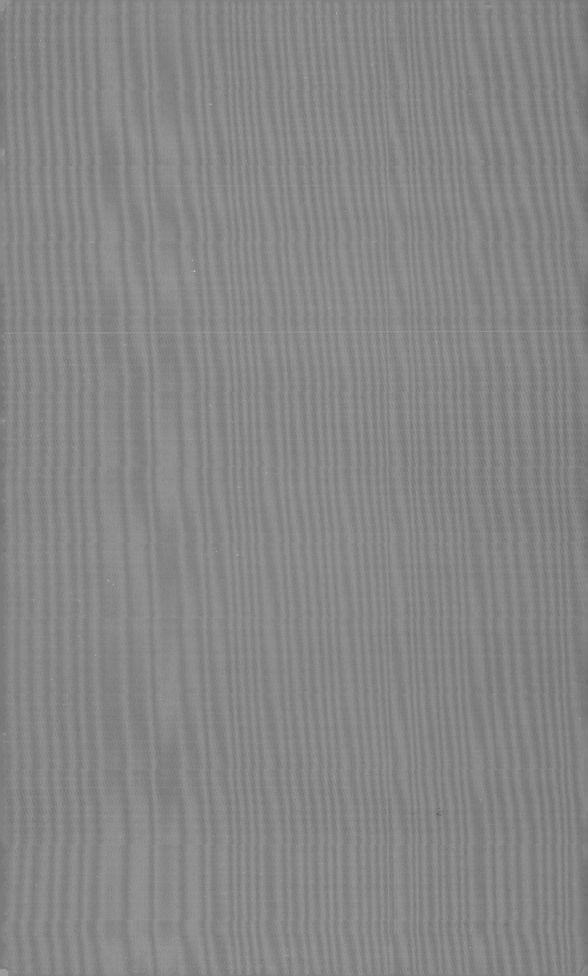